AF856157

2019 EDITION

iPad®
MADE EASY

© 2019 Flame Tree Publishing Ltd

All rights reserved. No part of this publication may be reproduced, stored in a retrieval system, or transmitted in any form or by any means (including electronic, mechanical, photocopying, recording or otherwise) without prior written permission from the publisher.

Publisher and Creative Director: Nick Wells
Project Editor: Polly Prior
Art Director: Mike Spender
Layout Design: Jane Ashley
Copy Editor: Daniela Nava
Technical Editor: Mark Mayne
Screenshots: Roger Laing, Chris Smith and Jamie Gunn

Thanks to: Josie Mitchell, Laura Bulbeck, Esme Chapman, Emma Chafer, Stephen Feather, Karen Fitzpatrick and Sonya Newland

FLAME TREE PUBLISHING
6 Melbray Mews
Fulham, London SW6 3NS
United Kingdom

All non-screenshot pictures are courtesy of © 2018 Apple Inc.: 1, 2, 3, 8, 9, 26, 88, 118, 240, 241, 242; cloudbite.co.uk: 101; gadgetmix.com: 24; JBL: 239; Speck: 237; Twelve South: 238; and Shutterstock and © the following photographers: baranq: 7, 184; Denphumi: 5, 54; Hanna Kuprevich 229; l i g h t p o e t: 6, 128; Mihai Simonia: 7, 216; 1000 Words: 5, 86; Y Photo Studio: 4, 14; robert_s: 12; wavebreakmedia: 6, 150; nixki: 20, 22. Other images courtesy of Flame Tree Publishing Ltd.

ISBN 978-1-78755-734-5

Manufactured in China

1 3 5 7 9 10 8 6 4 2

2019 EDITION

iPad®

MADE EASY

ROGER LAING AND CHRIS SMITH

FLAME TREE
PUBLISHING

CONTENTS

Time to get familiar with the iPad, its controls, all the essential apps you'll need and the everyday tasks that you'll use it for. Starting with the basics, you will learn all about the iPad's anatomy and the whereabouts of different buttons, as well as understanding what goes on inside your device. This chapter also takes you through other essentials such as using the App Store and syncing.

The iPad is the perfect device for browsing, downloading, arranging and reading books and magazines via the iBooks app – and this chapter shows you exactly how to do so. What's more this chapter introduces other reading apps such as Kindle and Zinio, and details how to adjust the appearance of text to ensure that you get the best reading experience possible.

When it comes to finding a comprehensive entertainment device, the iPad is king. This chapter describes how the iTunes, Podcast and Music apps allow you to use your iPad to browse, create and edit playlists and to make and share your own music. In addition you'll learn all about gaming on your iPad and discover apps that complement every aspect of your lifestyle, from shopping to cooking.

INTRODUCTION

Loved, desired and applauded since it was first launched, the iPad has revolutionized computing. Forget your laptop, ditch the desktop, the iPad is rapidly becoming the essential accessory for managing everyday life.

Above: The Retina display on the iPad offers incredible screen clarity, ideal for viewing video.

YOUR WORLD AT YOUR FINGERTIPS

The iPad is far more than a gadget. Once you have one it is almost impossible to remember life without it. Never before has there been a device that makes it this simple to read books, newspapers and magazines, browse the web, go shopping, play games, see movies, watch TV, listen to music, share photos, research ideas for business, write a report and organize the day. What's more, you can do all this and still communicate via email or chat with friends, family and work colleagues, whether close to home or across continents. With the iPad, your world is in your hand.

EVERYTHING YOU NEED TO KNOW

Apple is renowned for the simple elegance of their design. Following the principles set by their founder – the late Steve Jobs – they want to create technology that just works. While the iPad is user friendly, there is so much that it does that is not immediately obvious.

This book is designed to help you get the most from your iPad. It will guide you through all the ways you can use it for both personal and business use. We'll aim to make things simple and clear. Where it is unavoidable to use technical terms we will explain exactly what they mean.

Different Generations, Similar Features

Amazingly, since it first appeared in 2010, Apple has launched 20 different models of iPad, many with two options available – Wi-Fi only and Wi-Fi + Cellular.

Unfortunately, the naming of each model has been confusing. The original iPad was clear and so was iPad 2. But that was followed not by iPad 3 but the new iPad featuring the super-high-resolution Retina display, which Apple dubbed 'Resolutionary'. The new iPad was itself replaced within six months by a faster version referred to as iPad with Retina display. After that came the iPad Air (to reflect its lightness) followed by the iPad Air 2. There have also been four versions of the smaller iPad named iPad mini.

Apple released the iPad Pro in two sizes. The larger 12.9" Retina display and optional Smart Keyboard were seen as a potential replacement for the laptop. Its little brother, the smaller 9.7" was short lived and has now been replaced by the 10.5" iPad Pro. There are five iPad models currently on sale from Apple as of Spring 2019:

iPad (2018): The spiritual successor to the first ever iPad. It has a 9.7-inch screen with a sleek design and the first of its kind to support the Apple Pencil stylus. It's the most affordable iPad in the range.

iPad Pro 3rd generation (2018): The very latest iPad Pro models offer a squarer design, much thinner display bezels and support for Face ID facial recognition. It comes in 11-inch and 12.9-inch options.

iPad mini (2019): Apple has updated the iPad mini for the first time in years. It has a 7.9-inch screen, more powerful processors, a sleek design and support for Apple Pencil.

iPad Air (2019): This tablet has a 10.5-inch display, is lightweight and portable and features more power than the standard iPad (2018).

Below: The iPad mini is a smaller version of the iPad.

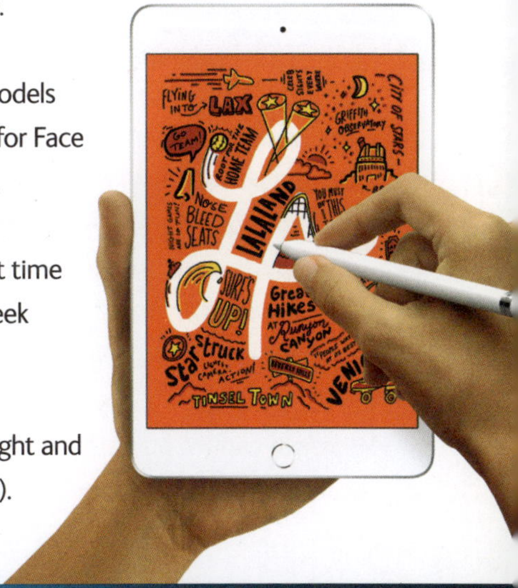

While there are physical differences between the different models – for example, iPad Pro has a more powerful processor and Apple Pencil compatibility, and the original iPad has no camera – many features are controlled by the operating system (iOS). The latest version is iOS 12. It runs on all iPads made from 2013 onwards, but even those older devices still support most features in this book. Where features are available only on specific models, this will be noted in the text.

SHORT SECTIONS

Pick up your iPad and flick through the screens and you'll often come across something new. Similarly, this book is not designed to be read in one sitting but to be a handy guide. For example, the section on gestures can be read on its own and you can practice them on your iPad until you feel confident that you can use them correctly. At the same time, it is a useful reference, if you need to remind yourself of some of the more advanced gestures later on.

STEP-BY-STEP

Throughout this book you'll find there are many step-by-step guides that take you through the precise actions you need to follow on certain tasks. This may be anything from connecting to your wireless network, setting up email or editing your photos to creating a new playlist for your music or troubleshooting app problems. Each step-by-step guide has clear, concise instructions on what to do and also explains any differences between the various iPad versions, so you can be sure you won't miss out.

HELP!

In the unlikely event you do get really stuck on a particular topic, we're here to help. Simply email your query to Flame Tree Publishing at *info@flametreepublishing.com.* While we cannot operate a 24-hour helpline for any iPad questions, we will respond by email as soon as possible.

YOUR GUIDE

If this is your first iPad, this book is designed to get you up and running as quickly as possible. There's plenty too for the more experienced user to discover. The author Roger Laing delves into some of the more advanced features and uses his experience as a technology writer to explain briefly and clearly how they improve your iPad experience and add to the fun.

Above: Editing photos is just one of the ways you can use your iPad.

DO MORE

Everyone has their own opinion on what's best about the iPad. It may be watching a movie or TV programme on a display that can vie with the best of screens. It could be playing games with a speed and power that rivals any console. It may be having a photo gallery to share with family and friends or the incredible range of apps, many of which have the potential to change the way you live and work. The good thing is you don't have to choose between any of these. The iPad has them all and more. This book will get you started; after that the possibilities are virtually unlimited.

Above: It is easy to use your iPad to watch films and TV programmes on websites such as BBC iPlayer.

SEVEN CHAPTERS

The contents of this book are split into seven chapters. Chapter one will show you how to get started with the iPad itself and the hundreds of thousands of apps available. Chapter two covers getting connected with email, video calling, social media and the like. Chapter three is all about photos and video – taking photos, editing them to add stunning effects, as well as viewing, storing and sharing them. It also offers practical advice on taking, viewing and editing your own videos, as well as buying and renting movies, and TV shows, etc. Chapter four is where to read all about the books, newspapers and magazines that turn your iPad into a digital reader. Chapter five is the entertainment channel, where you can discover how to listen, store and even make your own music or enter another world with games. Chapter six shows that the iPad is also a good work tool, which can help you organize your documents, your time, your contacts – in fact as much of your life as you allow. Chapter seven looks at the more advanced features that keep your iPad running smoothly – from customizing and setting your preferences to troubleshooting and security.

Above: Swipe right from the lock screen in iOS 12 and you have an enhanced Today page with the latest news, weather, calendar and other notifications.

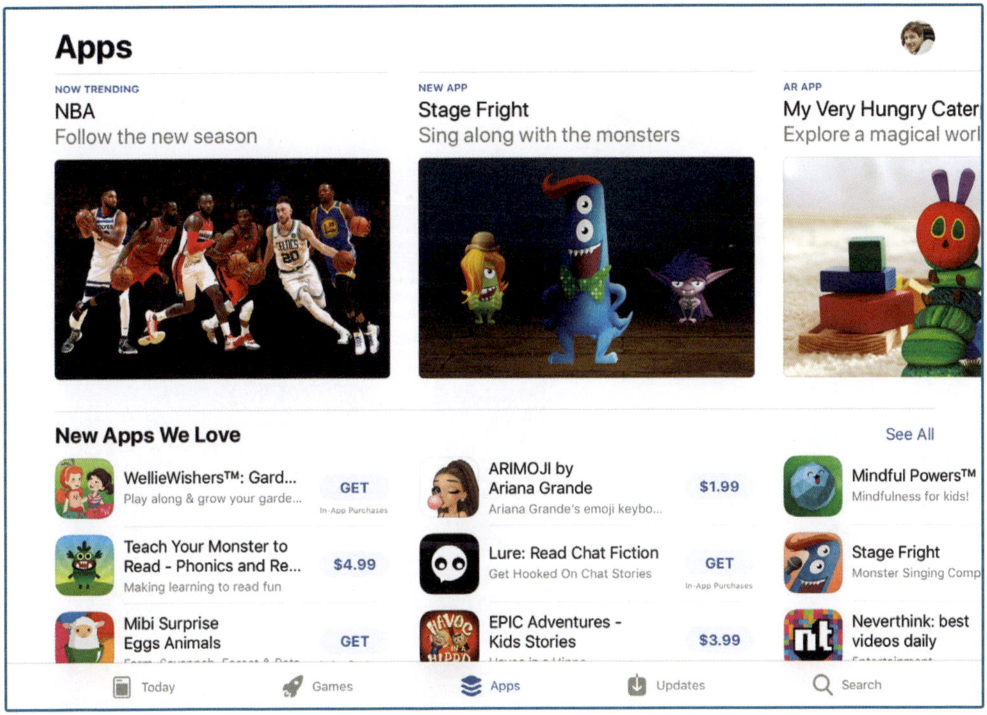

Above: Head to the App Store to browse and download apps and get the most out of your iPad.

HOT TIPS AND SHORT CUTS

Look out, throughout the book, for the Hot Tips, which provide quick and handy information on the way to get the best from your iPad. They also highlight many short cuts and quick techniques to help you become an expert iPad user.

APPTASTIC

Here in one handy list are the 100 essential apps that no iPad user will want to be without. They are linked to the relevant section in the book, so it's easy to refer back and get more information on the category they cover.

GETTING STARTED

WHAT IS AN iPAD?

Think of your iPad as the ultimate portable computer – light enough to take wherever you go, yet powerful and versatile enough to do whatever you need.

TABLET COMPUTER

The arrival of the iPad established the popularity of tablet computers, a type of mobile computer that typically has a touchscreen rather than a normal keyboard. Previously, several computer manufacturers had launched tablets but they failed to take off. Apple succeeded because they believed the tablet, which is bigger than a smartphone but smaller than a laptop, had to be better than either at key tasks – such as displaying text and video, organizing your work life and brightening up your personal life.

Above: Download, store and read hundreds of book and magazine texts on your iPad.

YOUR ENTERTAINMENT CENTRE

Whether it's a long read, listening to your favourite music, playing a game with friends around the world or sharing a memory of good times with your photos, the iPad does it all.

Books and Periodicals

Your portable library, the iPad is an ebook reader which can store hundreds of texts inside and also lets you buy more on the device. Apple has one app, Books, for reading and storing books. With many other apps from bookstores, magazines, newspapers and publishers, such as Amazon, you literally have access to millions of book titles worldwide and hundreds of periodicals.

Hot Tip

The small software programs that run on the iPad are called apps (mini-applications). Apple has approved more than a million apps for download through the App Store.

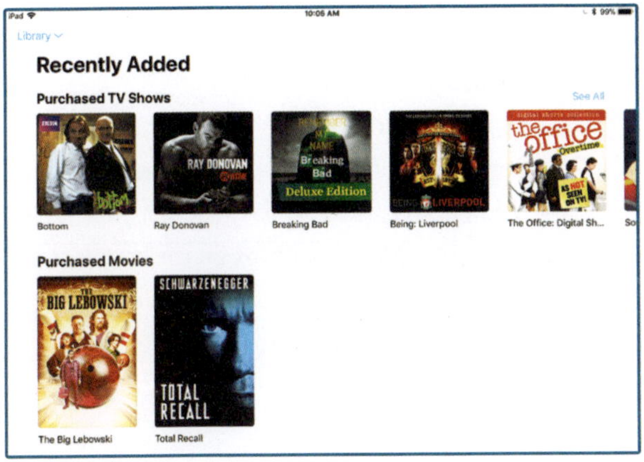

Above: The new TV app stores all of your video content purchased from iTunes or synced to your iPad.

Video

Whether it's watching films and TV shows purchased from iTunes or streaming from apps like Netflix, Amazon Prime, YouTube or BBC iPlayer, video viewing is a key feature of the iPad. The iPad has its own video app called Video (gradually being replaced by TV in most countries).

Once you've started the video player, using the touchscreen controls, you can view the video full screen for uninterrupted viewing. Not surprisingly, the app takes full advantage of the super clear Retina display available on all current models and can playback full HD video.

Music

The Music app is the home of your digital music library, whether it's transferred files from your computer or music streamed from the Apple Music subscription service. The app makes full use of that gorgeous display with a spacious layout, cover art, playlists and dedicated artist pages. Other music apps like Spotify and Google Play Music are very popular among iPad users.

Above: Photos organizes your photos and videos according to where and when they were taken.

Games

Games are another area where the iPad scores over the smaller screen iPhone. There are many games specially developed for the iPad, which has the speed and power to match the graphics of traditional games consoles. The Game Center functionality lets you play against friends and family and lets you join online leaderboards.

Photos

Open the Photos app to see all of the images taken with your iPad and those stored in your iCloud Photo Library, which keeps all your snaps up to date across all your Apple devices. You can flick through your photos on the touchscreen and tap to enlarge thumbnails. To save space, your photos can be stored at a smaller size on the iPad with the full resolution versions on iCloud. To turn on this feature go to Settings, select iCloud, then Photos and select Optimise iPad Storage.

Your photos and videos are automatically organized by where and when they were taken. The Years selection groups together all the photos taken each year. Tap to open Collections, where the photos are arranged by the place where they were taken (such as a French holiday) and tap again to open Moments, which groups together pictures taken around the same time and place (like an afternoon on the beach). Apple will even create custom video montages from your stills, accompanied by a soundtrack. They're called Memories.

Hot Tip

You get 5GB of free storage for your photos in iCloud and as your picture library grows you have the option to buy up to 2TB of storage. Head to Settings, Your Name, iCloud, Mange Storage, Upgrade to choose an option.

YOUR BUSINESS RESEARCH ASSISTANT

The iPad is a wonderful research tool that can help you find the important information you need, take notes or even full reports and share them afterwards.

Web Content

With Safari for iPad you have a browser that is similar to any you have used on a computer. It gives you access to all the same research sources – from Google search to Wikipedia and millions in between. With support for tabbed browsing, it's now easy to move backwards and forwards between the different pages you have visited.

Making and Storing Notes

Nothing is worse than having an idea you want to make a note of and no way to write it down. Fortunately, the iPad comes with its own Notes app. Use the notepad to jot down ideas, plan a project and write down a meeting report. For writing a To Do list, the better option is the iPad's list writing app, called Reminders. This lets you create a task list – from the weekly shop to packing for a holiday – for which you can set a reminder that will alert you when it needs to be done.

Sharing Information

Your notes and reminders can be synced with your other Apple devices, so you always have the latest version. You can also share your reminders with others through iCloud. Similarly, there are many file sharing services – from Dropbox to Evernote and Google Drive – which enable you to collaborate and work on documents with friends and colleagues, wherever they are, direct from your iPad.

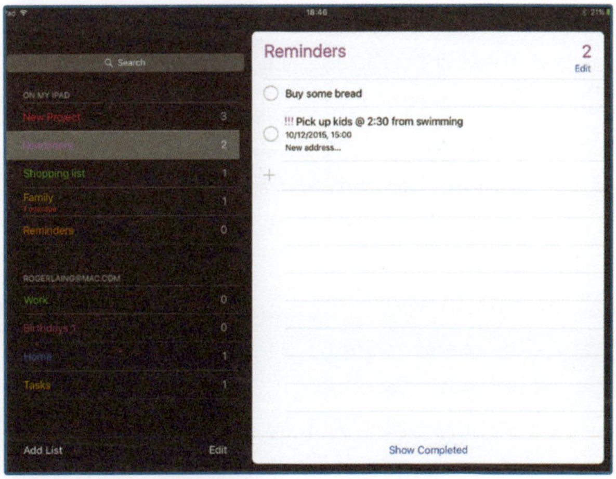

Above: Reminders allows you to make lists and set timed reminders. Sync your reminders with other Apple devices and share over iCloud to keep all relevant people updated, wherever they may be.

ANATOMY OF AN iPAD

While there are few obvious physical differences between iPads, there are some subtle and not so subtle variations between each generation. Here's your guide to the physical layout of the iPad.

FRONT

Home Screen

Your apps are displayed on the Home screen. Swipe right and you'll flip through further pages of apps. You can also organize your apps into folders. To do so, just press on an app icon until it starts shaking and then drag it on top of the icon you want to share the folder. A folder is automatically created, which you can rename. Tap on the folder and you can access the apps inside.

1 Headphone Socket

The 3.5 mm audio jack point works fine with headphones you use with other Apple devices, but others may need an inexpensive adapter to fit. The new iPad Pro doesn't have a headphone jack.

2 Sleep/Wake Button

- **Sleep mode**: press this button once and this will put your iPad to sleep. To wake the iPad, press the Sleep/Wake button once and swipe across the slide to unlock button.

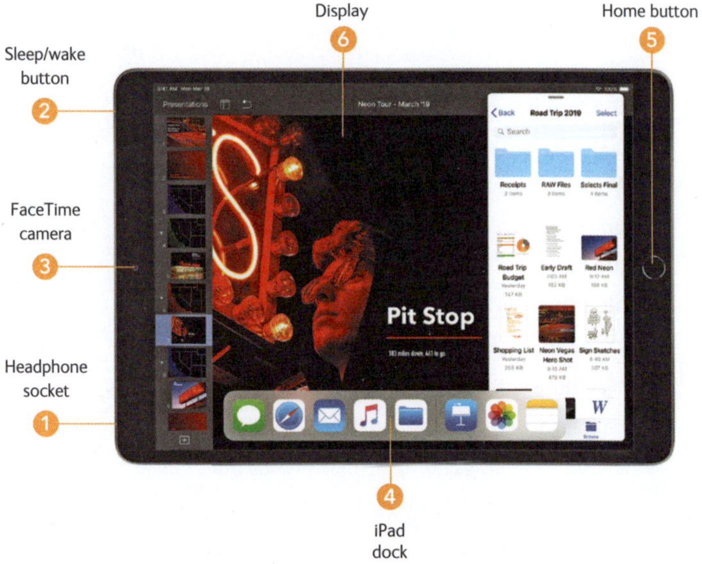

- **Shutdown**: turns the iPad off completely, saving your battery. To switch off, press and hold the Sleep/Wake button for a few seconds. Confirm your decision by using the slide to power off button to shut down.

3 FaceTime Camera

As its name suggests, this camera is mainly meant for using with FaceTime video chat, so other people can see you. On current models the front camera supports 1.2-megapixel stills and 720p HD (high definition) video. On iPad Pro models it is more advanced, with 7-megapixel stills and 1080p HD video.

> **Hot Tip**
>
> **One way to help preserve battery life is to set your screen to Auto-Lock when you're not using it. To do so, tap the Settings icon, select General, then Auto-Lock and set the interval to the time you prefer.**

4 iPad Dock

This dock bar appears at the foot of the Home screen and stays in place as you scroll between the pages. It means these apps are always available from any Home screen page. By default, the Safari, Mail, Photos and Music apps will be there, but you can customize the dock to include the apps you use most frequently. To add an app, press and hold until it begins to shake, then drag it to the dock. In iOS 10 you were allowed six, but now you can place in as many as you want.

The new dock also features recently used/suggested apps, allowing to switch between tasks quickly. Also new in iOS 11 was the floating dock. When you're in an app you can summon the dock with a slight swipe-up gesture from the bottom of the display. This is a really handy multi-tasking feature and is the gateway to using split view (*see* page 39).

5 Home Button

In an app, press this once to return to the Home screen. Pressing it twice reveals the apps that are running. On newer iPads, the Home button has a fingerprint sensor for Touch ID, which lets you unlock your iPad using your thumb or finger. The new iPad Pro doesn't have a Home button. You unlock with Face ID and use swipe gestures instead.

6 Display

There are multiple sizes available, some with higher quality displays than others.

- **iPad mini**: This is 7.9-inches diagonally. The newest version of the tablet is the fifth generation. It doubles display resolution from 1024 x 768 pixels to 2048 x 1536.
- **iPad**: The standard options available today have a 9.7-inch display, which has also improved significantly down the years. The resolution is the same 2048 x 1536.
- **iPad Air**: The first two iPad Air models also offered 9.7-inch displays. The latest version, released in 2019 has a larger 10.5-inch display with a 2224 x 1668 display.
- **iPad Pro**: Apple played around with the iPad Pro display sizes for a number of years, but settled on 11 inches and 12.9 inches with the latest models. They have display resolutions of 2388 x 1668 and 2732 x 2048 respectively.

Touchscreen

You control the machine and enter text by tapping and swiping the display. In addition, the iPad Pro has a connection for an optional smart Keyboard or you can use a digital stylus called Apple Pencil on the touchscreen.

REAR

1 iSight Camera

Each iPad model has a rear-facing stills and video camera of varying quality. As for the latest iPad

models, the iPad, iPad Air and iPad mini tablets have an 8-megapixel camera with 1080p high-definition video recording, while the iPad Pro has a 12-megapixel camera with 4K video recording.

2 SIM Card Slot

This feature is only available in Wi-Fi + Cellular models. It holds the Nano-SIM card your telecommunications company will give you to access their data networks. The cover is easily removed using the SIM card tool supplied or an ordinary paper clip. Your iPad can connect to fast 4G LTE networks. The most recent iPad Pro modles have an embedded Apple SIM which allows you to connect to data plans on selected cellular networks direct from the iPad itself.

3 Lightning Connector

The original 30-pin dock connector changed to the smaller Lightning connector. The dock connector allows you to hook up to your computer, power charger, camera connector and other accessories. The iPad Pro also has a smarty connector for linking to a wireless keyboard.

4 Speakers

The speaker grills are at the bottom edge of your iPad, so make sure that they are not obscured by the cover you use. The iPad Pro range has four speakers, two on top, two on the bottom.

5 Volume Buttons

With the rocker button, you press one end to turn the sound up and the other to turn it down.

Hot Tip

Cleverly, the iPad remembers two volume settings: one for the volume you set when using headphones and the other for the sound level when using the speaker.

6 Side Switch

This has been phased out on some newer models. On devices where it remains, it can do one of two things. By default, it is used to lock the orientation of the iPad, so it stays in either vertical (portrait) or horizontal (landscape) mode. If you go to Settings, you can change it to be a mute switch that turns the iPad's volume off.

INSIDE THE iPAD

With each new model the iPad has become faster and more capable. Here we look at the main features.

Above: The iPad unpacked! Complex and sleek, the iPad is also surprisingly environmentally friendly, boasting many eco features, including a recyclable aluminium and glass enclosure.

Memory (RAM)

As each new generation of iPad does more, more memory is needed for the operating system and apps. The iPad Pro now has 6GB of RAM because it deals with labour-intensive tasks. However, for most users, the 3GB of RAM with the new iPad mini is more than enough.

Processor

Each generation of the iPad has seen an increase in the power of the processor. With faster processors and more memory, the top end iPads can take advantage of new features in the iOS and smoothly open two apps on the screen at the same time. The latest iPad Mini, Air and Pro models feature Apple's A12 Bionic (A12X on the iPad Pro).

> **Hot Tip**
>
> **The A12 X Bionic processor gives the iPad Pro models 90% faster CPU performance over its predecessor.**

Storage Options

However much space you need to store your music, videos and photos, you'll probably end up wanting more. Each series has different sizes – 32 GB, 64 GB, 128 GB and 256 GB. The top-end iPad Pro has 1 terabyte (TB) of storage. Typically, this would allow you to store:

- **16 GB**: 2,000 songs, 7,000 photos, 22 hours of video
- **32 GB**: 4,000 songs, 14,000 photos, 42 hours of video
- **64 GB**: 9,000 songs, 28,000 photos, 86 hours of video
- **128GB**: 18,000 songs, 56,000 photos, 170 hours of video
- **256GB**: 32,000 songs, 110,000 photos, 310 hours of video

Hot Tip

Don't forget to allow space for the larger file sizes of HD games, movies and photos you may want to view on the Retina display.

Rather than carry everything around with you, you can use online storage services, such as Apple's iCloud, for your music, files and apps, downloading them only when you want them. However, that may not always be convenient. Downloads can be costly on 4G and you may not always have Wi-Fi access when you need it.

Wi-Fi/Cellular

All versions of the iPad are available with just Wi-Fi or with Wi-Fi + Cellular. With a SIM card and subscription from a mobile provider, you can use their data networks to surf the web, get email, etc. No voice services are included on any iPad models, so you can't make a call as you can with the iPhone (except over Wi-Fi through services such as Skype and FaceTime).

High-speed Cellular

The latest iPad cellular models support 4G LTE (4G is the fourth generation of mobile networks: LTE, or Long Term Evolution, is a type of 4G technology). 4G promises speeds about five times faster than existing 3G services. However, where 4G coverage is still spotty, the latest iPads also include support for the faster 3G wireless technologies.

Bluetooth

Bluetooth is the wireless technology that lets you swap data quickly over short distances. The version on the latest iPads is Bluetooth 4.2 is faster and uses less power than previous versions.

It will still work with your existing Bluetooth 5.0 accessories, such as wireless keyboards, photo uploaders, etc. However, you'll only get the full benefit of its energy efficiency if your devices support the new standard.

Smart Cover

The clever magnetic system of the Smart Cover switches your iPad on when you lift the cover and puts it to sleep when you close it. These are sold separately, but extremely handy.

Battery Life

Despite differences in screen resolution and processor power, battery life is the same across all iPads. Each model has about 10 hours of power if used with Wi-Fi.

Above:
The Smart Cover, as well as waking, sleeping and protecting your iPad, is also a handy stand for reading, watching and typing.

Above: From the main lock screen swipe from left to right to see the Today view. It hosts calendar events, notifications, suggested apps and more.

Hot Tip

In practice, battery life greatly depends on how you use the iPad. You can help the power to last longer by adjusting screen brightness and reducing, or turning off, notifications, location services and push email.

iPAD BASICS

Getting started with your iPad is simple and opens up a new world of communication and fun.

SET UP YOUR iPAD

When you get your brand new iPad, there's remarkably little in the box: just the iPad, power cord and not much else. There's no manual, which is one reason why this book can help to get you off to the best start. The set up process differs slightly depending on your iOS version, but here's how it goes for new iPads running iOS 12. You'll need an internet connection to get going.

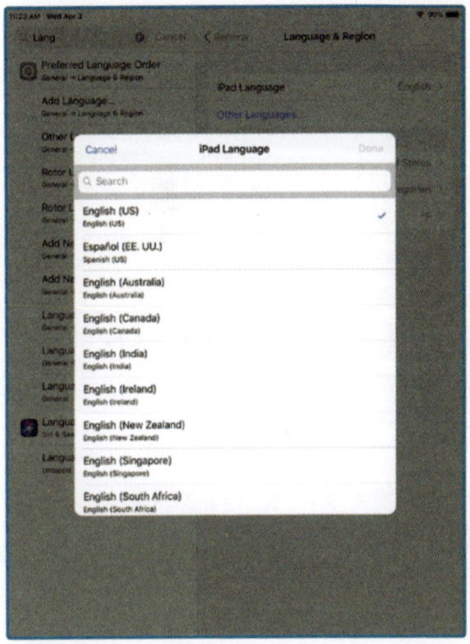

Above: Part of the iPad set up process asks you to select the language you want to use.

Step-by-step

1. A brand new iPad comes partly charged, so you can start straight away. Turn it on by pressing the Sleep/Wake button on the top and sliding the button across to start.

2. Pick the language you want to use, by tapping on it. A blue tick will appear beside it. Tap the blue arrow to continue.

3. If your iPad is running iOS 11 or later, you can use the Quick Set-up functionality. This allows you to skip many of the below steps by importing your saved Wi-Fi passwords, settings and favourite apps. When prompted bring your second device close to your new iPad and follow the instructions on screen. Given this book is aimed at newcomers to iOS, we'll assume that this feature probably isn't going to be one you'll use.

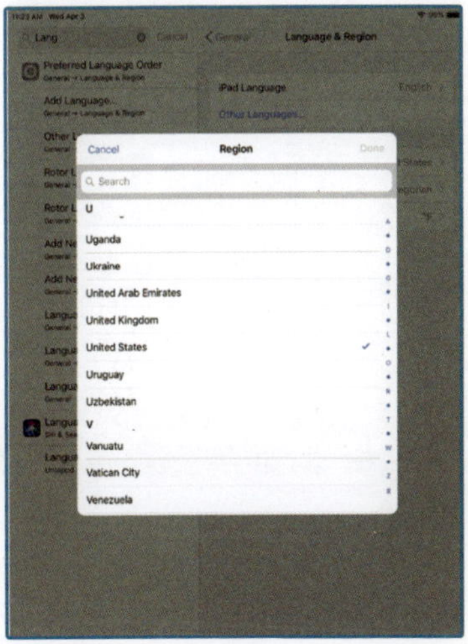

Above: You may need to choose your location by selecting the country you live in from the list.

4. If you're not using Quick Start, you'll be asked to connect to your Wi-Fi network next. A list will open of those available. A lock beside a name shows it is secured and you will need a password to use it. Tap on your chosen network name. Alternatively, if you purchased a Wi-Fi + Cellular option you can use your mobile connection to set up. Make sure you place the active SIM card in the tray before you turn on the iPad.

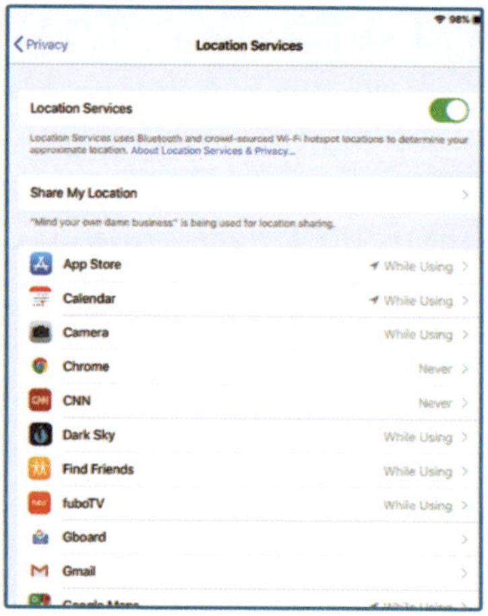

Above: Turn on Location Services to share your location through mapping and social media apps.

5. You'll be asked to set up the Touch ID feature. Follow the instructions and place a thumb or finger on the home button. This will allow you to unlock your device and authenticate purchases. You'll also be asked to create a passcode, which is used if you want to add more fingerprints. If you have an iPad Pro with Face ID, you can train the iPad to recognize your face here too.

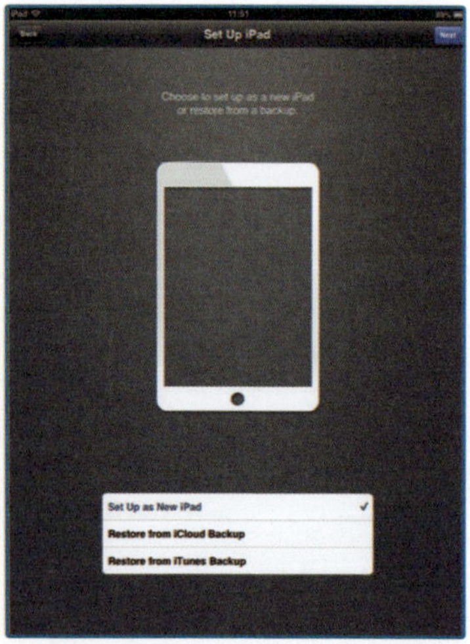

Step 6: Choose whether you want to set up your device as a new iPad or transfer data from an old iPad.

6. Now, it's time to activate your iPad. If this is your first iPad, select Set Up as New iPad and tap the Next button in the top corner. If you are transferring your data from a previous iPad, select one of the other options to transfer from iCloud or iTunes.

Step 7: Set up an Apple ID, or sign in with an existing Apple ID, so that you can download apps from App Store and access iTunes.

7. To get the most from your iPad, you need an Apple ID, which is also used to set up your iTunes account. Sign In with an Apple ID if you already have one. Otherwise, Create a Free Apple ID takes you through the process.

8. Next you'll be asked to set up the Siri voice assistant in iOS 12.

9. Depending on what version you're using Apple will ask you to set up a number of features. You may want to share your location through mapping and social media apps. To be able to do this, tap Enable Location Services here and then tap Next. In iOS 12 you can also set up a Screen Time app to help you with monitoring your usage.

10. The usual terms and conditions appear for you to agree before you can proceed.

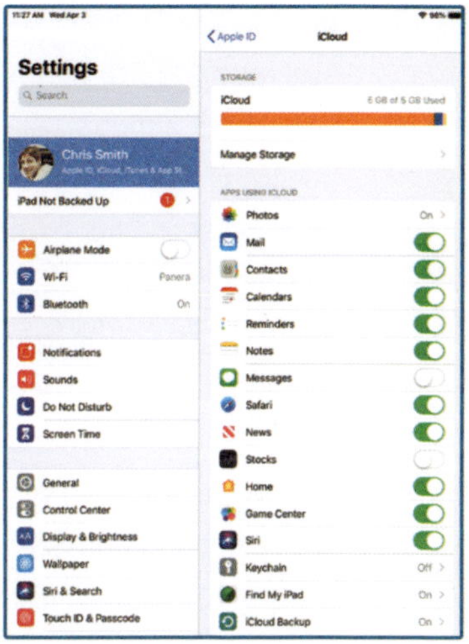

Step 10: iCloud is an extremely useful way of storing, backing up and sharing data across different devices.

11. During this process you'll also be asked to activate features like Apple Pay (*see* page 244), iCloud backups for your data and iCloud Keychain which syncs passwords for your accounts across multiple devices.

12. Before completing set up you'll be asked whether you want the iOS software to update to the next available version automatically.

Mobile Connections

If you have a cellular iPad, you will need to install the SIM card, provided separately by the mobile network company. Open the SIM card holder on the side of the iPad – using the pin provided – and put in the SIM card. Turn the iPad on and tap the Settings icon then Cellular Data and check this is set to On.

Hot Tip

If you are unsure about any services offered, tap the link at the bottom of the screen for help.

Wi-Fi

All iPad models can use Wi-Fi. Increasingly, hotels, cafés, restaurants, airports, railway stations and the like offer free Wi-Fi. There are also networks of public hotspots – Wi-Fi access points – where you can connect. Some are subscription based, others are free. To connect, tap the Settings icon on the Home screen. Tap Wi-Fi and then On. Under Choose a Network you'll see a list of those available. The signal strength is shown by the number of bars on the wireless symbol. The lock shows that it is a secure network and needs a password to access it. Tap the one you want to use to activate it.

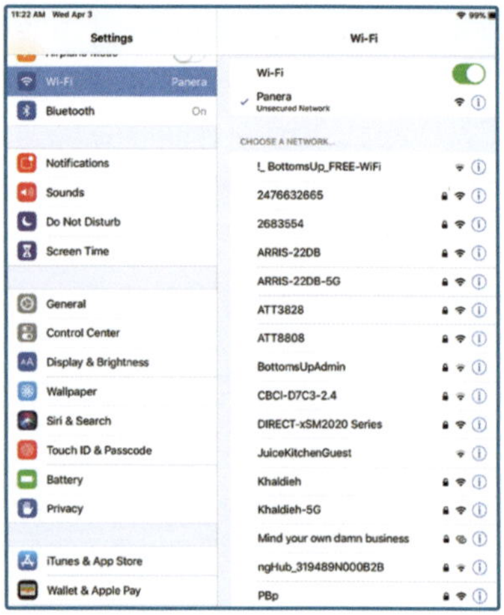

Above: To activate a Wi-Fi connection choose a network from the list and enter the password.

Notifications

While it's good to know what's going on and needs your attention, previous versions of Notifications were distracting. Now you decide when, where – or if – notifications appear.

Access the Cover Sheet

- If the device is unlocked, put your finger at the top of the display and swipe it down. The **Cover Sheet**, a representation of the lock screen, slides into view, showing any alerts that require attention. They can be from news apps, emails, messages or anything in between.

- Tap **individual items** to view them. This will take you to the app that created them and show you, for example, the message or email that you were notified about.

- Notifications can also appear on your iPad's **Lock screen**. Slide your finger on the notification and it will **unlock the iPad** and go to the **relevant app**.

- You can **select** which apps send notifications and whether they appear on the Lock Screen by **tweaking your settings**:

Hot Tip

If notifications show on your Cover Sheet or Lock screen their preview contents (e.g. the first few lines of an email) could be seen by anyone. Change this by tapping the Settings icon, then Notifications and Show Previews, and then choosing Never.

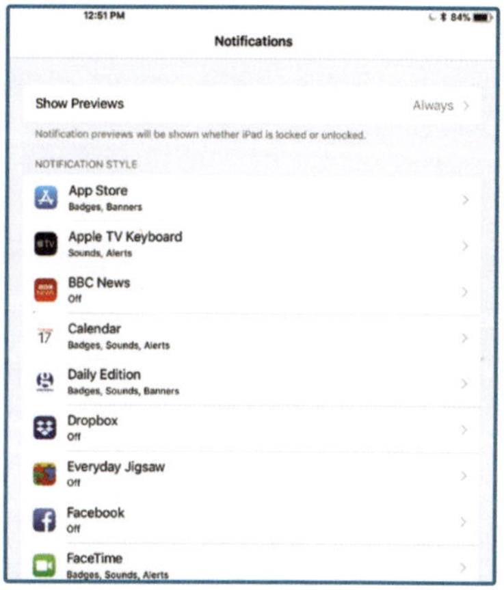

Above: By tapping the Settings icon on the Home screen and selecting Notifications, you can edit which apps you wish to receive them for.

1. Tap the **Settings icon** on the Home screen and select **Notifications**. A list of your apps will appear.

2. Tap on an app and you will see toggles for different settings. Switch **Allow Notifications** to off (it will turn grey) to **turn off notifications** from this app completely. Alternatively, you can turn off **Show on Lock Screen** to stop notifications from this app appearing on the Lock screen.

Bluetooth

There are several wireless accessories that enhance your iPad – such as an external speaker or wireless headset – most of which connect via Bluetooth.

- Tap the **Settings icon** then **Bluetooth** and then switch it **On**.

- Under **Other Devices** is a list of nearby **Bluetooth devices**. To connect they must be paired with your iPad. Select your device. You may be asked for **a passcode to pair** (if unsure try 0000). Not all devices require this, and others have dedicated buttons to enable Bluetooth pairing.

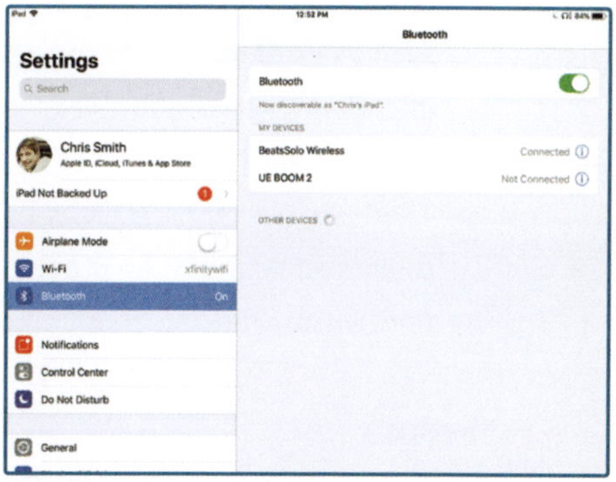

Above: You can turn on Bluetooth within the Settings app to pair your iPad with wireless accessories such as a wireless keyboard.

Print

While the iPad saves paper, as you can carry all your documents electronically, there are times when you do need to print something out – whether it's a report or directions.

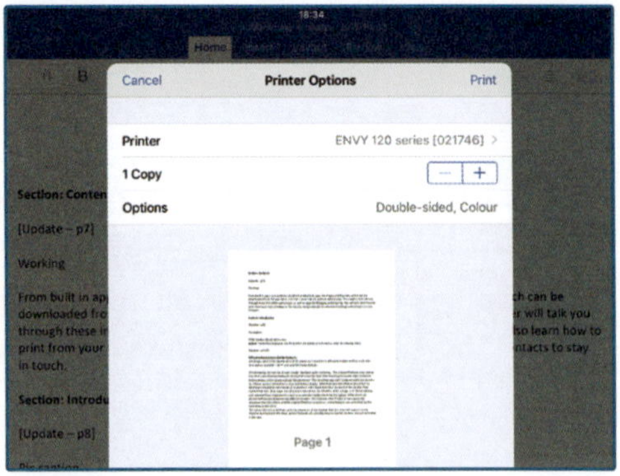

Above: You can print documents within some apps by tapping the share icon, then Print and selecting the options you want.

- Built in to the iPad is support for printing wirelessly to **AirPrint-enabled printers**. All that's necessary is for the printer to be on the **same wireless network** as the iPad. You can **print direct** to AirPrint-enabled printers from built-in iPad apps such as Mail, Photos, Safari, Notes and Maps.

- To print a document within an app, tap the Share icon (an arrow protruding from a box) then **Print**. Sometimes, in apps like Pages, the print setting is hiding in the '**More' menu**, represented by three dots. Press **Select Printer** and choose one from the list. Set the printer options (these are generally fairly limited and differ between apps) and tap **Print**.

- If you don't have an AirPrint-friendly printer, all is not lost. There are **third-party apps**, such as **Printopia** (Mac only) or **Fingerprint** (Mac or Windows) that turn your computer into a print server and will let you print from your iPad or iPhone.

- There are also apps, such as **PrintCentral** (Mac or Windows) for printing from your iPad to any wireless printer, provided it is on the **same** Wi-Fi network. They also connect to printers attached to your computer.

Search

You know the exact piece of information you need is on your iPad but can't remember where. Search will hunt through all the built-in apps, an individual app or all apps at once to find it. The Search box appears in the Today view, which also features prevalent information from your calendar.

To access the Search box from the home page or lock screen swipe right. To access it from any page (like a Safari web page), flick down from the top of the screen and then swipe right. As you start entering text in the Search field, results begin to appear.

Above: Swipe right on the home page or lock screen to reveal the Search box at the top.

NAVIGATING YOUR iPAD

The iPad is remarkably simple to use, considering the technical complexity behind it. Here's a handy primer on the gestures to use to speed your way around your iPad.

Gestures

- **Tap**: The most common gesture, the touch equivalent of the mouse click.
- **Double-tap**: Tap twice in quick succession. Primarily used for zooming in on a web page or section of text.
- **Tap and hold**: Works similarly to the right-click on a mouse. In text, for example, this will give you options for cutting and pasting words or whole sentences. Tap on the screen and hold your finger in place and a small pop-up menu appears.
- **Scroll**: The touch equivalent of using the scroll wheel on a mouse to navigate down a web page quickly. Press your finger lightly on the screen then run it up or down to move through the list or web page. On some apps, such as Contacts or Music, there is an alphabetic scrollbar on the side. Press the letter you want and the page will automatically scroll to that part of the list.

- **Flick**: An extension of the scroll, this allows you to work your way through a long list, such as Contacts, more quickly. Press your finger gently on the screen then flick up or down. The faster the flick, the quicker the scroll.

- **Swipe**: Another of the primary navigational aids. Swipe left or right to move through your Home screen pages and your images in Photos. Swipe up from the bottom of the screen to view the Control Centre. This also shows the multi-tasking view with cards representing all open apps.

- **Pinch**: To zoom in or to open something put your index finger and thumb together on the screen and slowly move them apart. To zoom out do the reverse. The faster you move your fingers, the quicker the zoom. The zoom in and out motions can also be used to go to view thumbnails of all currently open taps in Safari.

- **Rotate**: Turn everything upside down. Just put two fingers on the screen and make a circular gesture clockwise or anti-clockwise.

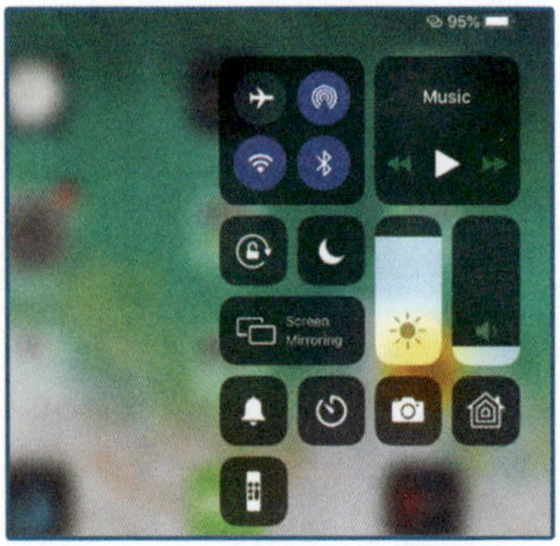

Above: Swipe down from the top right corner of the screen to access the Control Centre. From here, easily access your controls, including AirPlane Mode and Wi-Fi. In iOS 11 and earlier, you access this by swiping up from the bottom of the screen.

iOS 12 Gestures

With iOS 12 Apple brought some iPhone-style gestures to the iPad, adding to those included in iOS 11. Learning them will make it easier to navigate around your iPad.

- **Access Control Centre**: Swipe down from a tab in the top right corner to access a Control Centre with access to quick settings.

- **Summon the Dock**: The dock containing pinned and frequently used apps is hidden when working within apps. You can summon it with a short swipe up from the bottom of the display.

- **View Open Apps**: Perform a swipe up from the bottom of the display into the middle to show the apps you currently have open. This will enable you to switch between, or close them down. Double clicking the home button also works here.

- **Return To Home Screen**: Perform a long swipe up from the bottom of the display.
- **Move between apps**: Use four fingers to swipe left and right between the apps you have open.

Status Symbols

Just like your computer's menu bar, the iPad has a number of status icons at the top of the screen that show what's going on. Icons for your mobile and Wi-Fi connections are on the left, with other services on the right.

Signal strength: You'll only see this if you have a Cellular iPad. The more bars, the stronger the network signal. One bar shows little to no service, five bars and all is well.

Carrier: At the end of the signal strength indicator is the name of the mobile data network provider, such as EE or 02-UK.

Wi-Fi strength: This radar-like symbol shows when you're connected to a Wi-Fi network. The more visible bars, the stronger the reception is.

Personal hotspot: The two interlinked circles show that your iPad is sharing its high-speed mobile data connection to link a computer or other device, such as an iPod Touch, to the internet.

Airplane Mode: This switches off any communication systems likely to interfere with a plane's controls and lets you can carry on using other apps, such as iBook. It turns off GPS, Bluetooth and Wi-Fi, but you can override individual settings.

Above: Activate Aiplane mode by toggling to On in the Settings menu. Note the plane icon in status bar.

VPN: Shows you are using a Virtual Private Network (VPN) as a secure connection across the internet to your office systems.

Syncing icon: This rotating circle appears when the iPad is trying to make a connection over your Wi-Fi or Bluetooth network.

Battery status: When your battery is charging, this icon shows a small lightning bolt. Beside it the percentage figures show how much battery power is left.

Location Services: This arrow appears when an app, such as Maps, is using Location Services.

Bluetooth: This is turned on and is being used by your iPad to pair with another device, such as a wireless keyboard.

Alarm clock: Get ready for your early morning wake-up; this shows you have set an alarm in the Clock app.

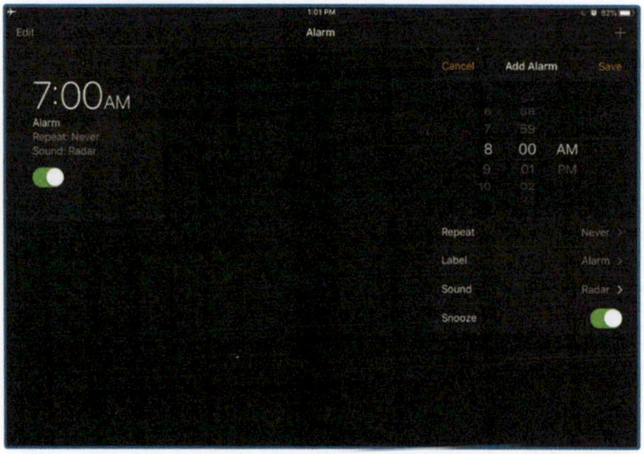

Above: Set an alarm by scrolling through the numbers wheel until it shows your chosen time.

Do not Disturb: The do not disturb or moon icon shows that no notifications will appear on screen and that no sounds will be made while your iPad is locked or sleeping. This feature is not available on iPad 1.

Lock: The small padlock in the centre at the top of your screen indicates that your iPad is locked.

Orientation lock: Wondering why your apps won't change from portrait to landscape? If this icon is in the status bar, it means that the orientation has been locked. To unlock it, double-press the Home button, swipe to the right and tap on the orientation button, so the lock disappears.

Multitasking

With multitasking you can switch between tasks without having to close them. You can, for example, be using one app – such as your email – and click a link that then opens another, such as Safari. Later iPads go further with the Slide Over and Split View features (*see* pages 38–39). Picture in Picture (available on iPad Pro series, iPad Air or later) scales down FaceTime or the video you're watching to a corner of the display so you can open a second app.

Multitasking Screen

In iOS 12, the multitasking screen has been separated out from the Control Centre. Now it simply features your open apps. Here's how to access it:

- **To open it**: Double tap the home button or swipe up from the bottom of the displays, stopping half way. You'll see thumbnails of each open app and others by swiping left and right.

- **To switch to another app**: Simply tap the preview of the app you want and this will open it full screen.

- **To shut down any of the open apps**: Tap and hold the app's preview page and swipe up until it disappears at the top of the screen.

- **Dock**: In iOS 11, the floating dock remains present so you can tap an app to open it from here too.

Above: Double click the home button to access the multitasking menu on your iPad.

Control Centre

This is a great way to quickly alter key settings and in iOS 12 it's easier to access than ever. Swipe down from the tab in the top right corner and you'll see the Control Centre icons to the right of the screen. You can access the camera, clock, audio controls etc. If you have an Apple TV you can mirror the screens, and you can access quick controls for music currently playing.

Using Two Apps at Once

On newer iPad models, Apple has made multitasking easier by enabling us to use two apps at once. In iOS 11and iOS 12, these features are more powerful thanks to the ability to drag and drop content (like photos, text, etc.) from one app to another. For example, dragging an image from the Photos app directly into a new email window.

- **Slide Over**: This handy feature puts a smaller version of a second app on the right side of the screen. To use Slide Over open the first app, then summon the Dock with a brief swipe up. Choose the second app you wish to hold and then drag that icon up and towards the right of the screen. Release the icon. Now you can work within both apps.

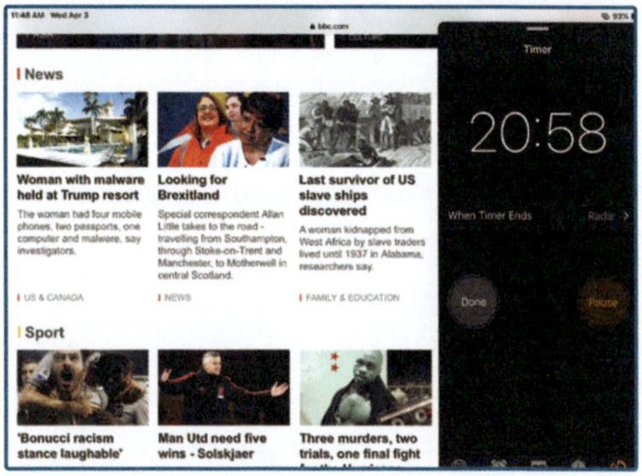

Above: Split View enables you to work in two apps at the same time and adjust how much screen each of the apps takes up.

> **Hot Tip**
>
> **Using a long press on certain Control Centre icons lets you access additional functionality (e.g. long pressing the camera icon allows you to shortcut to selfies, video and more).**

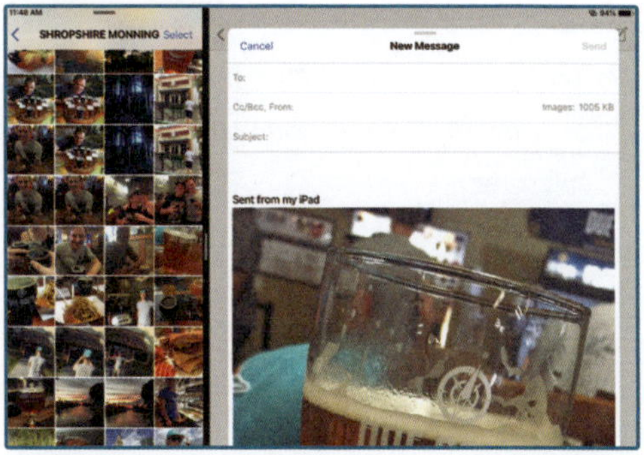

Above: Use Slide Over to add a second app to the screen. Here you can see Mail and Safari. You can also drag the web address from the bar in Safari into the New Message window.

- **Split View:** This is a similar concept but enables you to split the screen 70/30, 50/50 or 30/70. Drag the second app from the dock and pull it to the far-left or far-right of the screen and release it. Drag the dividing line left or right to alter the proportions.

USING YOUR iPAD

Once you get used to the touchscreen keyboard, it's as quick and easy to use as any conventional computer keyboard. Also, if you decide you don't want to type, ask Siri to do it for you.

On-screen Keyboard

What gives you the power to work on the iPad just as efficiently as any laptop is the virtual keyboard. In apps that use it, simply touch the area of the screen where you want to write and the keyboard appears. Unlike most keyboards, the iPad's doesn't type the letter when you press the key, but waits until you lift your finger off. There is a benefit. If you press the wrong key, simply slide your finger to the correct one before taking your finger off.

Three-in-one Keyboard

The main keyboard just has the letters and basic punctuation, with two shift keys for entering uppercase letters. To enter numbers or some of the less frequently used punctuation marks, tap the key marked .?123 to switch keyboard. To return to the first keyboard, press the ABC key, or to access the third keyboard, which has the least frequently used keys, tap #+=.

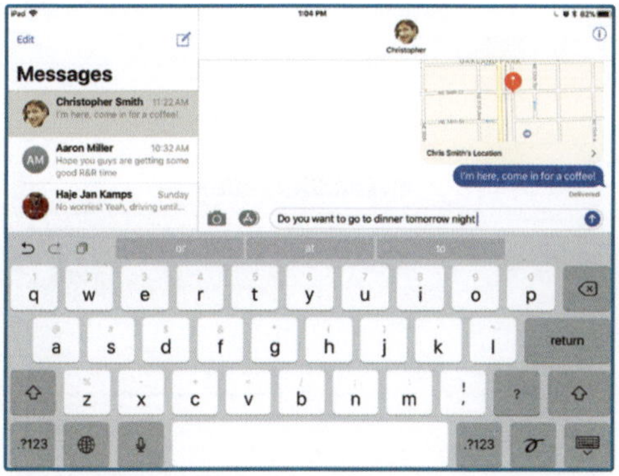

Above: In iOS 11, you can see numbers, punctuation and some symbols placed above letters.

Easy Punctuation

iOS 11 debuts a keyboard design that makes typing punctuation, numbers and symbols even easier. You'll see them shaded above the letter keys. All you need to do is press down on a key and drag down with a finger until the symbol replaces the letter. Then release your finger.

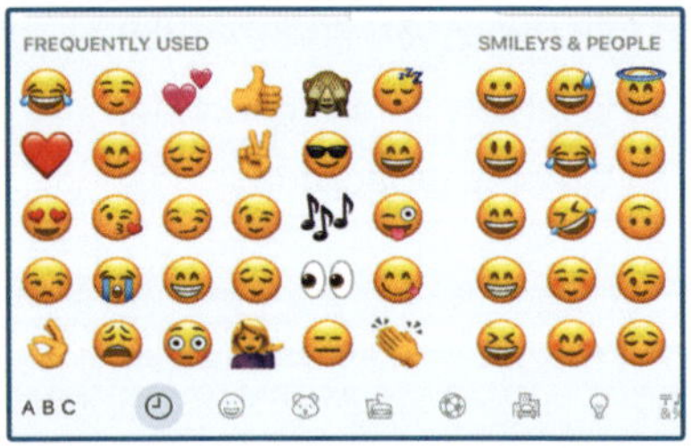

Above: The emoji keyboard offers quick access to characters that can add colour to your text.

Cap That

Although it won't happen very often, there may be times when you need to type in all caps. To do so, double-tap the shift key. It will turn blue to show the caps lock is on. When finished, tap once more to disable caps lock. If this doesn't work, you will need to enable the caps lock. To do so, go to Settings, General then Keyboard and switch Enable Caps Lock to On.

Emoji

Emoji are the small characters that can be added to supplement text or even replace it. There's everything from facial expressions, food and drink, to musical instruments and road signs. To access them hit the smiley face icon in the bottom left of the keyboard.

Editing Text

No matter how good your typing is, mistakes will always happen. With the latest operating system you'll see the icons for cut, copy and paste at the top of the keyboard.

- **To correct your text**: Tap where you want the cursor to be and press the backspace key (a left-pointing arrow with an X inside).
- **Magnifier**: It can be fiddly to get the cursor where you want it. You can tap-and-hold the text until a magnifier appears. Move this around the text and when you find the precise point you want, let go.
- **To select a word**: Tap the cursor, and the selection buttons appear. Double tap

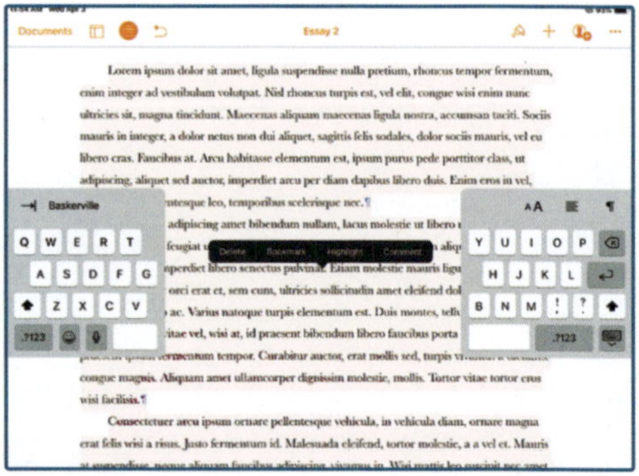

Above: To reveal more of your screen, split the keyboard in two by placing two fingers in the centre and sliding them apart. Reinstate a single keyboard by putting one finger on each side and sliding them together.

a word, and it is selected and highlighted in blue with two grab points at either end. Drag these either way to select more text. Double-tap selects the whole paragraph.

- **Once the text is selected**: Option buttons appear for cutting or copying it. The Paste option will replace the highlighted text with the last text cut. Depending on the app used, other features, such as sharing, styling or text formatting, may be available.

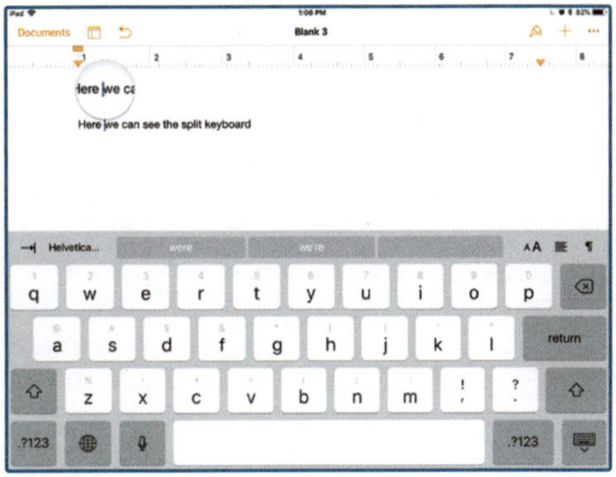

Above: Use the magnify tool to highlight a word or selection of words with greater control and precision. Option buttons will be displayed, allowing you to copy, cut and paste as desired.

Shake It All About

A quick way to delete a message you've written, get back an email you've archived, or to undo an edit you've made is to shake your iPad lightly. A dialogue box will appear to ask if you would like to undo the last action – tap Undo if you would.

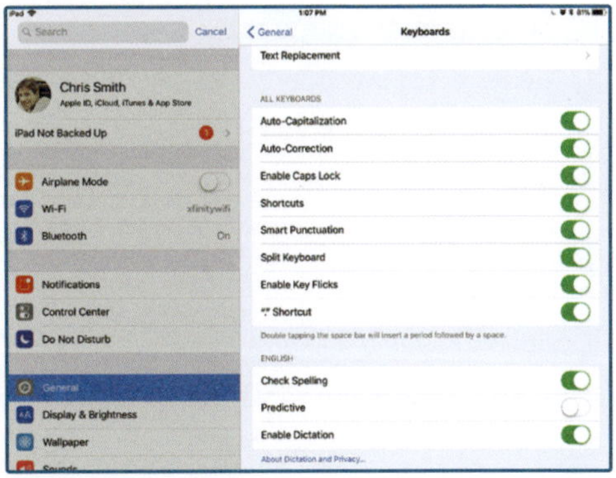

Above: To stop your iPad from predicting what you want to write toggle Predictive to off in the settings menu.

Predictive Text

Rather like someone watching over your shoulder, the iPad will try to be helpful and guess what you're typing. Its suggestions will appear at the top of the QuickType keyboard. Press the relevant suggestion to accept it.

The accuracy of the iPad's suggestions should improve the more you type, as it builds up a dictionary of words you commonly use. However, some people do find this feature deeply irritating. To stop it, go to Settings, General, Keyboard and turn off Predictive.

Voice Dictation

Siri first appeared on the iPad 3 and has been on every iPad since. You can use Siri to dictate what you want to write. With time and a little practice this can be easier and more convenient than using the on-screen keyboard to type your text.

1. Check that voice dictation is turned on. Press the Settings icon, select General, followed by Keyboard. Then scroll down to tap Enable Dictation.

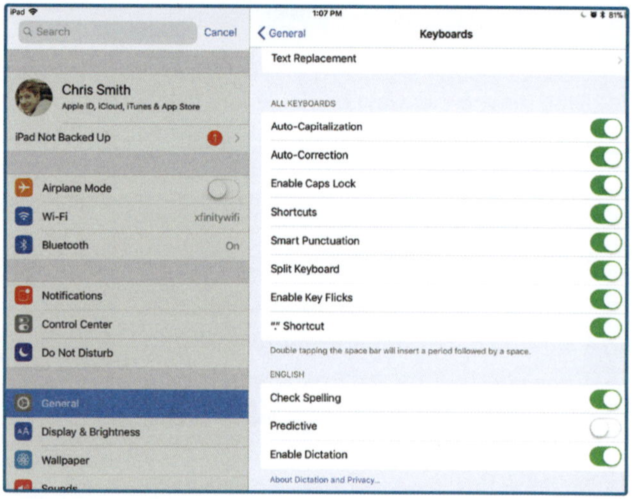

Step 1: Turning on Dictation in the keyboard section of the General Settings menu.

3. Open the app you want to use, such as Pages for a document or Mail for email.

4. Tap the screen, so the on-screen keyboard appears. In the lower left-hand corner is the voice dictation logo, which looks like an old-fashioned radio microphone.

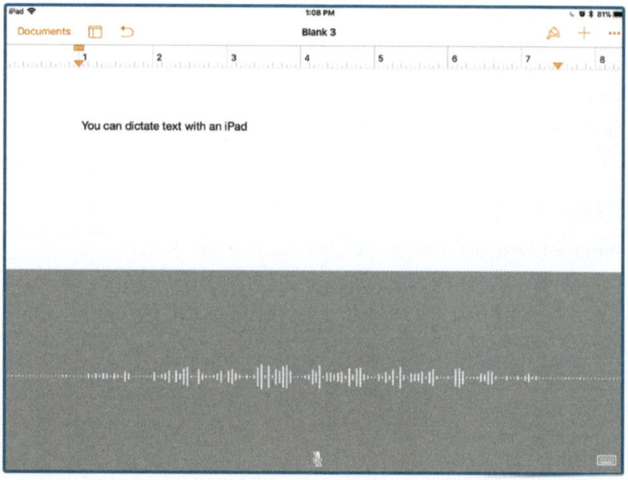

Step 4: Touch the microphone icon at the bottom of the on-screen keyboard to begin dictating your text to Siri.

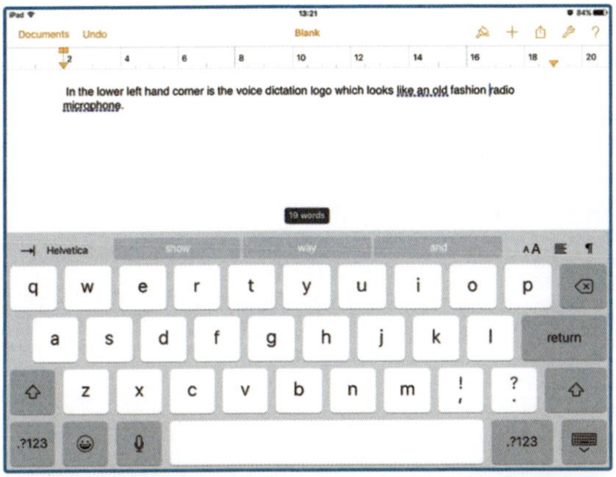

Step 7: You can make corrections using the on-screen keyboard.

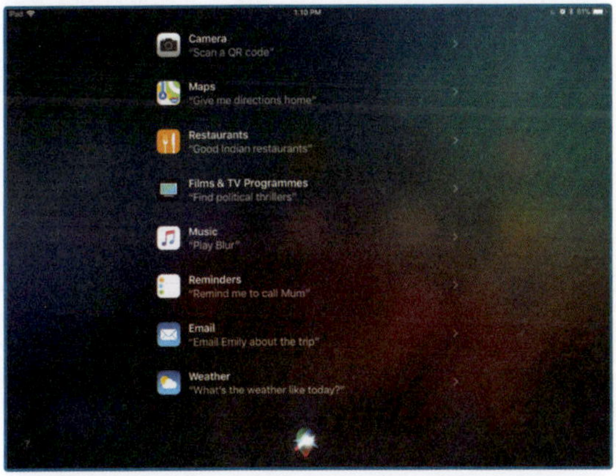

Above: Siri works with many more apps in iOS 11. This list is just some of the options you have to use Apple's voice-activated digital assistant.

5. Tap this and start speaking. You will need to include punctuation commands, such as comma, new paragraph, etc. Take care to pronounce special symbols, such as the 'at sign' – @ – seen in emails, clearly.

6. When you've finished dictating, tap the keyboard icon again. Your text will appear soon.

7. If you make a mistake, or the dictated text is wrongly transcribed, simply tap where you want to edit and the on-screen keyboard appears. Use this to make your corrections. Siri's done well in the example above – only the end of 'fashioned' has been left off.

8. To add more, repeat the steps.

Hot Tip

Any app that uses the on-screen keyboard should allow dictation, as the feature is built into the iOS, not the program.

Hot Tip

The more you use dictation, the better it gets as it adapts to your accent.

APPS

Your iPad comes with just 25 or so apps already loaded, covering the basics from writing notes to playing music. When you want to do more, such as tracking the stars or mind mapping, you can be sure there is an app for it.

GET AND USE APPS

There's no shortage of apps for your iPad. Currently, there are more than one million free or paid-for apps in the App Store that are specifically designed for the iPad.

Above: When the App Store is open, five useful buttons are displayed on the lower toolbar.

Finding New Apps

You can find new apps through Apple's App Store, which can be accessed through the App Store app, which has a blue icon, preloaded on the iPad.

Apple ID

To use the App Store, you have to be connected to the internet (via Wi-Fi or mobile) and have an Apple ID. You probably entered this when you activated your iPad. If not, go to Settings > Your Name > iTunes & App Store and enter your details or create a new ID. You'll be asked to set up payment details too.

Using the App Store App

Accessing the App Store from the iPad itself lets you download new apps directly. Tap the App Store icon to open it and you'll see there are five buttons on the lower toolbar.

- **Today**: The homepage for the App Store is curated by Apple's editors to bring you a compelling selection of trending apps across all genres, exciting new titles, collections and so on.
- **Games**: The landing point for the latest and greatest games, arranged into curated categories and the current charts for free and paid titles.

Hot Tip

You can restore apps that you have deleted. From the Today tab, tap your profile picture and select Purchased and then select Not On This iPad. Find the app you would like to restore and then tap the Cloud icon to download it. You won't have to pay again.

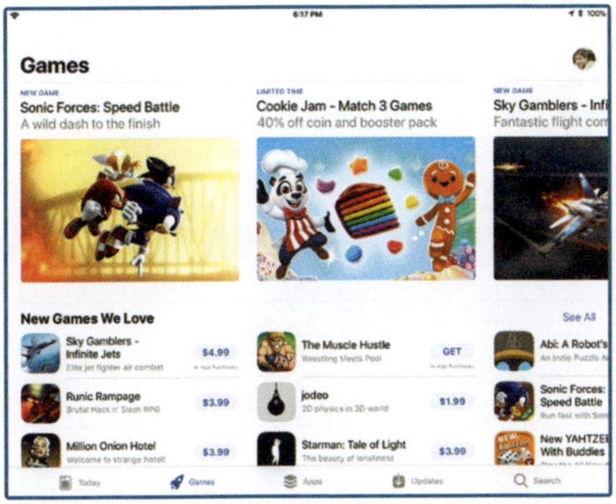

Above: Tap the Games tab to see the best new games available.

- **Apps**: Similar to Games but for more general purpose apps. You might see sections like 'New Apps We Love', alongside charts for free and paid apps, as well as categories. These include: lifestyle, photography, sports, travel, and music, to name a few. There are many categories to choose from so this is the best place to browse.
- **Updates**: If any of the apps you have installed on your iPad have new versions available, you'll see them represented by a red numbered badge next to the Updates tab. From here you can update them individually or choose to Update All. If you have a Wi-Fi + Cellular iPad this is best done when using a Wi-Fi connection.
- **Search**: If you're searching for a specific title, you can type the title here. Suggestions will load as you type.

Choosing Your Apps

There are specially selected lists of new and popular apps. Often these are related to seasonal or topical events, ranging from winter holidays to Halloween and major sporting occasions. To find out more about an app, click its icon to access a dedicated page with details of what it does, screenshots, and customer ratings and reviews for each version. On the iPad this opens in a pop up window when you tap the icon.

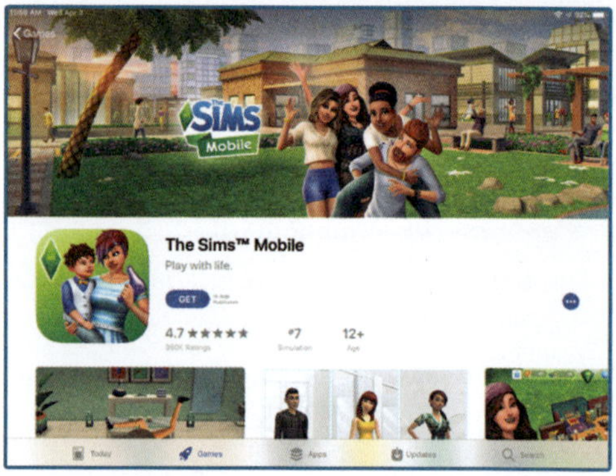

Step 1: Tap an app's icon to open a new page dedicated to that app, featuring reviews and download information.

Downloading Apps from the iPad

1. Once you've found the app you would like to get, downloading it is very quick and easy. Tap an app's icon in the App Store and information about it will appear in a new window.

2. Scroll down to read a description or use the tabs to see ratings and reviews by other customers or related apps from the same developer that you might be interested in.

3. Tap the price button and then tap Buy. If it's not a paid-for app, tap the Get button (previously labelled Free) then Install.

Hot Tip

Tap an app to pause the download (useful if there are other apps you want to get first). Tap again to resart.

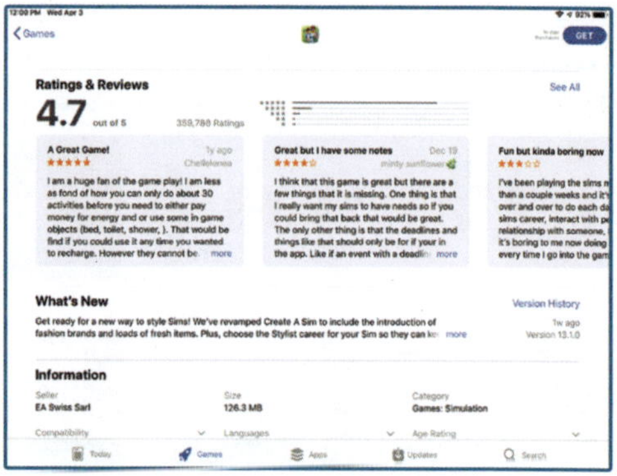

Step 2: The app's information page allows you to read ratings and reviews before you decide to download an app.

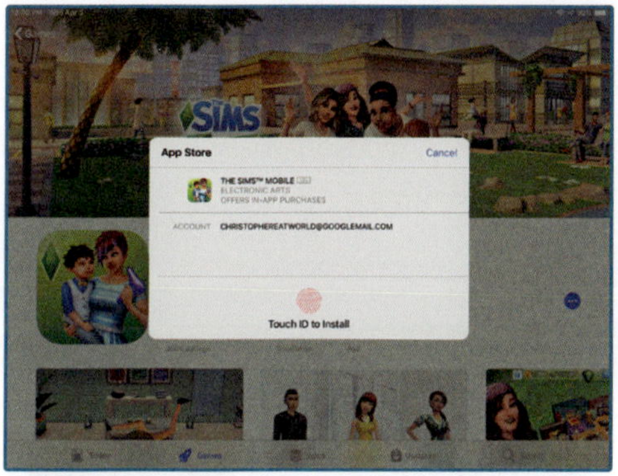

Step 3: Once you have decided to download an app, tap the Buy or Get button and you'll be asked to confirm.

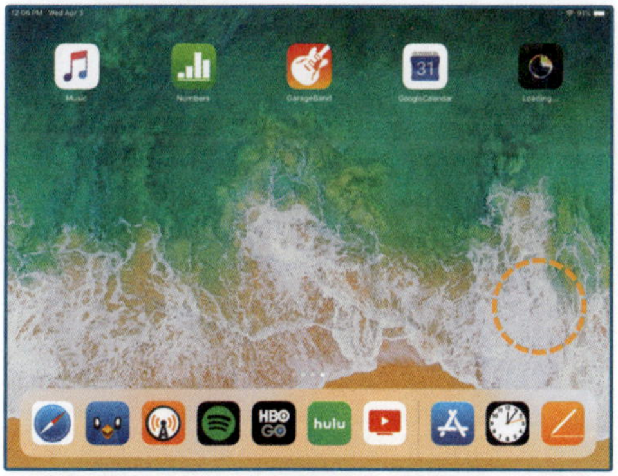

Above: Once downloaded, the new app can be accessed from the first available spot on your Home screens.

4. To stop you buying the same app twice the button will say Open, Install or Update after your purchase has gone through.

5. You may be asked to enter your Apple ID and password. Tap OK when ready. If you've enabled Touch ID for this purpose you can tap your finger to the home button to authenticate the installation.

6. The button is replaced by a progress bar. You can move off the page and open other apps while this is happening. Once the download is complete, the app appears on your Home screen and is ready to open.

7. If the app download is interrupted, it will start again automatically the next time you connect to the internet.

Hot Tip

Sync all your apps to your iPad automatically, no matter where they were originally downloaded. Tap the Settings icon then Your Name > iTunes & App Store and go to the Automatic Downloads section. Slide the switch beside Apps to On.

Open and Close Apps

Simply tap the app's icon to open it. To close it and return to the Home screen, just press the Home button. In fact, the app is just suspended. To fully close it, double-press the Home button to open the Multitasking screen, place your finger on the app's preview page and swipe up.

Arranging Your Apps

With so many apps available, you may soon have several pages of apps, but you can rearrange them to suit your preferences. Lightly press and hold the app's icon until it starts jiggling, then drag and drop it where you want it. If you want to move it to the next page of apps, drag it to the edge of the screen. When finished, press the Home button to stop the icons jiggling.

Above: Double-press the Home button to bring up the Multitasking screen and close apps by swiping up on their previews.

Organizing Apps in Folders

Several related apps can be grouped in folders. Tap and hold the icon of one app and drag it on top of another you wish to group it with. When you lift your finger, a folder will open with both apps inside. The folder is automatically given a name based on the apps included. To change this, tap in the box to access the on-screen keyboard and type

Above: Arrange apps on the Home screen of your iPad by tapping and holding an icon until it starts jiggling, and then dragging and dropping to rearrange.

a new name. Press the Home button when you are finished.

To ungroup the apps, tap the folder to open, then tap and hold one of the app's icons until it starts jiggling. Once in Edit mode, drag and drop each app icon out of the folder.

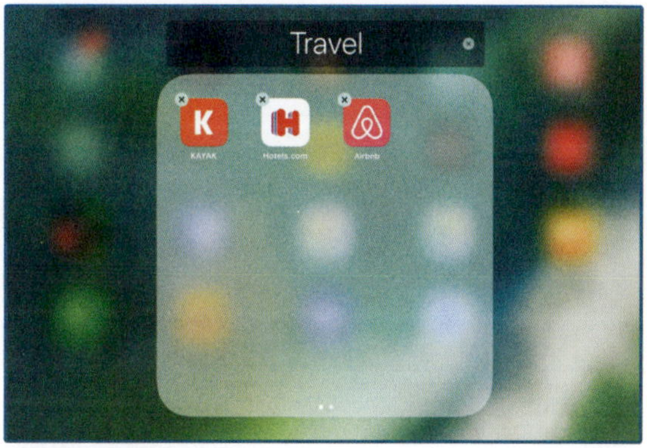

Above: Ungroup apps by tapping open a folder, holding an app icon until it jiggles and then dragging apps out the folder.

Remove Apps

To delete an app, tap and hold its icon, then press the small X in a white circle that appears in the top-left corner. Be sure you want to do this, as any data entered – such as financial information in an accounts app – will also be permanently removed.

Running iPhone Apps

Some iPhone apps can work just as well on the iPad. Because they are not specifically designed for the iPad they will usually run in a small window in the middle. You can enlarge the app by tapping the 2x button in the lower-right. If it's blurry or blocky, restore it to its original size by tapping the 1x button.

Hot Tip

If you tap and hold an app and the small black X doesn't appear, it means it is one of the default apps, pre-loaded on the iPad. Some of these can be deleted (like News) and some can't (like Messages).

Changing App Settings

Most apps keep the options for changing the way they work inside the app itself. Confusingly, though, some apps have a second set of options inside the iPad's Settings app. To access these, tap the Settings icon and select the app from the list on the left. The available options are shown on the right.

SYNCING

It's easier than ever to keep your personal information, music, video files and apps on your iPad in sync using iTunes, iCloud or other online cloud services.

SYNCING WITH ITUNES

As well as keeping all your information up to date, syncing is a good safety measure. Each time you sync your iPad with iTunes, a backup can be made of all your information. You can restore all your data from these backups. It also allows you to transfer music and videos.

Syncing by USB

1. Connect your iPad to the computer by USB cable. Open iTunes on your computer and your iPad appears as an icon in the top-left of the screen.

2. Click the iPad icon and you'll see the Summary tab with information about your iPad, along with several options. These include checking for software updates, choosing where you want to back up and general settings, such as automatically opening iTunes when the iPad is connected.

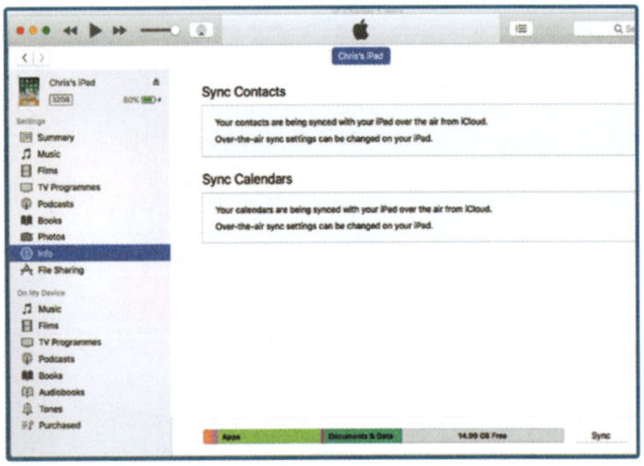

Step 1: To sync your iPad with your computer connect via USB cable.

3. Select the Info tab for options to sync your contacts and calendars with related Apple apps on the iPad.

4. Select the Music tab and check Sync Music. As the iPad has a smaller capacity than your computer, you probably don't want to sync your entire music library. Instead check Selected playlists, artists, albums and genres. Then go through the different categories and check the box beside the ones you want to transfer.

5. Go through the other tabs – Films, TV Programmes, Podcasts, Books, Photos – and select what you want to sync. When finished, click Apply to start the sync.

Syncing Wirelessly

To sync using Wi-Fi, ironically, you first have to connect your iPad with iTunes using a USB cable.

1. Click your iPad in iTunes and scroll to Options on the Summary tab. Check the box next to Sync with this iPad over Wi-Fi and click Apply.

2. Your iPad has to be on the same Wi-Fi network as the computer and the computer must also have iTunes open. If you don't see your iPad in the list of devices, quit and restart iTunes or restart your iPad. Then configure your sync options.

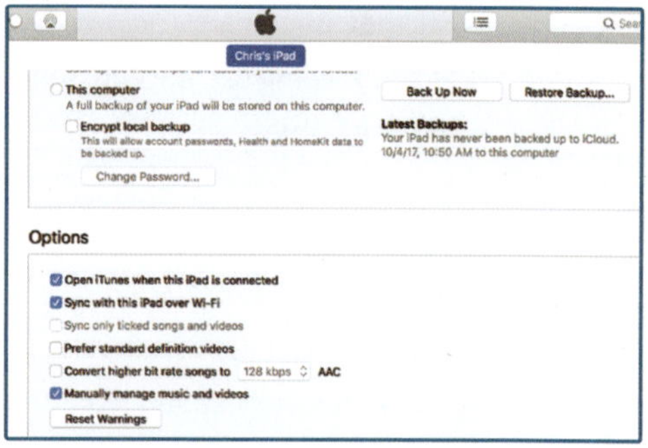

Above: Set up wireless sync using iTunes, so that you can sync your devices over Wi-Fi.

iCLOUD

Apple's online service enables you to keep everything in sync and store your music, photos, documents and apps securely online.

Setting Up iCloud

1. To set up and configure iCloud: tap Settings then tap your name beneath the search bar. Sign in with your Apple ID and password, or create one if you haven't yet done so.

2. Tap iCloud and choose which iCloud services you want to use: slide the switch to On.

3. iCloud Drive lets you safely store PDFs, images and any other kind of document in iCloud and sync it with your iPad using the iCloud Drive app.

4. Photos: the photos on any iOS device you have will show up in the Photos app on your iPad.

5. Mail, Contacts, Calendars, Reminders, Notes and News: these sync with relevant apps. Safari: this syncs your bookmarks, any open tabs and reading list. Backup: sends your data wirelessly to iCloud.

6. Keychain: keeps your passwords and credit card information safe and accessible. Find My iPad: locate your lost or stolen iPad. Home: if you have smart home devices these can be synced.

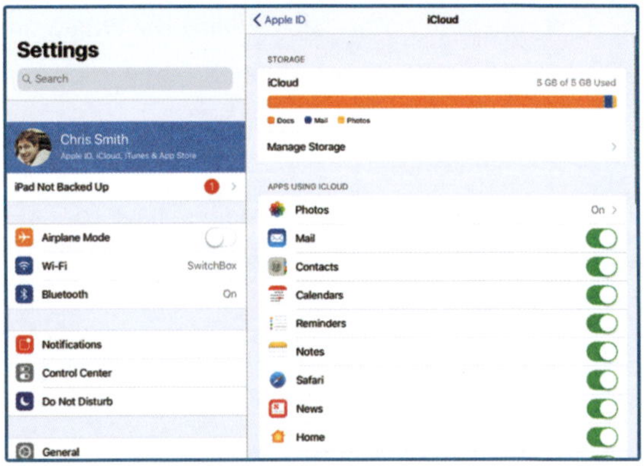

Above: To choose which iCloud services you want to use, toggle switches to On or Off accordingly. Safari will sync your bookmarks; Photos will allow you to see your photos from another iOS device on your iPad; and Notes will let you access your notes whatever device you have with you.

OTHER CLOUD SERVICES

While iCloud works well with the Mac and iOS devices (iPad, iPhone and iPod touch), not all its features are available on those that don't use Apple software. Fortunately, there are many other cloud services that work just as well with the iPad.

In the Cloud

Cloud services are online storage and syncing facilities. Your content is uploaded to the company's data centre, known metaphorically as 'the cloud'. Your stored content can be accessed via the internet, or downloaded wirelessly to your computer or iPad, whenever you want.

Cloud Apps

Many cloud services have an app for the iPad. Using this, you can access your documents and files stored in the cloud and keep them in sync. Several also have desktop software for your Mac or PC that works in a similar way. Cloud services you can use direct from your iPad include: Google Drive, OneDrive from Microsoft, Dropbox and Evernote.

FILES APP

New in iOS 11, Apple Files is one of the most fundamental changes to the iPad's software since its launch. It's a single repository all of your files, across iCloud Drive and third-party services. Everything can be accessed across iOS devices.

Using the Files App

To use Files you'll need to enable iCloud Drive on your iOS devices (see step 3, opposite). Once this is done, you'll see any files synced in an iCloud Drive app within the Files app. You can browse these, tap the Cloud icon to download them, and open and edit them.

Add Other Cloud Apps to Files

If you store your files via another service (such as Google Drive, Dropbox, Evernote, Box or OneDrive) you can integrate them into the Files app. Here's how:

1. Download the third-party app from the App Store and log in to your account. Then head back to Files and you should see a number 1 badge next to the Locations tab. Tap it and toggle the app in question to On.

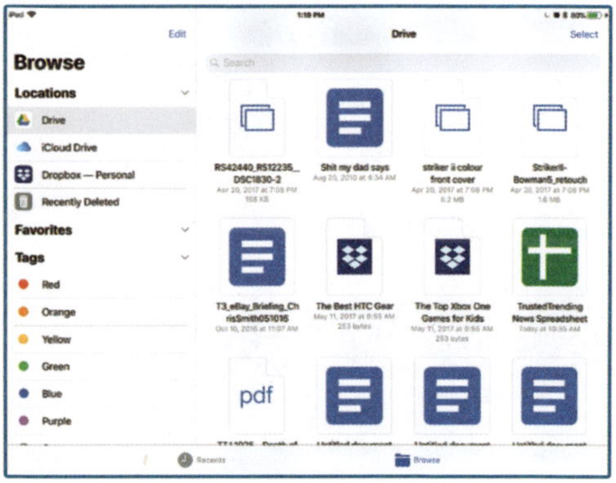

Above: You can add third-party apps to Apple Files, making it a single repository for all of your stuff.

2. Select the account in question to see your files. Then tap a file to view it. If you have the correct app (for example, Microsoft Word, Pages or Google Docs) installed you'll be able to edit it.

3. Once you've finished editing all changes will be synced back to all other devices automatically, meaning you'll be able to access the most up-to-date versions of all your files. You can easily share these by long pressing on a thumbnail in the document list and tap Share from the pop up menu.

GETTING CONNECTED

SURFING THE NET

Through the built-in Safari browser and your Wi-Fi or mobile connection to the internet, you can surf the web, view your favourite sites, update your blog and download files.

ACCESS WEBSITES

The high-quality screen makes browsing clear and bright, and with the Retina display on the latest iPads the web has never looked so good.

Browsing

- **Safari** on the iPad is a little different from the one on your **Mac** or **PC**. To open it, **tap** the Safari icon in the dock of commonly used applications at the bottom of the screen.
- When you open Safari, it will show the **last web page** you viewed, if any, or a favourite page you select.
- In the **top bar**, tap the screen and type the web address (**URL**) you want to visit. As you type, you'll see suggestions of previous pages you've visited, which you can **select** by tapping the address in the list. Tap the blue arrow on the keyboard when you've finished.

Hot Tip

Made a mistake? Clear the address bar at any time by tapping the X button on the far right.

Above: To visit a website use the onscreen keyboard to type the web address and press go.

Tab That

Just like your desktop browser, you can have several web pages open at once, in separate tabbed windows. To open a new window, tap the + button in the top right corner and enter the web address. Switch between the windows by tapping the tab you want. To close just that page, tap the X button in the left corner.

Cloud Button

If you've been surfing the web using Safari on your Mac, you can carry on from the same place on your iPad by tapping the View open tabs icon (two squares on top of each other) in the Safari toolbar. This will show you the tabs that are currently open on your other iOS devices and Mac, provided they are also set up to use iCloud.

FASTER BROWSING

Provided you have a cellular model, newer iPads support 4G data technology, which enables much faster browsing and quicker download speeds for videos, updating apps or simply retrieving an email attachment.

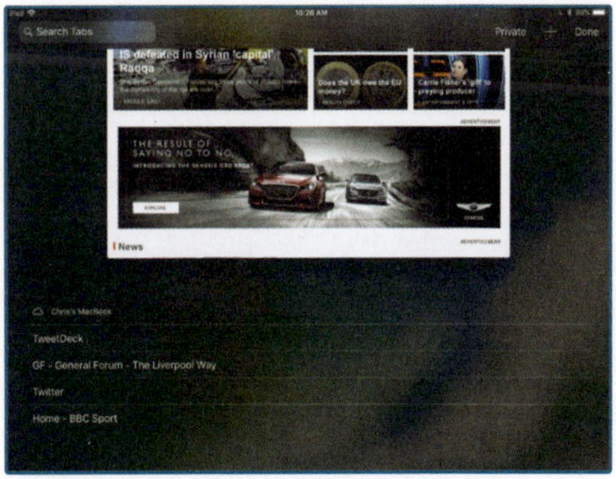

Above: Tap the View open tabs icon to access sites which are currently open on your Mac or other iOS devices that have iCloud activated.

4G LTE

The latest iPads with mobile connections support the next generation of mobile broadband – 4G LTE (Long Term Evolution). The advantage of 4G is that it is about five times faster than 3G and more reliable. This relies of course on the network coverage of your mobile provider – some have better coverage than others. Not only are browsing and downloading faster with 4G, but there's also less choppiness when you stream a video or watch TV – that is, fewer stops as the iPad struggles to keep up. Even without 4G, the new iPads support the latest and fastest versions of 3G. With their powerful antennae inside they are unlikely to lose the connection.

NAVIGATING THE WEB

Just like your computer browser, Safari lets you move backwards and forwards between open web pages using the left and right pointers on the top bar. However, there are other novel ways to navigate individual pages.

Viewing Web Pages

- **Scroll the page**: Drag your finger up and down the screen. The scrollbar on the right shows where you are. For faster scrolling, flick your finger up or down the page.

- **Unpinch**: This lets you zoom in on part of the page. Put two fingers together on the screen where you want to enlarge the page and move them apart. Put two fingers either side of the screen and move them together (pinch) to reverse this.

- **Zoom in to images** and text by double-tapping the screen. Zoom out by repeating the double-tap.

- **Once zoomed in**, tap the screen and drag the page left or right. A horizontal scrollbar at the bottom of the screen shows where you are on the page.

Uncluttered Websites

Some web pages are so full of text and ads that they can be difficult to read. Safari Reader can present a stripped-down version of the page. It's not available on all sites, but if you tap the Reader button to the left of the address field, ads are removed.

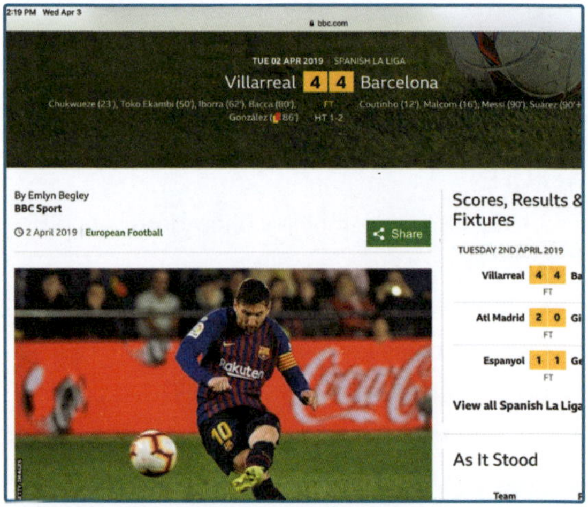

Above: You can navigate web pages by pinching and unpinching to zoom in and out, and dragging up and down to scroll.

Private Browsing

If you don't want to leave a trail of the websites you've visited – such as the jewellery store where you have been looking for presents – turn on private browsing.

Hot Tip

The Reader button doesn't appear with every web page you view. It has to be supported by the website you're visiting, which many commercial sites won't do, as they want their ads to show.

1. Tap the View open tabs icon (two squares) then tap Private and the + sign to open a new browser window. Now sites you visit won't appear in iCloud tabs or be added to the History on your iPad. You also lose the convenience of Safari saving any website login details.
2. With Safari in private mode, the top and bottom bars are dark grey rather than the usual lighter tones.
3. For further privacy you can also clear your history (the list of sites you have visited), as well as cookies and other website data. Tap the book icon next to the URL bar, then tap Clear.

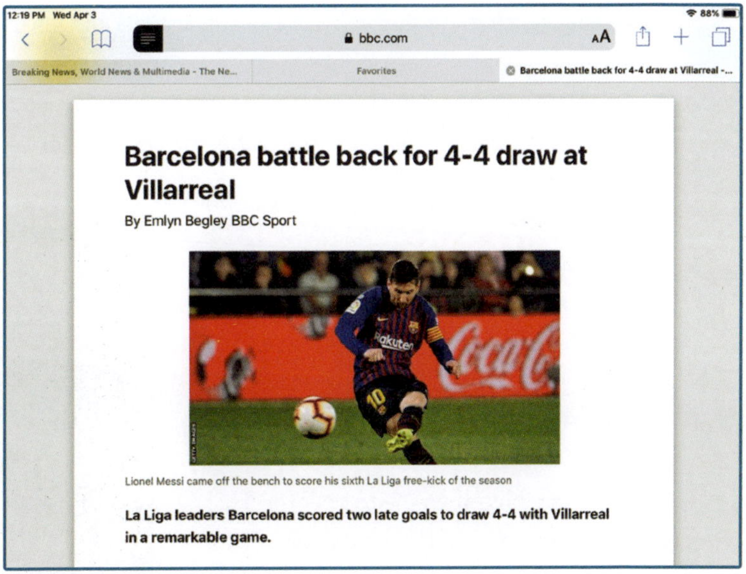

Above: Select the Safari Reader button to display an uncluttered version of the webpage which has ads removed, leaving only text and pictures.

SEARCH

Search the web, using your preferred search engine, direct from the iPad.

> **Hot Tip**
>
> **If you don't feel like typing your search query, press and hold the Home button until Siri appears. State what you're looking for – e.g. pizza restaurants – Siri repeats the request and returns the results (on iPad 3 and later).**

1. **The Search box**: This is now part of Safari's address bar. Simply tap the bar and use the pop-up keyboard to enter what you are searching for.
2. **As you type**: A list of suggestions will appear as you type. If none are correct, finish entering your text and tap the blue arrow (enter) on the keyboard.
3. **Search term**: You can also look for your search term on the web page you're currently viewing. Scroll to the end of the list of suggestions and tap On This Page.
4. **Google**: This is the default search engine used by Safari. To change this, tap Settings, Safari, then Search Engine and select the one you'd prefer.

SAVE THE WEB

As you browse the web, Safari offers several ways to share the pages you like or save them for reading later.

Sharing

Tap the Share button on the top bar for various ways to spread the word about a web page. Mail the link, text it or post it to your status on Facebook and Twitter. For easy

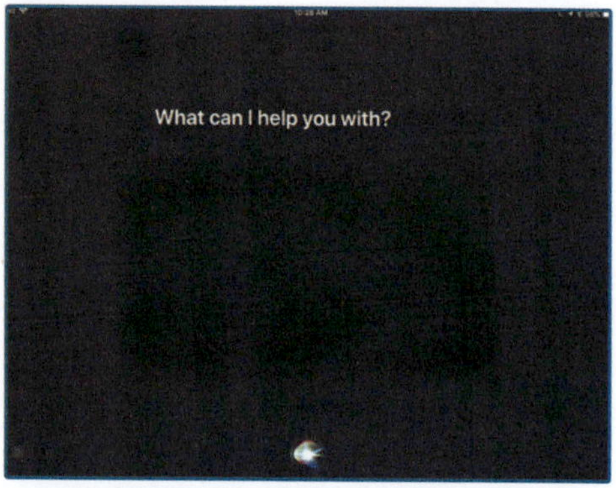

Above: Press and hold the Home button to search the web by dictating your request to Siri.

access, add it to your Home Screen or Reading List, save it as a PDF to Books or some other cloud service and bookmark, or print it, if an AirPrint printer is available.

Reading List

If you don't have time to read something that interests you, view it later. Tap the Share button, then touch Add to Reading List. The page isn't stored on your iPad but is synced with iCloud, so you can access the page, using any of your iOS devices, via the internet.

Hot Tip

Instead of repeatedly filling in your personal contact details on web forms, use AutoFill. Enable it by tapping Settings, Safari and selecting AutoFill preferences.

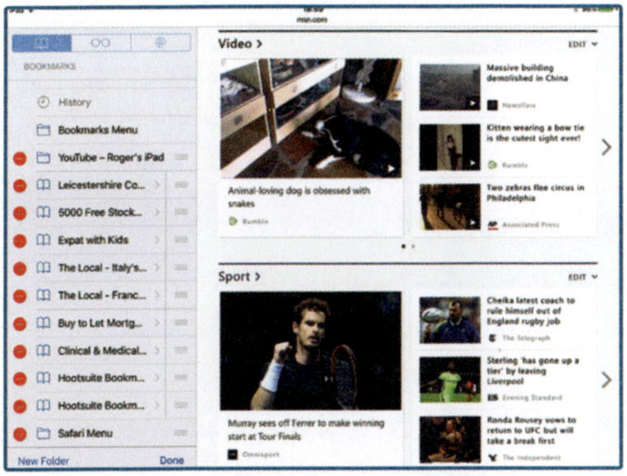

Above: View, visit and reorder your bookmarked pages by tapping the open book icon in the top bar.

To view your Reading List, tap Bookmarks and then the spectacle icons for Add to Reading list. Once you have visited the page, it no longer shows in the Unread list but can still be accessed by selecting Show All.

BOOKMARKS

To add a page to your bookmarks, tap the Share button, then Bookmark. To access your bookmarks, tap the open book icon on the top bar. Using iCloud, you can synchronize your bookmarks between your iPad, computer and other iOS devices.

To change your bookmarks, tap Edit in the top corner. Press the red '–' sign to delete one. To reorder your bookmarks, tap and hold the three-line grab handles and move them up or down the list. When finished, tap Done.

MESSAGING

Need to send a message to a friend? Using the built-in Messages app, you can text anyone who has an iPhone, iPod Touch or iPad for free – and even send pictures or video.

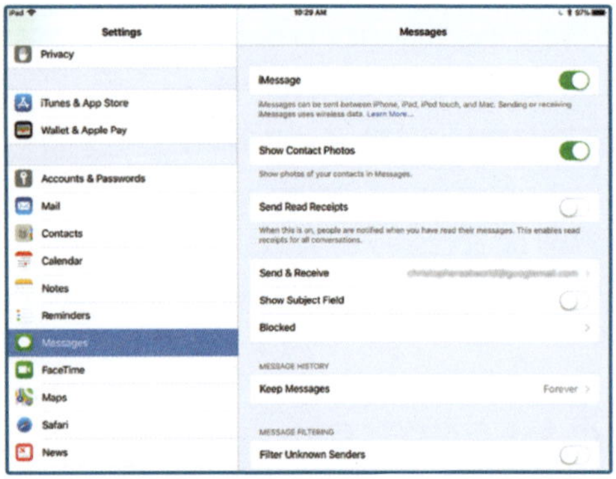

Step 1: Check iMessage is turned on by selecting the Messages option within Settings.

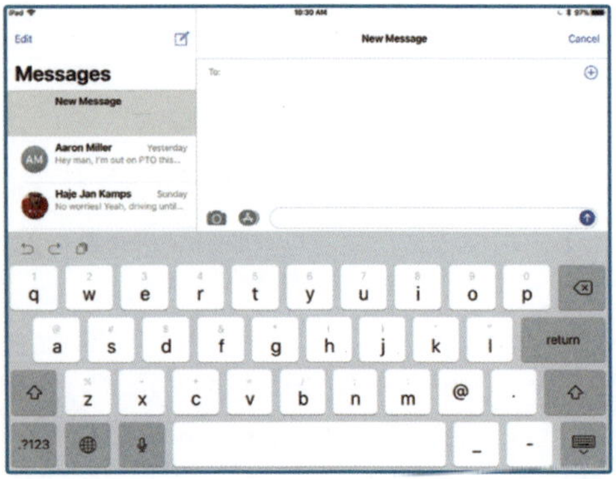

Step 4: Tap the New Message icon, start typing in the To box to bring up other iMessage users.

TEXTING

iMessage, the name that Apple has given to its messaging system, is on all iOS and macOS devices.

How to Text: Step-by-step

1. Go to Settings, Messages and make sure that iMessage is turned on.

2. Launch the Messages app. If it's not already entered, you'll have to give your Apple ID and password to activate the service. Then tap Sign In.

3. By default Apple will use the email address associated with your Apple ID to send messages.

4. Open Messages and tap the new message icon at the top of the screen. Start writing in the To: line and a box of relevant contacts will appear.

5. Tap the contact's name. If they're an iMessage user you'll see their name and contact details in blue. Type your message and press Send.

6. In true messaging style, your conversation is shown as a series of speech bubbles: your message on the right, your friend's reply on the left. When someone is replying to you, there's a bubble with three dots in the chat window.

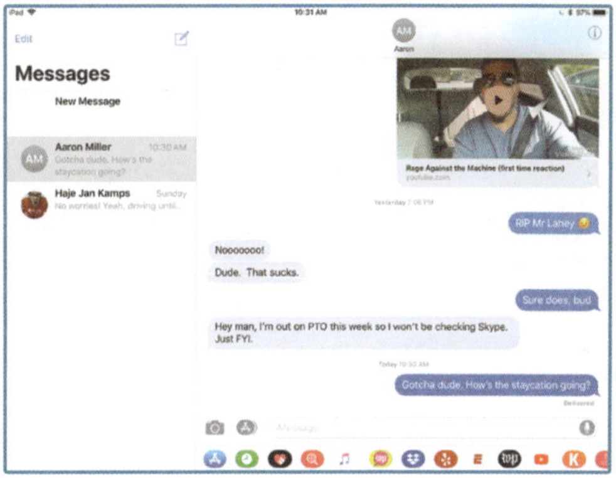

Step 6: Sent and received messages are shown in speech bubbles – responses are in grey and your messages are in blue.

Go Multimedia

To add a picture tap the Camera icon. The pop up box will give you chance to take a photo or video photo or video or take a selfie. You can select the Photos app from the app drawer to select from recent images or all photos available from your iPad.

Apps in iMessage

iMessage is such a powerful tool Apple has given it its own App Store. You can send friends a song you like from Apple Music, directions from Apple Maps, sports scores from ESPN, files from Dropbox, Movie show times from Fandango and more – but you must have the app already installed. Within an iMessage conversation, tap the App Store icon below the compose box to see available apps, or tap the relevant app in the drawer to access content from existing apps.

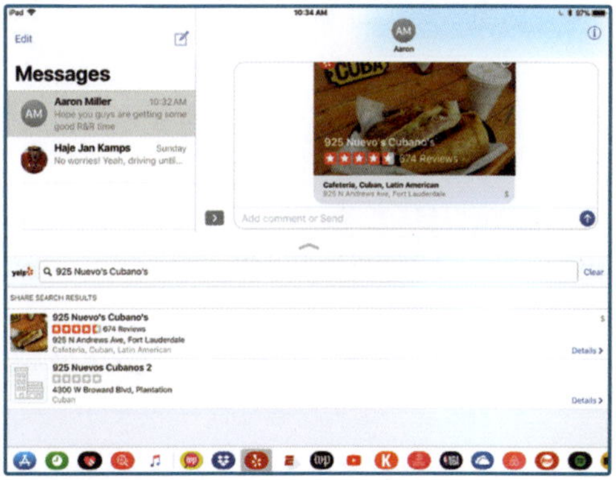

Above: Apps in iMessage make it easy to share information like restaurant recommendations to your contacts.

Cleaning Up

To forward your message tap and hold, then press More, select additional items, then tap the Forward arrow. Do the same again and choose the Dustbin icon to delete messages. To remove the whole conversation, select it from the left-hand menu, swipe your finger right to left and tap Delete.

EMAIL

If you can't bear to be parted from your email, the Mail app lets you connect to your online mailbox and will even notify you when you've got mail.

SETTING UP ACCOUNTS

To access your email, you first need to set up details of your email service. Although you can now use iCloud to sync your Apple Mail with the iPad, it is best to set up other email accounts directly on your iPad.

Syncing Your Email via iCloud

1. Using the Mail app you can sync your Apple email addresses with the iPad using iCloud.
2. Go to Settings, tap your profile, then select iCloud.
3. Make sure the toggle button beside Mail is on and showing green. Now all your emails to your iCloud address are synced with the iPad.

Add Email Accounts Direct to Your iPad

You access your emails through the Mail app, but you set up the account using the Settings app.

1. Tap Settings, then Passwords & Accounts and Add Account.
2. You will see the most popular web-based mail services listed, including Gmail, Outlook.com, AOL etc. There's also Microsoft Exchange, which is used by many schools and companies.
3. Tap the button for your email service if it's listed. You'll get a pop up screen from your provider. Enter your email address, password and agree to the terms.

4. Toggle things like Contacts and Calendars to on if you want to integrate those too and press Save.

5. If your email provider isn't listed, select Other and enter your account details. You can get them from your Internet Service Provider.

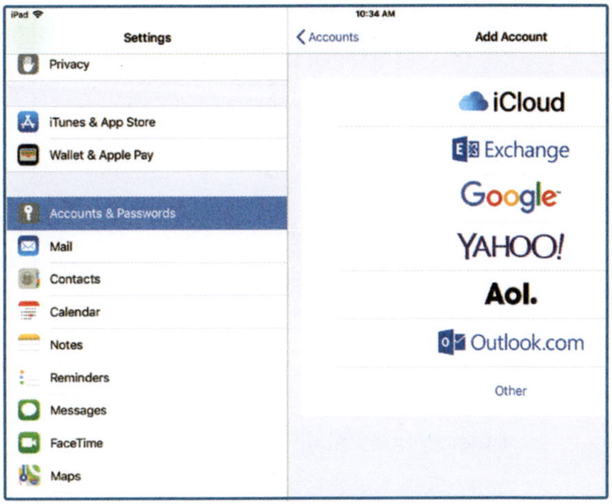

Above: Choose your email provider from the list, or tap Other to add your account details.

CONFIGURING MAIL

There are several ways to customize Mail to make it work in a way that suits you, so that you can keep up-to-date with your emails without being overwhelmed.

Preferences

Select how you want to organize your emails in Settings, then Mail.

- **Preview**: Change how many lines of text from each email are shown in List view.
- **Show To/Cc Label**: This shows if you are the main recipient of an email or if it was copied to you.
- **Swipe Options**: Lets you set what actions – such as Mark as Read – are taken when you swipe left or right.
- **Flag Style**: Change whether you want this as a colour or shape.
- **Ask Before Deleting**: This is a useful precaution if you often delete emails accidentally.

- **Load Remote Images**: Turn this off to save bandwidth, if you often download your email over a mobile connection.
- **Organize By Thread**: Turn this on and all replies to an email will be grouped under the original message.

Other options let you send a blind copy of every outgoing email to yourself; indent text quoted in a reply; and set the default email account to be used by iPad apps.

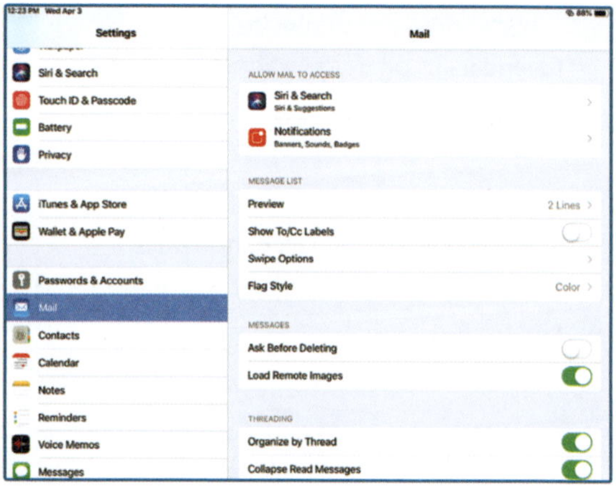

Above: Choose how your emails are organized by toggling options On or Off in the Mail settings list.

Configuring How Email is Received

Where it's supported, you can have new emails pushed to you automatically or fetched from the server at a set interval you determine.

Above: Choose whether to receive your emails by Push or Fetch, and how frequently this will happen.

1. Tap Settings, then Accounts & Passwords and then Fetch New Data.
2. If you have an email service where the server will automatically 'push' any new emails received to you, such as iCloud or Microsoft Exchange, then select Push.

3. If not, select Fetch. Then choose how frequently you want Mail to check for new emails, ranging from Every 15 Minutes to Hourly to Manual.

4. Select each account and then choose which schedule you would like to apply. Selecting Manual effectively turns off automatic email checking and requires you to refresh your inbox in the app.

Hot Tip

Signature adds your personal sign off to every email you send. Go to Settings, Mail, then choose Signature and enter your text. This is also where you delete the annoying default signature added by Apple: *Sent from my iPad*.

WORKING WITH EMAIL

Use the built-in Mail app to send and receive your emails when you are connected to the internet.

Using Mail

Mail shows all your inboxes – the mailboxes for incoming emails – in one list with the Accounts shown underneath.

- At the top of the list is **All Inboxes**. This is a **single inbox** for all the emails you receive from any account. Alternatively, you can select the inbox for an **individual account**, such as your main personal or work account.

- The list appears **automatically** when the iPad is in **landscape view**. In **portrait view** flick your finger from the **left** of the screen to show the list; flick from the **right** side of the screen to close it again.

Receive Mail

1. When you tap the inbox, there's a list of all your emails. Each one shows the sender's name, when it was sent, the subject line and a preview of the first few lines of the message.

2. Drag the list down to check for new messages. Tap the message preview, and the full message opens in the main window.

3. If you tap Details you can then choose the sender's name. This allows you to add them as a new contact, add the email address to an existing contact or add them to your VIP list.

4. A message at the top shows how many items are grouped together into a thread, because they all have the same subject line.

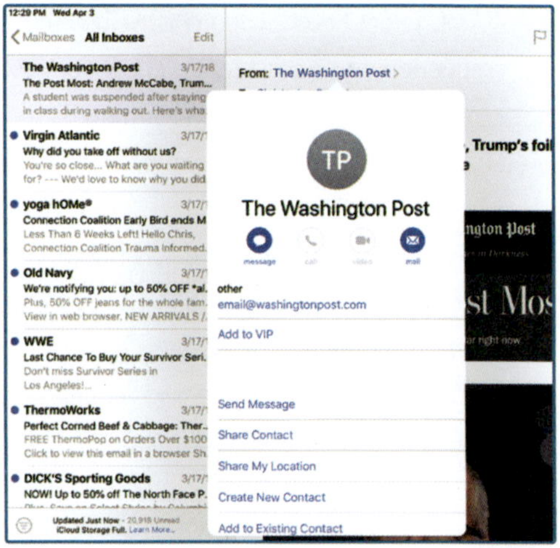

Above: Tapping the name of an email sender gives you the option to add the address to your contact or VIP lists.

5. Flick to scroll through the message or messages if it's a thread. Double-tap or pinch to zoom in on the text or images. Touch and hold an image for options to save, copy or share it.

6. If there's a word in the message you're not familiar with, look it up. Double-tap to select the word, using the grab handles if necessary, and then tap Define in the pop-up menu bar.

7. To zip back to the start of the email, tap the iPad status bar at the top of the screen.

Organize Your Messages

Along Mail's top bar are several icons that help you organize your messages.

- **Flag**: Tap this and select Flag to show the message is important (it will appear with an Orange circle beside it in the list) or Mark as Unread (which is shown by a small blue circle), or Move to Junk.

- **Folder**: Tap, and the list box shows the folders (mailboxes) for that account. Select a folder, and the message is moved there.
- **Bin**: This moves the message to the trash (for some accounts you may see a filing box icon. This archives rather than deletes the message).
- **Arrow**: Tap this for options to Reply, Forward or Print your message.
- **Compose**: The Compose icon on the far right launches a blank 'new message' window.
- **Edit**: Use this to apply an action to several messages at once. Tap the Edit button at the top of the Inboxes List, then touch the messages you want. Press the Delete, Move or Mark as Unread buttons as required.

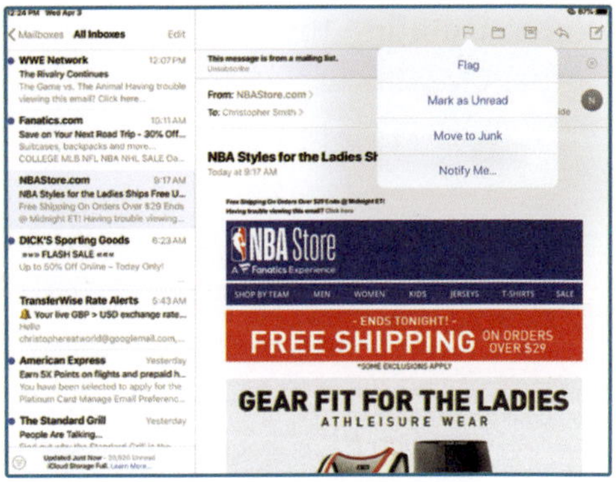

Above: Tap the flag icon in Mail's top bar to Flag an important message or Mark as Unread.

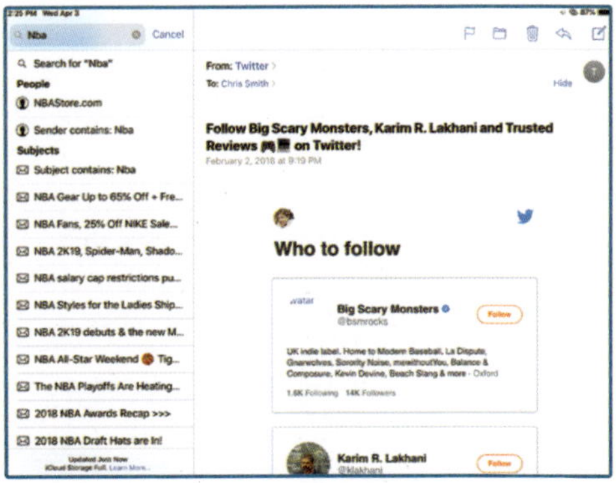

Above: To find an email, type a phrase in the search box and choose where to search.

Search

This is handy if you want to find that elusive email or group several on the same topic. Tap in the Search box at the top of the screen and enter your phrase. As you type Mail suggests ways you can refine your search. From the results, click the Edit button and select the emails you want to delete/archive, move or mark, as appropriate.

Delete Messages

To delete a message, flick its title in the message list. If the email is open, you can also use the delete button in the top bar. To delete several emails at once, click the Edit button, select the messages and click the red delete button.

Deleting the Archive

Given the huge amounts of space some services offer for email storage, some email providers, such as Gmail, don't delete messages but archive them.

1. Flick across a message in the list and the normal Delete button is shown as Archive. Tap this and the message is removed from that inbox but still remains in the All Mail folder.
2. To delete the message, tap Settings, then Passwords & Accounts. Tap the relevant account, then the account name, select Advanced and under Move Discarded Messages Into: select Deleted Mailbox.

Hot Tip

If you forward an email, you can include attachments from the original, which you can't if you just Reply to a message.

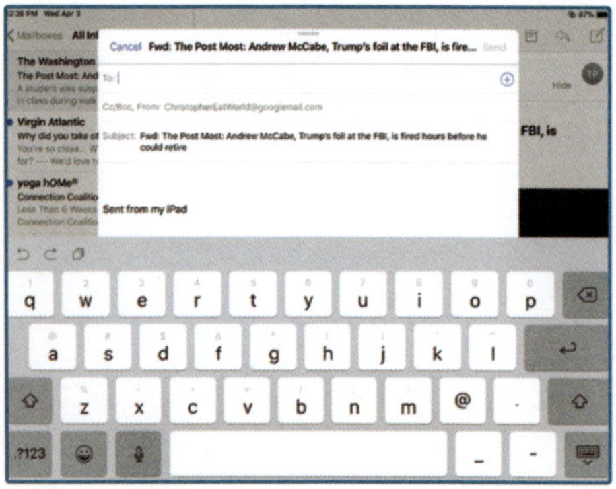

Above: Forward a message by clicking on the curved arrow at the top of an email and select the Forward option.

Send Email: Step-by-step

1. To write a new email, tap the Paper and Pen icon at the top of Mail or if you're replying or forwarding a message, select the curved arrow at the top.
2. In the New Message box that opens, add the recipient's email address. You can type this in or tap the + sign to select them from your Contacts list.
3. If you choose the wrong name, simply tap it and press the backspace key on the keyboard to delete it.
4. Add anyone you're copying the message to. Use Bcc (blind copying) if you're sending it to lots of people and you don't want to show all the addresses. To access the cc/bcc options, tap that field.
5. Tap From and choose the account you are using to send it. Then you can write your email.

6. To format the text, tap and use the grab handles to select all the text you want to include. Tap BIU and then choose Bold, Italic or Underline.

7. To add an attachment, tap where you want to add it and select the Camera icon on the keyboard to insert a Photo or Video or the paper clip to attach a document. Select the source, then the item and tap the Use button.

Hot Tip

You can resize photo attachments, which is useful when sending your email over a mobile connection. Once the photo is attached, tap Images, then Image size in the header section.

8. If you want you can also add a drawing. Press and hold in the message field to bring up the black formatting bar. Select Insert Drawing. This is better for iPad Pro users with an Apple Pencil, but anyone can sketch, for example, a little map to help guide someone.

9. When you're happy with your message, press the Send button in the top-right corner. If you're not yet ready to send, tap the Cancel button and choose the Save Draft option.

VIP MAIL

Messages from people you choose as important to you appear in their own VIP mailbox. They will also have a VIP star icon beside their name in the message preview.

- **To add a sender to your VIP list:** Tap their name in the From field in an email and select Add to VIP from the pop-up box.
- **To manage your VIP list:** Tap the 'i' icon and choose Add VIP. Here you can add more people and set up alerts for the arrival of VIP mail.

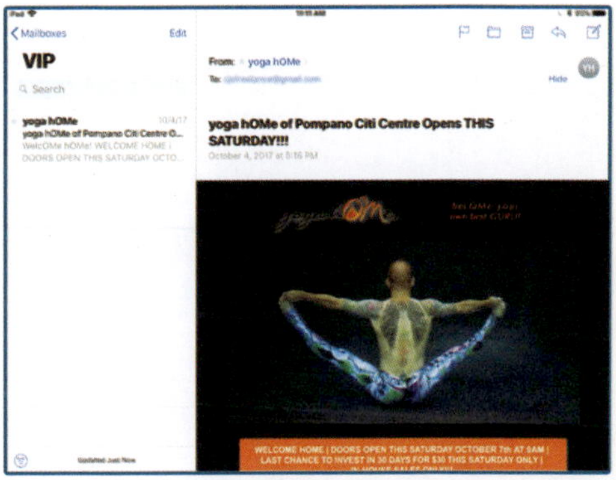

Above: Tap the VIP mailbox to add and remove contacts to your VIP list and set up alerts.

VIDEO CALLING

All iPads but the original 2010 model have a built-in camera to have great video chats with other Apple users via FaceTime or use Skype to reach more of your contacts.

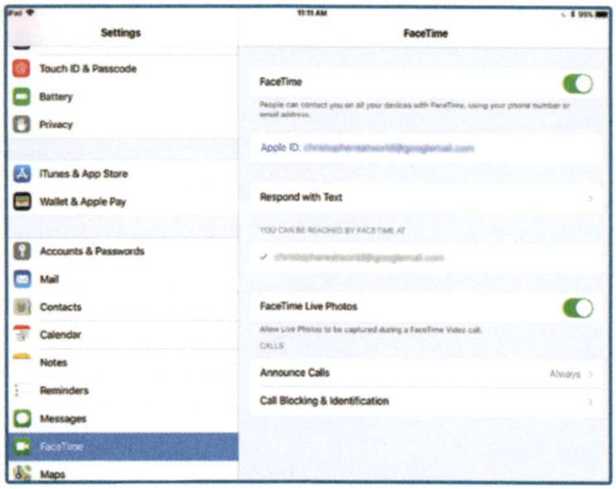

Above: Activate FaceTime by selecting the FaceTime option in your settings list and toggling to On.

FACETIME

With the iPad's FaceTime app you can make free video calls over the internet from anywhere in the world.

Setting up Your Video Calls

As well as a camera-equipped iPad, you'll need to be connected to the internet to use FaceTime. The person you are calling must also have an iPad, iPhone or iPod Touch with forward-facing camera or a Mac computer with camera and FaceTime.

1. Before you start, activate FaceTime by going to Settings, then FaceTime.

2. FaceTime identifies you through your Apple ID, the email address and password you use for accessing the App Store.

3. Next, select which of your email addresses to use as your contact point with your FaceTime account.

4. If you also have an iPhone you can accept calls on your iPad if it's on the same Wi-Fi network. Go to the Settings, then tap the FaceTime menu and turn on Calls from iPhone.

FaceTime Calls: Step-by-Step

1. To make a FaceTime call, tap the FaceTime app to open it. A list of previous calls is on the left. Enter the name, email address or number of the person you want to call in the search box or tap the + icon to view your contacts.

2. To make a call, tap the name of the person (or the 'i' if choosing from the previous calls list), then the camera icon for a video FaceTime or the phone for just audio.

3. When they answer, there will be a pause while the video chat is set up. Once connected, your face will shrink to a small thumbnail, while the person you are calling is pictured in the main window.

4. During the call, drag your picture to a different position if it's in the way.

5. Tap the microphone icon on the menu to temporarily mute sound (the picture won't be affected). Tap again to restore it.

6. Tap the camera icon to switch from the front camera, showing you, to the back camera, which will show what's around you.

7. To finish the chat, tap the telephone icon marked End.

Step 3: Video images of yourself and your contact appear once the call is set up.

Step 5: Tap the microphone icon to mute sound, and tap again to unmute.

Group FaceTime

In iOS 12, Apple added the ability to enjoy Group FaceTime video and audio session with up to 32 people. To start a Group FaceTime conversation, open the app and click the + button to access your content. Search for and select a contact. Then repeat for all other contacts. Those eligible to receive the call will be in blue. Then you can choose audio or video in green to start ringing. Your fellow users will also need to be running iOS 12 or macOS Mojave on a Mac.

SKYPE

Unlike FaceTime, Skype offers free video and voice chat that lets you stay in touch with friends and family no matter what computer or mobile device they use.

Hot Tip

You can switch apps during a chat, if for example, you want to look something up. Press the Home button, and the video will be minimized into a smaller window. When you want to return to full-screen tap the arrow within the FaceTime box.

Using Skype: Step-by-Step

Once you've downloaded the Skype app from the App Store you can either sign in using an existing account or create a new one using your email address or phone number. If you have a Microsoft email account (such as Hotmail or Outlook) you can use those login details to sign in to Skype.

1. Open the app and enter your Skype sign in or follow the steps to create a new account. Once you're signed in you'll be asked to allow Skype access to your microphone, camera and contacts.

2. You can tap the contacts icon with a + button and enter a name or email address in the Search box to find someone.

3. Once you have discovered them, select their name and in the screen that opens tap Add Contact. Enter a message asking them to accept you as a contact and tap send.

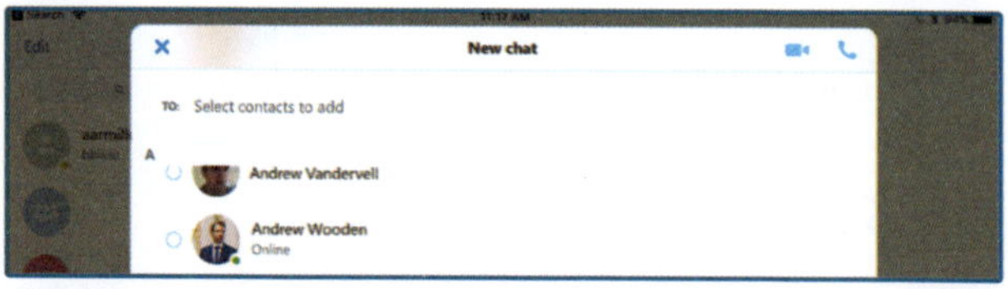

Step 2: Tap the contacts icon with a + button to use Skype Search for people you want to add to your contact list.

4. Once you have built up a contacts list, tap the contact you want to call. You'll see video and voice call options or you can begin typing in the Chat window.

5. Tap the video recorder icon to video call a contact, or tap the phone if you would prefer a voice call. The controls are much the same as for FaceTime, with the menu bar at the bottom and the main window displaying the video with your picture inset (except on the first generation iPad).

6. To send a text message during your video chat, tap the message icon – a speech bubble – and type it in the pop-up box that appears. Tap the message button again to close the window.

7. Once finished, you can end the call by tapping the phone receiver icon.

8. You can see your most recent calls and chats in the Recent tab at the bottom of the screen.

9. By default, Skype will show you as online when you login. You can change this status by selecting the My Info icon. Click on Status and you have the option to say you're Away, Do not disturb or Offline. If you set it to Invisible you'll appear to be offline to all your contacts but you can still use Skype as usual.

Phone Home, Cheaply

As Skype-to-Skype voice calls are free, they are a very popular way for people to stay in touch, wherever they are in the world, without running up huge phone bills. Low-cost calls can also be made to ordinary landline phones and mobiles by signing up to Skype's unlimited plan or buying pay-as-you-go credit.

Hot Tip

You can chat with anyone, anywhere using the Skype app with a Wi-Fi or 3G connection on any iPad. But while you can send and receive video using the front or back camera with the iPad 2 or above, you can only receive video on the first generation iPad.

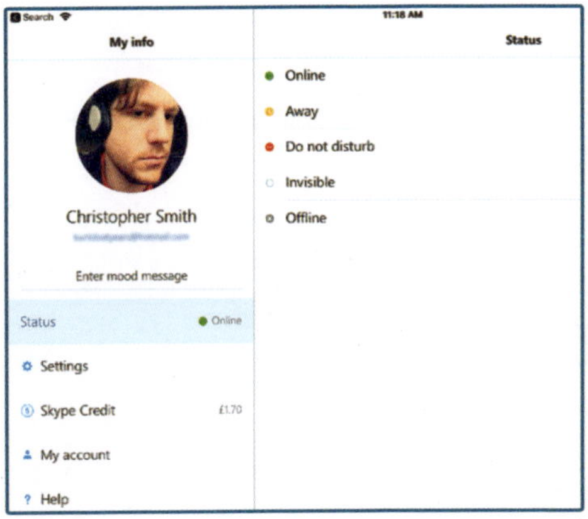

Above: If you do not want to always appear 'Online' but still use Skype, change your status to invisible.

SOCIAL MEDIA

The popularity of social media is such that Apple has great support for Facebook and Twitter on the iPad. You can Tweet, update your status, post a photo, your location or a link direct from several apps.

FACEBOOK

As one of the most popular sites on the web, with more than one billion users, it's natural that Facebook is easily accessible from your iPad.

Setting up Facebook

Facebook account access was built into the iPad software until iOS 11. This 'baked in' access made it easier to post on and share to Facebook. If you're on iOS 11 you will need to download the Facebook app from the App Store for access. Enter your username and password to sign in and skip ahead to Using the Facebook App, opposite. If you're using an older iOS, read on.

1. To set up Facebook, tap Settings and then Facebook. If you haven't already installed the app, do so by tapping Install.

2. Enter your Facebook Username and Password and tap Sign In. The pop-up window explains what you allow by signing into Facebook from the iPad's operating system. In essence, this is agreeing to:

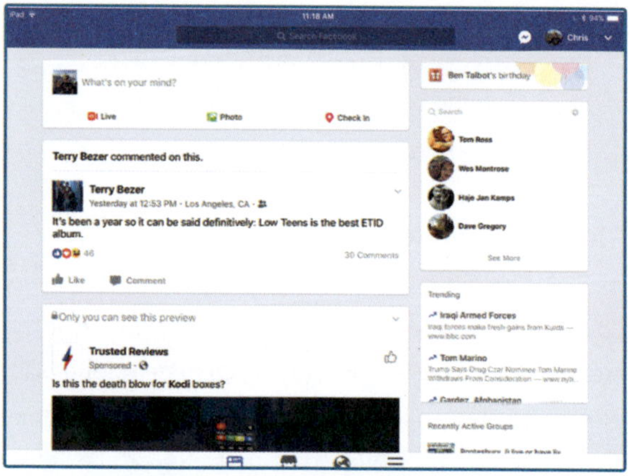

Above: The Facebook app for iPad allows you to access many of the usual features.

- **Merge** your Facebook friends' details with your Contacts, so that if they update their details, their entry in your Contacts is also immediately updated.

- **Download** your Facebook events to your calendar.

- **Allow** you to post photos, update your status, and send messages and other content to Facebook.

Hot Tip

To keep up with what is happening on Facebook go to Settings, then scroll down to Facebook and tap Notifications then Allow Notifications.

- **Enable** other apps on your iPad to access your Facebook account. To do so, they first have to ask your permission and make clear what information they will use and how. You can withdraw your permission at any time.

3. Touch Sign In if you agree.

4. Having allowed Facebook to access your Contacts and Calendar, you can refuse either one or both, by turning off the button beside the relevant icon in the Allow These Apps to Use Your Account section.

5. If you tap Update All Contacts, your information will be shared with Facebook, so they can update photos and usernames.

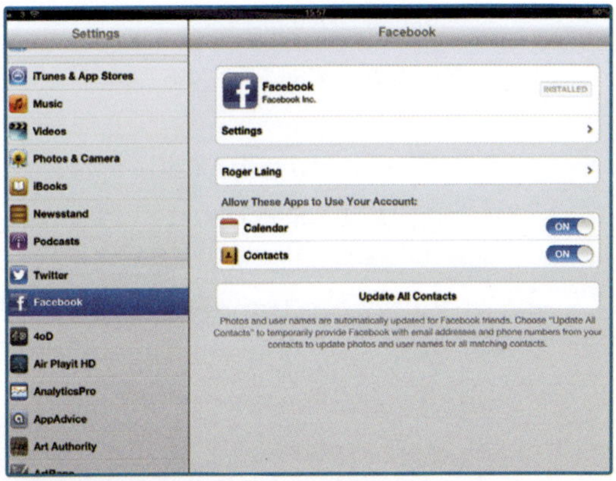

Above: Choose whether you want Facebook to have access to your Contacts and Calendar by toggling the buttons to On or Off.

Using the Facebook App

- **Update your status:** At the top, above your News Feed is the Status Update box. Write your message, then tap the Post button. You can also add content like photos and videos, live videos, check into a location, add a 'feeling' and tag your friends, among other things.

- **Share URLs**: When you're browsing the internet with Safari and come across a link you'd like to post on Facebook, tap the Share button, then Facebook.

- **Send pictures**: To send photos directly from the Photos app, select the image (or images) you want to post, tap the Share button and then Facebook. In the Update box you'll see the image. You can add a caption in the 'Say something...' section. Tap the album icon at the foot of the screen to select a Facebook album.

- **Share your current location**: In the Maps app, tap the pin that marks where you are, then the Share button and select Facebook. Alternatively, in the Facebook Status Update box add your location by tapping the Check In icon in the bottom-right corner. Choose who you want to share it with by tapping the Friends icon and selecting from the list. You can also write something in the box that says 'What's on your mind?'

Ask Siri to Update Your Friends

If using iOS 10 or earlier on an iPad 3 or later, Siri can update your Facebook status for you. Hold the Home button to launch Siri, say 'Post to Facebook' and dictate your message. Anything said after Facebook will be posted to your wall.

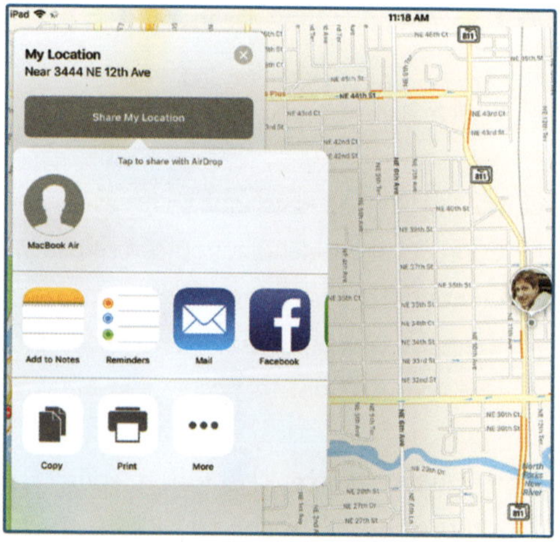

Above: Share your location over Facebook by tapping your location in the Maps app and choosing the Share button and then selecting Facebook.

Facebook Messenger

Facebook Messenger is a great option for chatting with your friends. It may be preferable to iMessage because more than 50% of people are Android users who can't access Apple's app. Facebook Messenger used to be built into the main app, but now you'll need to download a dedicated app from the App Store. Use your Facebook login details to sign in.

Hot Tip

To be notified when you receive messages from Twitter go to Settings, scroll down to select Twitter (the app must be installed), then tap Notifications and turn on Allow Notifications.

TWITTER

Twitter is a social networking and micro-blogging service, where every post is 280 characters (previously 140) or fewer. In versions prior to iOS 11, Twitter account access was 'baked-in' to the iPad. Not anymore. You'll need the Twitter apps.

Setting up Twitter

Just like with Facebook, you'll need to download the Twitter app from the App Store to get started. You can't tweet without it in iOS 11.

You'll also need a Twitter account. If you have one already, enter your details. If not, set one up by tapping Get Started and following the instructions. If, like many people, you have several accounts – one for your personal Tweets, another for a business or a hobby – then tap your profile picture, then the three dots in the top-right and 'Add an existing account'. You can then enter the details.

Tweeting: Step-by-step

1. Simply tap the Twitter app to open it and click the Tweet box with a quill at the bottom right of the screen. Your Twitter profile pic is already entered in the message box.

2. To send from a different account, if you have one, tap your profile pic and select the one you want from the list.

Above: Twitter allows you to share brief thoughts, photos, animated GIFs, create polls and much more.

3. Now you can start typing to enter your tweet. As you type the number at the bottom right shows how many available characters remain.

4. Tweets can include more than words. You can select the Photos icon to include images from your phone or the GIF to add a short looped video known as an animated GIF file. You can even create a poll for your followers to vote on. When finished, tap Tweet to post your tweet.

Tweeting Photos and Your Location: Step-by-step

If you have a photo you must share with your Twitter followers, it's easy to do through your iPad.

1. In the Photos app, select the image and tap the Share button, then Twitter. This opens the Tweet box, with the photo loaded. Now you can add your message.

2. If you enabled Twitter to enable your location during set-up, the tweet will list that location while composing. You can tap the GPS pin to customise it further or turn off location.

3. Alternatively, simply Tweet your location from

Step 1: Tweet a photo by selecting an image from your Photos app, tapping the Share button, and choosing the Twitter option.

within Maps. Tap the pin marking your location, then select the Share button and choose Twitter.

4. Tap Send to post to Twitter.

Hot Tip

If you have more than one Twitter account, tap your profile icon, then the three dots and from here you can Add an existing account or Create a new account. Once added, long press on your profile icon to easily switch between accounts.

Alternate Facebook and Twitter Apps

If you don't like the official apps or simply want to access some features you won't find in the official portals, you might want to try Friendly for Facebook or Tweetbot for Twitter from the App Store. Tweetbot, for example, gives you more power to mute content you don't want to see. There's also a better statistics view and a night mode for evening reading. You can also find a column view on the iPad that allows you to browse your timeline and your mentions at the same time.

The Friendly app gives you access to multiple social media accounts from a single app. If you don't want to install any apps, you can also access Facebook and Twitter via the Safari web browser.

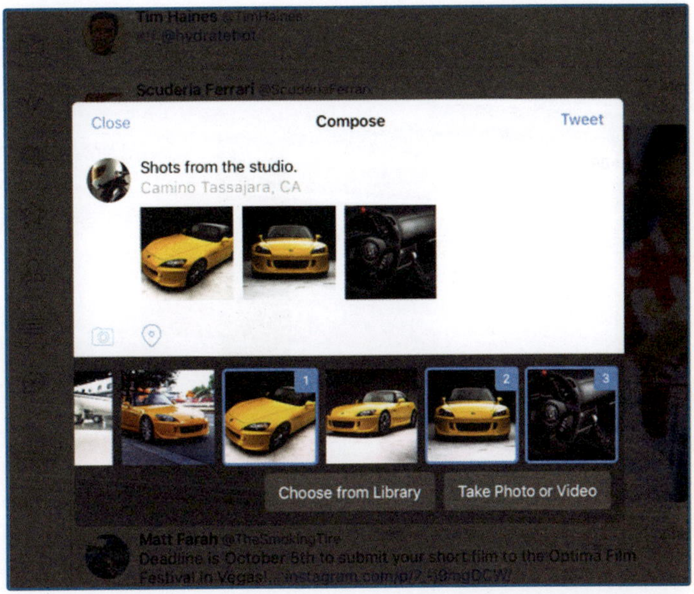

Right: Apps such as Tweetbot can be downloaded from the App Store if you want a more comprehensive Twitter experience.

LOCATION SERVICES

Whether it's forecasting the weather where you are, or finding the nearest pizza restaurant, more and more apps are using the iPad's Location Services.

FIND YOURSELF

Location Services combine information from the iPad's built-in compass with Wi-Fi, mobile and GPS data to locate you. Tap Privacy then Location Services to control which apps have access to your location and when.

Find My Friends: Step-by-step

The iPad can be used to keep tabs on friend and family locations. Don't worry, no one can be tracked without giving their permission.

1. You can download the Find My Friends app from the App Store.

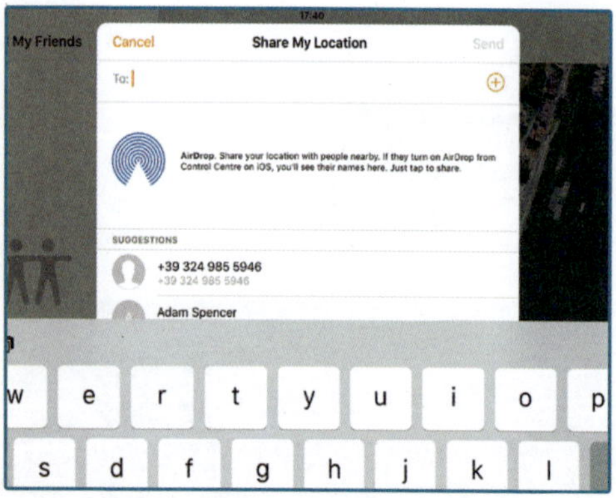

Above: Enter your contacts' names or email addresses or select them from the list to request them to share their location with you using the Find My Friends app.

2. Agree to allow the app to access your location, and follow the prompts to switch on Share My Location.

3. Ask a friend to share their location by tapping Add and entering their contact information. Then press Send.

4. When your friend accepts, you can see their location but they can't see yours. To do so, they have to ask your permission. If they do, you'll see it under Requests.

Temporary Sharing

This is great if you and your friends are planning to meet up for an evening. They can track you to make sure they go to the right location. This is now done through iMessages instead of Find Friends.

1. Start a conversation with the friend or group of friends you want to share your location with, tap the thumbnails at the top of the conversation and select Info.

2. Tap Send My Current Location to do that or tap Share My Location. In the box that opens up you can choose to share your location for an hour, until the end of the day or indefinitely.

> **Hot Tip**
>
> **On iPads with Wi-Fi and Cellular (3G and 4G), the built-in GPS will be used to determine your location more accurately, which can run down your battery faster.**

EXPLORE WITH MAPS

The Maps app enables you to go local, and find the nearest restaurant or cinema, or international. It provides step-by-step directions and traffic conditions as well as a Flyover view and public transport directions for a limited number of major cities.

Getting Started with Maps

A Wi-Fi or mobile internet connection s needed for Maps to draw down the mapping information. It also relies on Location Services for many of its features. Make sure these are on by going to Settings, Privacy, and turning on Location Services and then Maps.

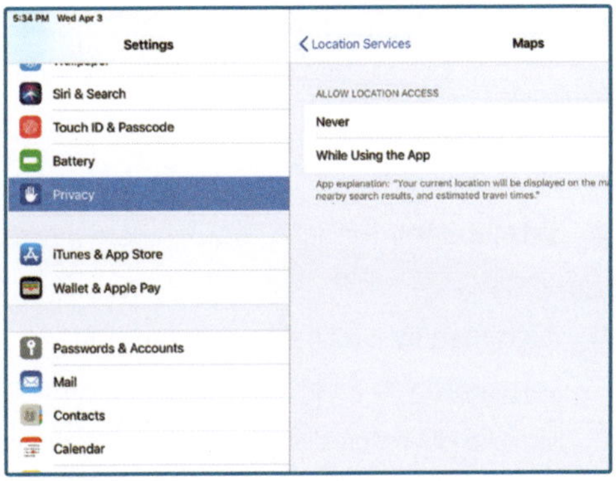

Above: Activate Maps by making sure it is switched on to use Location Services.

Find a Location

1. Tap the Maps app, then type the name of the place you're looking for in the Search bar. You can search by geographic features, place names, street addresses, landmarks and so on.

2. If you don't know exactly what you're looking for the Nearby service below the search box features categories like Food, Shopping and Fun. Tap one to see a list of popular nearby locations. Or, if you're looking for somewhere close by tap the compass arrow to zoom in on your current location.

3. Maps will show locations on the map. Tap one that interests you to open a host of details in a tab. This tells you more about the location. There's a short cut to directions, contact details a website, photos and perhaps reviews. You can share the location or add it to your Favourites.

Hot Tip

Apple Maps is much improved, but many people still prefer Google Maps. You can download it free from the App Store.

Change the View

Tap the information icon in the top-right corner and you can change the way you look at the location.

- **Map:** This is the standard style.
- **Transport:** To view public transport.
- **Satellite:** For overhead photographic views.
- **3D:** When in satellite view, tap the 3D Map button to zoom in on the map and tilt it. If HD resolution satellite pictures are available for the location, the 3D button changes to a Flyover button.

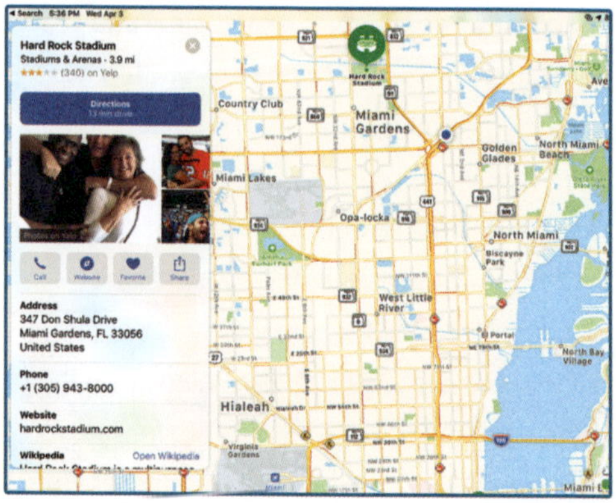

Above: Tap a location on the map to find out more information about it, including photos, reviews and directions. You can also share the location with others.

- **Flyover:** The short Flyover videos take you on a tour around landmarks. If you type London into the search bar, for example, you'll see a Flyover option appear.

Get Directions

1. To get directions to a location, by car, on foot or using public transport, find your location then tap the Directions button. This will automatically plot a course from your current location, however you can change this by tapping From My Location.

2. At the bottom you'll see Drive, Walk and Transit options. Tap one to see suggested routes, distance and estimated time of journey.

3. Select Driving Options in the bottom left if you want to avoid things like motorways and toll roads.

4. Tap Go to select one of the suggested routes. This will load the step-by-step sat nav instructions.

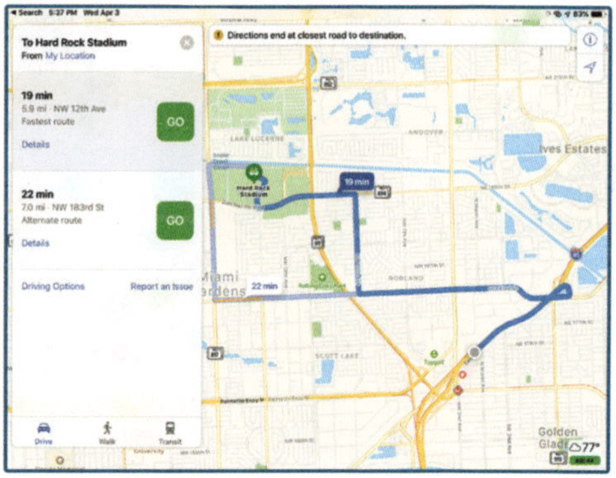

Above: Maps will display alternative routes to your destination, with times and distances noted.

Check Traffic En Route

Apple Maps helpfully colour codes traffic conditions on your route. If you see a blue line it's all clear, but yellow and red sections represent traffic. Yellow warning signs also represent incidents like roadworks and accidents.

Step-by-step Navigation

Maps offers step-by-step GPS navigation, similar to the sat-nav in a car or handheld system. Once you've selected a route you'll be taken to the directions screen. Providing you've used a Wi-Fi connection to set up the location you won't need data along the way, GPS will take care of that.

Hot Tip

Siri can find locations, tell you what points of interest or services are nearby and get directions for your trip (iPad 3 and above).

รวมพล
วันที่ 9 ธันวาคม 2555
ภาคีเครือข่าย

PHOTOGRAPHS & VIDEO

YOUR PHOTOS

The iPad is the complete photographer's kit – able to capture great photos and display them in their full beauty on a high-definition screen.

TAKE GREAT PHOTOS

Apple updates the iPad cameras with most new models. The latest iPads can shoot video in HD or 4K, and they can take 8- or 12-megapixel photos depending on which model you buy (see page 22). As a hand-held camera the iPad is bulky, but it benefits from both a front and backward-facing lens, and it can provide good results.

Taking a Picture: Step-by-step

1. To take a picture, tap the Camera app and you should see the image. If you're in the picture, you're using the forward-pointing camera.

2. To switch to the rear camera, tap the camera icon with the curved arrows. Make sure that the mode is set to Photo and not Video or any of the other settings such as Time-lapse, Square or Panoramic.

3. A rectangle briefly appears where the exposure is set. This is done automatically but you can adjust it manually. Tap the light icon next to the rectangle, then slide up or down to change it.

Step 3: Tap anywhere on screen to focus on that part of the picture, as indicated by a yellow frame.

4. When using the rear camera, tap the image with two fingers together and

push them apart to zoom in on the area you want to shoot. This also works in video on later iPads. Alternatively there's a vertical zoom bar on the left.

5. When ready, take your shot by pressing the round button on the screen. Alternatively, you can use the up and down volume button on the side of the iPad.

Above: The Panorama setting lets you capture a wider field of view. Hold the iPad steady and pan across.

6. Your pictures can be viewed in the small square box beneath the capture button. Tap the image to bring up the controls. These let you view, share and edit your images. Tap the back arrow in the top left to return to the camera.

Live Photos

With Live Photos the camera shoots a couple of seconds of video either side of you pressing the shutter,so instead of just the smile, for example, you get the pose and the smile. If you want this to look good you hold the iPad still for a couple of seconds before clicking the shutter. Tap the Spirograph-looking icon on the right side to enable.

High Dynamic Range

The HDR initials on the capture screen stand for High Dynamic Range. This uses the camera's exposure setting to take two photos, one at the high exposure, one at a low exposure. The result should be balanced lighting in photos with vivid colours.

Panorama

If there's a scene you wish to capture that doesn't fit within the frame, select Pano. Click the shutter and pan from left to right while holding the iPad. Try to keep the iPad level along the yellow line. Click the shutter again when done.

EDIT YOUR PHOTOS

However good or bad a photographer you are, the iPad's image-editing tools can make your pictures look better.

Photos App

It's all too easy, in the rush to capture a moment, to end up with a less than perfect photo. The Photos app gives you the basic tools to make your pictures better – whether they are images taken with the iPad itself, streamed through iCloud or uploaded from your digital camera.

Hot Tip

After you save your edits you can still go back to the original, so don't worry if you make a change you wish you hadn't. Tap the image, then Edit and tap Revert.

- **To start editing**: tap the Photos app with its easily recognizable colourful flower icon.
- **To Edit**: Select the photo you want to change, tap to view it and then tap the Edit button.
- **Editing tools**: Buttons for the main editing tools appear on screen:

Above: Use the Apple Photos app to edit your photos by rotating, cropping, enhancing and removing red-eye from images.

1. **Auto-enhance**: the magic wand icon will adjust the colour and contrast of your image.
2. **Remove Red Eye**: Tap each eye that needs correcting.
3. **Rotate and Crop**: This lets you alter the angle of the picture to straighten the image. You can also resize your pictures by tapping the Crop button and then adjusting the frame. If you're planning to print your photos, you can constrain the crop ratios to match. Tap the Constrain

button (it looks like frames inside each other) and select the proportions you want.

4. **Photo Filters:** let you apply different colour effects, such as Mono or Chrome.

5. **Adjustments**: Sets light, colour and black-and-white options.

6. **Markup**: Tap the the menu dots and tap Markup. This enables you to annotate the image. Tap the + icon to add text. Any changes can be undone using the back arrow.

- **Save your changes**: Tap Done. If you don't like the results tap Cancel, then Discard Changes.

ADVANCED PHOTO EDITING

Make your pictures as eye-catching as possible, with iPad apps that offer the sort of sophisticated editing techniques usually found on more powerful computers.

Pixelmator App

Pixelmator provides advanced editing tools that are simple and effective to use on the iPad. It also supports Apple's Handoff feature, which means you can start editing on your iPad and then transfer the photo to the Mac and carry on right where you left off (or vice versa).

- **Buy and install** Pixelmator from the App Store, then tap to open. To start you need an image. You can import one from iCloud or the Photos app or take a photo with the iPad.

- **Import an image**: Tap the + sign in the corner, then either tap Photos or iCloud Drive and follow the prompts.

- **Create a new image**: Tap the + sign then Create Image. Tap Show Categories to see the available templates, from collages to posters.

Hot Tip

If your images from iCloud Drive aren't showing up you need to set it up. Go to Settings, iCloud, iCloud Drive and turn on Pixelmator.

Above: Use the Pixelmator's editing tools to transform photos by altering properties and adding effects.

Above: With the Effects tool you can simply retouch photos or turn them into artistic creations.

- **To take a photo**: Tap the + sign then Take Photo. Point at what you want to shoot. If you like the image tap Use Photo.

Editing Photos with Pixelmator

Once you've selected the photo you want to edit, tap the paint brush icon to open the photo-editing menu.

- **Select Crop**: Do you want to cut some of the noise out of your photo? Using the grid you can focus in on the detail that's important, while keeping the aspect ratio the same. To change it click Undo or Revert to Original.

- **Select retouch**:

1. **Repair**: lets you remove unwanted elements.
2. **Lighten or Darken**: Change areas of an image according to your preferences.
3. **Clone**: Copy part of the image from one area to another.
4. **Sharpen or Soften**: Change the focus on the photo to make it clearer or more blurred in different places.
5. **Fix red-eyes**: Easily and quickly get rid of red-eyes.
6. **Saturate or Desaturate**: Alter colour strength.

- **Effects**: Want to age your photo or make it more artistic? Tap Add Effects and swipe your finger through the thumbnails to choose which option to apply.

Applying Edits

With several of the tools, you tap and hold the area of the image where you want to apply the change, then move the circle to increase or decrease the effect.

Other Photo-editing Apps

There are many excellent photo-editing apps available from third-party developers. Among them are Adobe Photoshop Fix for retouching photos and Snapseed, which saves over the original photo rather than duplicate it to make it easier to revert to the original image.

ORGANIZING YOUR PHOTOS

Arranging your images in albums makes it easier to find the ones you want and show them off.

Create Photo Albums: Step-by-step

You can use the built-in Photos app to set up your albums.

1. Tap to open, then select Albums and tap the + sign in the top-left corner. In the New Album box enter a name, then tap Save.

2. The Photos view shows all the images on your iPad. Scroll through and select the images you want to add to that album. As you select each one, it is marked with a blue tick in the lower-right corner. Tap Done to add the photos to the new album.

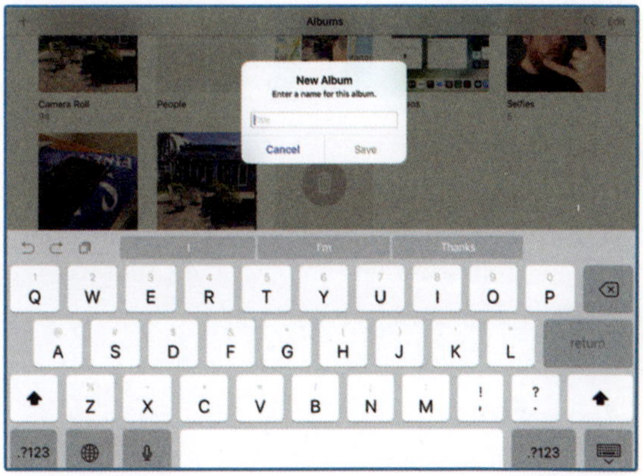

Step 1: Create a new album by selecting the + sign from the album screen and entering the name into the New Album box.

3. If you already have an album and want to add more images to it, open the album, then tap the Photos button for a view of all your images and press select. Choose the photos you want, as above, and tap the Add To button.

4. Alternatively, tap the Photos button, press Select, choose your photos, press Add To and scroll through the albums to find where you want to place them.

Smart Albums

Some albums are automatically created for you. So you'll see there are albums for the latest selfies, screenshots, photo bursts and panoramas.

Manage Your Albums

When viewing your album list tap Edit. To delete an album tap the X in the corner or to rearrange the order touch the album and drag it to another location in the list.

Above: Photos has a tab from iOS 10 onwards called Memories, which create slideshows of your photos, such as 'Best of Last 3 Months'.

ADDING EFFECTS

From stretching and twisting your face to creating your own comic book images, there is a range of apps to add special effects to your photos.

Fun with Photo Booth

This works with either the front or rear camera. Tap to open Photo Booth and choose the effect you want. Depending on the one you choose, you can pinch, swipe or rotate the image to alter the intensity of the effect.

1. Tap the camera to take the shot, which will be preceded by white flash. The picture appears in the photo roll at the bottom of the screen.

2. Tap the picture, then the Share button and you have a range of options to email, copy, print or save it to online storage accounts like Dropbox.

Instagram

The photo-sharing app has been a massive hit with iPhone users since it launched. It lets you take a photo, choose a filter to change its look and feel, then post it to Instagram for friends and family to view. Surprisingly, though, given the iPad's superior screen, there's no native iPad app, so you have to use the iPhone version.

Add Text to Your Photos

There are loads of great apps to help you add text to your images before sharing them. We enjoy After Photo, Quick, PicLab and Typorama. They all have multiple fonts, colours and style to choose from.

Comic Book Effect

Create your own comic strip with ComicBook! It turns you and your friends into stars of your own comic book in seconds, and you can publish direct to Facebook.

Other Effects

There are iPad-specific apps to add virtually any effect you can think of – from vintage film-star looks to pop art – and then combine them in unusual ways to create collages, moodboards, posters and the like.

Above: Photo Booth allows you to alter an image in many different ways by choosing various effects.

VIEWING PHOTOS

The iPad's display is great for showing off your photos, and if you have one with the Retina screen, they'll look even better.

PHOTO DISPLAYS

The iPad is a wonderfully portable digital photo album that can deliver slide shows or be an electronic picture frame that can change photos automatically.

Hot Tip

Retina is just Apple's marketing term to convey the extraordinary quality of screens with a high pixel density, where the average human retina can't make out individual pixels.

Album Photos

1. Open Photos, tap the Albums button, and you'll see various ones listed. These also correspond to any picture folders you sync from your computer.

2. Tap on the album, and you'll see all the individual photos. Tap on any photo to view it up close. Tap the album name in the top-left to return to a view of all the photos.

3. Tap Albums at the top-left corner to return to the list of albums.

4. Alternatively, put a finger at the top and bottom of the screen and pinch them together to pull the photos back into album view.

Step 2: Tap on any individual photo in your album to view it close up.

Slideshow

To make more of your photos, add music and fancy transition effects to create a slide show.

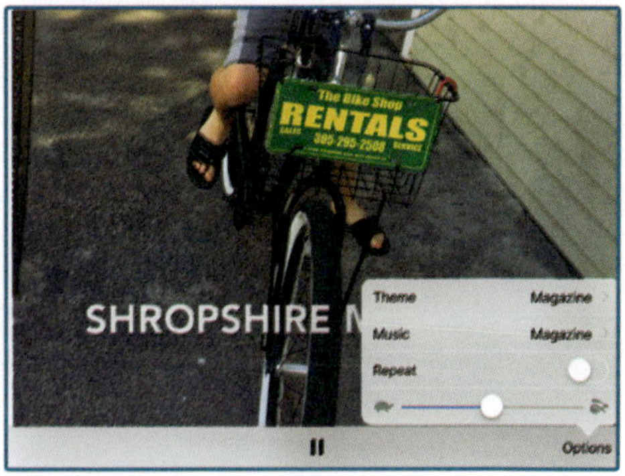

Step 3: Select slideshow options such as the theme for the transitions and music.

1. In Photos, select the album or group of photos you want then press the Slideshow button.

2. Tap the first picture and press the pause button while you select the effects you want.

3. Tap options. Themes lets you change the transitions between slides, while Music allows you to choose from the preset sounds or access your iTunes music. You also have options to repeat the slideshow and change the speed it plays at.

4. Tap the Play button to start the Slideshow again. To stop the slideshow, tap anywhere and press the pause button.

> **Hot Tip**
>
> **If the picture frame is on public display, you might not want that photo of you asleep in a deck chair popping up. To avoid this, create your own photo album specifically for use with LiveFrame.**

Picture Frame

Apps like LiveFrame can turn your iPad into a digital photo frame.

1. Download LifeFrame from the App Store and open it. This will show a range of potential sources on the left hand side.

2. To use photos you've taken on your iPad select My Device. Otherwise you can sync Google Photos, Instagram, Facebook, Flickr and Dropbox accounts.

3. After selecting My Device you'll be asked to choose from All Photos, the last day, week, month, year or make a custom album selection. When you have made the selection, press the Play button to begin a slideshow, complete with time and date.

Deleting Photos

However embarrassing a photo is, it may not be possible to delete it from the iPad. You can only delete photos you've taken on the iPad, that have been uploaded via the camera connection kit, saved from your email or a website using Safari, or are in your Photo Stream.

- **To delete a single photo**: Tap the photo you want to delete, then the dustbin icon and press the red Delete Photo button. If the photo is in your iCloud Photo Library it will be deleted from all your devices.
- **To delete a group of photos**: Tap the Select button followed by each photo you want to delete. Those selected are marked with a tick. Tap the Delete button, then confirm by pressing the Delete Photos button.
- **No delete option**: In some albums there is no delete option, as these photos are copies of images synced with your computer. To delete them, go to your computer and remove the photos from any albums that sync with the iPad.

Left: Delete groups of photos by tapping the Select button and choosing the photos to delete. Each one will be marked with a blue tick. Once you have finished selecting, tap the Delete button.

SHOW PHOTOS ON A BIGGER SCREEN

The iPad screen uses a special technology – In-Plane Switching (IPS) – for better viewing from different angles. However, for a bigger display, wirelessly transmit your photos to other screens, such as your TV.

Mirror Your Pictures with AirPlay

To do this, you'll need a second generation Apple TV or later. Despite its name, it is not a TV but a receiver that connects to your TV with a high-definition cable. Special AirPlay wireless technology mirrors what's on your iPad to the receiver, which displays it on your TV.

- **To connect successfully** you need an iPad 2 or later, and both your Apple TV and iPad have to be on the same wireless network.
- **To show off your photos**, open Photos, tap Albums and then select the one you want to display. Tap on the photo, then the Share icon and select AirPlay (a square screen with an upward-pointing arrow at its base).
- **Select Apple TV** and your photo will appear on the TV screen. You can flick between images, zoom in, pause and move from landscape to portrait view, and the changes will be reflected on the big screen.

Above: Use AirPlay to show your photos on Apple TV by tapping on a selected photo, selecting the Share icon, then Airplay and the Apple TV option.

Physically Connect Your iPad Display and TV

An alternative way to mirror what's on your iPad screen to a TV or other display is through a physical connection. You'll need an Apple Digital AV adapter. Plug this into your iPad and then connect it to an High Density Multimedia Interface (HDMI) cable from the TV or other display.

ADDING PHOTOS

There are numerous ways to put photos onto the iPad to take advantage of its high-quality display.

SAVED PHOTOS

Whether it's direct from the camera, if you have a camera-equipped iPad, or images from the web, you can save them all to the Photos app.

Add Photos with the Camera

Photos taken with the iPad appear automatically in the All Photos album if you use iCloud Photo Library. If you don't they will appear in the Camera Roll album instead. You can access them directly by tapping the square icon in the bottom-left of the Camera app.

Hot Tip

If you use Photo Booth to apply special effects to your photos, these will also appear in the Camera Roll/All Photos album.

Add Photos from Other Apps

- **Safari:** As you browse the web, you'll come across images you want to save. Tap and hold the image you want. In the box that opens, select Save Image and it will be downloaded to Photos.

- **Messages:** Tap the image you've been sent to open it full-size then tap again and select the Share button in the top-right corner and select Save Image.

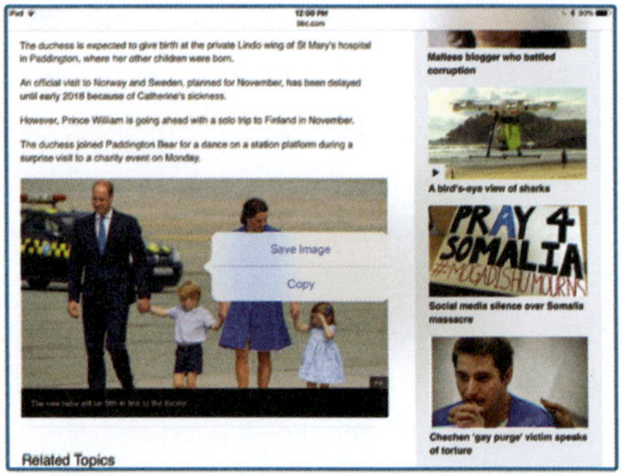

Above: To download a photo from Safari, tap and hold the image and then select the Save Image option.

- **Email:** Select the email with the image attached. Tap and hold the image in the email then select Save Image from the pop-up box.

Screenshots

Want to capture an image of what's on your iPad screen – such as your highest ever score on a favourite game? Press the Sleep/Wake button at the top of the iPad and the Home button at the same time then release. There'll be a flash of white light, a camera click and the image will be saved to a dedicated folder in the Photos app. In iOS 11and up, a thumbnail of the screenshot will appear in the bottom of the display. Tap it to edit, annotate, print or share.

UPLOADED PHOTOS

To transfer photos direct from your digital camera, you need a separate adapter. Alternatively, upload them first to your computer and use one of a growing number of third-party apps to transfer them wirelessly to the iPad.

Lightning to SD Card Camera Reader

If you have iOS 9 or later, this £29/$29 adapter allows you to connect your digital camera's SD card to your iPad. It is one of the few ways you can upload photos and videos direct from your camera. If you have a 30-pin dock connector on an earlier iPad model, try to track down the iPad Camera Connection Kit which will be compatible.

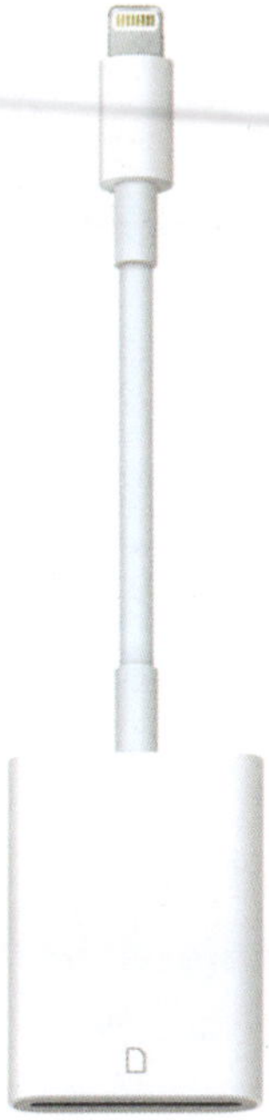

Above: Download photos directly from your digital camera using an SD memory card adapter.

Importing Photos with the Adapters

Once you've made the physical connection, open Photos, if it hasn't already opened automatically.

1. Tap individual photos to select them, then press Import. To upload all the photos, tap Import All.

2. Tap the photos you want to transfer, touch the red sync button and select where you want your photos to be transferred to/from.

3. In Photos, tap Albums, Last Import to see the photos.

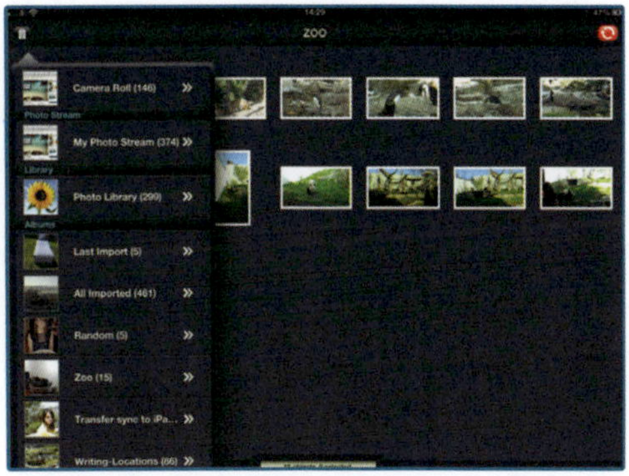

Step 1: Download the PhotoSync app to transfer photos to your iPad from other devices wirelessly.

Wireless Transfer

There are several apps, such as PhotoSync, used here, which let you wirelessly transfer your photos to the iPad. You can import them from either your desktop computer, laptop or another iDevice, like an iPhone. PhotoSync will sync your images with online photo storage sites, such as Flickr, Dropbox and Facebook.

1. Install the app on the iPad and any other iOS device you are using, as well as your Mac or PC.

2. Go to Settings, Privacy, Location Services (just Location Services on iPad 1) and turn on PhotoSync, so the app can access your photo library.

3. Transfer your photos directly using the Wi-Fi network or Bluetooth, or via your web browser.

SYNCED PHOTOS

To make sure you have all your latest photos on the iPad, sync your photos using iTunes or automatically download the most recent shots via iCloud.

My Photo Stream

This links up all your iOS devices or computers running iCloud so you can share any photos automatically using My Photo Stream.

1. My Photo Stream should be turned on by default. If not, go to Settings, Photos and switch on Upload to My Photo Stream. Now if you take a photo on your iPad, it will appear in all others that have My Photo Stream running.

2. The My Photo Stream album stores 1,000 of your most recent photos on iCloud for 30 days.

3. Remember to move them from here to another album, share them or delete them before they are replaced as part of the normal rotation of photos.

iTunes

Traditionally, the main way to add photos is to sync them through iTunes (although you can't do this if you turn on iCloud Photo Library).

1. Connect your iPad to the computer, via USB cable or wirelessly, and click iTunes. Your iPad will show in the top bar. Click this and select Photos.

2. Make sure there's a check mark beside Sync Photos, then click on the drop-down menu to choose your picture library, such as Photos.

3. It's unlikely that you'll want to sync all your photos or indeed have sufficient space. So click Selected albums and Automatically include photos from the period of time you want. Then go through the list of Albums and select the ones to sync.

4. When finished, click Apply or Sync.

Step 2: Check Sync Photos and then choose the library you wish to sync with.

Hot Tip

As you select each photo album, keep an eye on the Capacity bar underneath. This will change, indicating how big it is and the amount of free space left.

SHARED ALBUMS

The iPad is a great digital hub for collecting, managing and adding special effects to your photos before sharing them online.

iCLOUD PHOTO LIBRARY

Copy your photos to Apple's online storage service, iCloud, and they can be automatically pushed out and received wirelessly on your computer (Mac and PC) and iOS devices. To turn on iCloud Photo Library go to Settings, Your Name, iCloud, Photos. To set up iCloud, *see* page 52.

iCloud Photo Sharing

Create albums of photos to share with your friends and family.

Hot Tip

iCloud provides unlimited free storage for music and apps, etc. that you buy through iTunes, as well as for your My Photo Stream. However, there's only 5GB of free storage for your documents, Mail, iCloud Photo Library and backups, although you can purchase more space as needed.

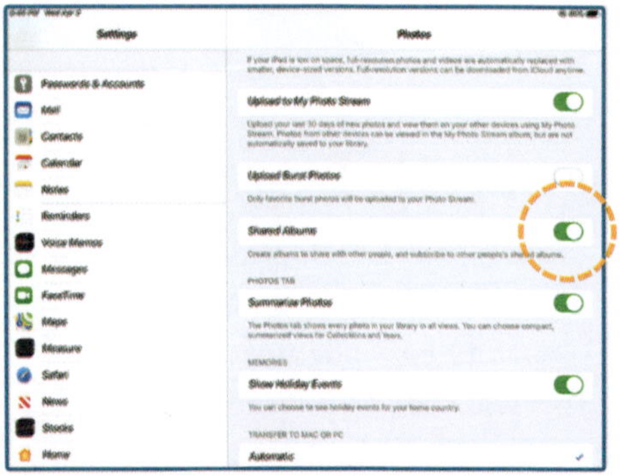

Step 1: Activate Shared Albums by toggling the switch to On in the Photos section of iCloud settings.

1. First, tap Settings, your profile, then iCloud, Photos and turn on Shared Albums.
2. Open the Photos app, then the Select button. Select the photo(s) you want to show off to others (blue ticks will indicate those selected) and tap the Share button in the top-left corner.
3. Tap Shared Albums, add any comments you have, then share to an existing shared album, if there is one, or select a new one.

4. You can invite people to view your shared album using their email address (or the mobile phone number they use for iMessage).

5. If your contacts use iOS 7 or OS X Mavericks or later, they can add their own photos and videos.

6. Alternatively, you can publish your album to a website for anyone to view. To do so select the shared album, tap People then turn on Public Website. Tap Share Link to announce the site.

SHARING DIRECT FROM YOUR iPAD

To make it easier to share your photos, via text, email or social media, all the different options have been brought together under one Share button.

Photos App

There are several ways to share images from the built-in Photos app. Tap to open it, select the image to share and press the Share button – a square box with pointing arrow.

- **Mail**: Tap this to open a new email message with the photo already attached. Tap Images to select the size of image you want to send.
- **Message**: Again, the photo is automatically added to your message. All you need do is add the contact address, your message and press Send.
- **Shared Albums**: Press this to add an individual photo to shared albums stored on iCloud.

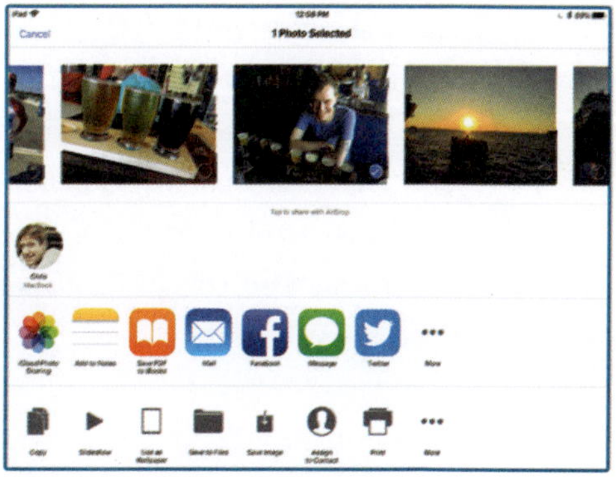

Above: Share your photos by tapping the Share icon in the top-right corner. Choose how you want to share your image from the options shown, which include sharing via Facebook, Twitter and Email.

- **Facebook**: If you have the app installed, posting a photo to the world's biggest social network is also incredibly easy. Tap the Facebook icon and the picture is already attached. Tap the album icon at the bottom to choose the name of the Facebook album to which the photo will be added.

- **Twitter**: Tap the icon and a tweet box opens with a thumbnail of the photo attached to a tweet. You can then type a message in the 'What's happening?' box. To tag someone in the photo you will have to go to the Twitter app.

Drag and Drop

A new feature in iOS 11 allowed you to drag a file from one app into another. The best example is for sharing photos. Using Split View or Slide Over you can drag a photo from the Photos app directly into a message, email, note and may more.

ONLINE ALBUMS

Move your pictures from the iPad to photo-sharing sites such as Flickr and Google Photos.

Google Photos

One of the best ways to view a photo library on the iPad is to use a third-party cloud app like Google Photos, especially if you have an Android phone that doesn't pair with iCloud. That way, you can view all of your photos without taking up space on your iPad. Google Photos offers unlimited storage for photos stored at normal resolution.

Above: The Google Photos app lets you access your photo library online, and share photos with friends.

Flickr

As it's one of the biggest online photo-sharing sites, several photo-editing apps, such as Photos, let you post directly to Flickr. In addition, there is a Flickr app for the iPad that allows you to view previously uploaded images.

PHOTO SERVICES

Get creative with your iPad and use your photos to create online journals, greeting cards and much more.

Journals

With apps like Day One, you can create your own photo journal and diary capturing your life as you live it. All your memories and photos can be synced through through iCloud or Dropbox or via the Day One Mac desktop application.

Photobooks

Apps such as Snapfish take your photos – including pictures taken with your iPad camera – and turn them into photo albums, story books for your children or travel journals.

Greeting Cards

Surprise gran with a greeting card featuring the family. Apps such as Punchbowl let you incorporate photos from the iPad into a series of templates to create personalized cards for all occasions.

Above: Turn your photos into jigsaw puzzles by downloading the Jigsaw Puzzle app.

Calendars

Make your holiday last a year. Shutterfly for the iPad will let you memorialize your trip by turning your travel shots – or any photo – into a calendar.

Puzzles

Jigsaw Puzzle turns your photos into jigsaws – ranging from four pieces if it's for children to 1,024 pieces for the patient/experienced puzzler.

YOUR VIDEOS

Shooting and editing video is so easy on the iPad that you will soon be creating movie clips to share on the internet. Go viral, and your clip could be the latest online sensation.

VIDEO RECORDING

Point and tap is all you need to do to start recording your video, provided you've got an iPad 2 or later, but there are a few things to bear in mind in order to get the best results.

Shooting Video

The video recorder is built in to the Camera app you use to take photos.

1. To start, simply tap the Camera app and rotate the camera options until Video is highlighted in yellow.

2. Point the camera at the scene you want to capture and tap the recording button in the centre-right of the screen.

Step 2: Start recording your video by tapping the red recording button to the centre-right of the screen.

3. As recording starts the red circle changes to a square. A timer with flashing red dot showing how long you've been recording appears.

4. To finish recording, tap the record button again. Watch your movie clip by tapping the vhumbnail beneath the capture button.

Focusing Your Video Recording

While the iPad has its own autofocus, you can target a particular area. Tap the screen on the area you want to focus on and the iPad will make the necessary adjustments.

Which Video Camera to Use

The iPad has come with two cameras since the iPad 2.

- **The front-facing camera**: Primarily intended for FaceTime video chat calls, this has a lower resolution than the rear camera. If you do want to use the front camera – perhaps to introduce your clip – switch lenses by tapping the camera icon with two circular arrows above the capture button.

- **The rear camera**: Newer iPads have good rear cameras that allow you to shoot photos in high definition and, in some cases, even 4K video. These later iPads have auto-stabilization features designed to compensate for any shakiness.

Hot Tip

You can view your video equally well in portrait or landscape mode (although landscape is better for sharing to YouTube), choose one or the other before you begin and don't switch midway through filming.

EDITING VIDEO

Tidy up your video by using the Camera app to trim unwanted footage from the beginning and end of your clip – or use iMovie and Clips for more extensive movie-editing.

Simple Editing

1. Once you've shot your video, tap the Camera Roll in the bottom corner to view the clip or select one previously recorded from your videos album in Photos and tap Edit.

Step 2: Tap the screen to show a timeline of your video, with the cursor marking where you are in the clip.

2. When the video opens you'll see there's a scrubbing bar at the bottom – that is a timeline of your video, with the cursor showing where you are in the clip.

3. If you press and hold the left or right edge of the scrubbing bar, it will gain a yellow border and allow you to move in and out to shorten the clip.

4. When you have the section of the video that you want to keep, tap the Done button.

5. If you try to increase the clip's length but the trim handle doesn't move, it means there are no additional frames to add.

More Advanced Movie Editing

With Apple's iMovie app (available from the App Store) on the iPad, you have many of the useful video-editing features that are available in the full version of the program that runs on Mac computers.

Hot Tip

It's best to have your iPad in horizontal view when running iMovie as you can see more of your timeline and the editing controls.

Import Video

The iMovie app lets you polish up your video footage, combine clips, and add titles and special effects in the transitions between scenes.

1. Open iMovie, tap the + button to Create Project. Then choose between a Movie and a Trailer to create a new folder for your video. A Trailer uses a series of customizable title

title screens, themed music and transitions. You can choose from romance, scary, superhero and others.

2. You'll see a tab on the left-hand side where you can import stored media. There are Moments, Video, Photos and Albums. If you have iCloud Photo Stream enabled you'll see photos from your iPhone too.

3. Tapping one of the folders will load the available media. As well as any video clips, you can also add photos. Tap the items and press Create Movie.

4. The clips will appear on a timeline in the order you selected them. From here, you'll be able to trim, rearrange, add music and more. You can also add more from the Media section at any time.

5. Alternatively, capture video direct from within iMovie by tapping the video camera icon from the My Movie screen. This accesses the iPad's iSight camera and you can shoot your HD video as before. You can switch cameras to film yourself and change the quality of the recorded footage.

Step 3: Add a photo from your photo library to the end of your timeline. Multiple copies are added so the photo lasts on screen.

6. The white vertical line, known as the playhead, shows where you are in the video. The image by the playhead is displayed in the preview window above.

7. Flick your finger left or right to scroll through the timeline. Pinch your fingers to zoom in and out or press the triangular Play button under the preview window to start the video.

Edit Video

Having added the video clips to your project, you can edit them into your own movie.

- **Rearrange a clip**: To change the order in which they play, tap and hold the clip you're moving and drag it to the new location. The existing clips move to make space.

- **Delete a clip**: Tap the clip you want to remove, and tap Delete in the bottom corner. If you change your mind and want to add it back, it will still be in the list of available video clips.

Above: Delete a clip by double-tapping and selecting Delete.

- **Trim a clip**: This is done in much the same way as in the Camera app. Tap the clip in the timeline and then drag the yellow endpoints to a new start and finish position.

- **Split a clip**: Tap the clip you want, and drag it until the playhead is right over the spot where you want to split it. Tap the video, and it will be outlined in yellow. Swipe your finger down the playhead as though you were slicing it in half. Now you can add another clip or insert a different transition.

Edit Transitions

The on-screen move from one clip to the next is called a transition. There are five types:

- **Cut transition**: Marked by a white line on a black square this is called None in iMovie because, although there is a break between clips, there's no transition effect. On screen, one clip will just flow into the next but the transition will still be shown in the timeline in case you want to change it.

- **Theme transition**: Marked by two white boxes on a black background. To choose the theme to apply, tap the Project Settings button – the cog wheel – in the top-right corner and make your choice.

- **Dissolve, Slide, Wipe and Fade:** The final four offer more visual means of moving between two clips. Tap them to see a preview, control the length of the transition, control sound effects and more.

Hot Tip

If Cross-Dissolve isn't available in iMovie, it's because the clips either side aren't long enough to support it.

Select Transitions

By default, there's a transition between each video clip and photo in the project.

1. To change it, tap the transition icon in the timeline.
2. From the Transition Settings that open below select the style you want. To change how long it lasts, tap the duration required.
3. Tap on the yellow triangles to open the precision editor. This lets you move the endpoints where you want the transition to begin and end. Tap the triangles to return to the timeline.

Step 3: Tap the yellow triangles below the transition button to open the precision editor.

Add Titles

Another way to give a more professional finish to your videos is to overlay titles.

1. Tap the clip and select Title from the bar that appears below. Boxes showing the different styles appear above.
2. Tap your chosen text style and use the on-screen keyboard to add your title.
3. On some themes you can add a location. Tap Location and enter the details.

ADDING SOUND TO YOUR VIDEO

From recording your own commentary to adding a song from your iTunes collection, there are several ways to add sound to your video.

Background Music

If you are adventurous, you can record your own music with an app like GarageBand; you can also select iMovie theme music or add any song from your Music library.

1. To turn Theme music on tap the Audio tab from within the Media section in the upper-right.

2. You can choose from Theme Music (iMove presets), Sound Effects and your music. There are Playlists, Albums etc. Tap the chosen track, hit Use and it will jump onto your timeline.

3. Only one music track can play at a time. If you add a music track when there is already one in place, it will play after this if the video is long enough. If it's not it will replace the original music.

Step 1: Tap the musical notes icon and select Theme Music to begin adding background music to your videos.

4. If you have background music looping turned on (that is the track keeps repeating throughout the video) then you can only have one track.

5. To set the volume of the background music tap the Waveform button in the middle bar and you'll see a mix of yellow and red peaks. Red shows the audio is too loud and likely to be distorted.

6. Change the volume until these peaks disappear, by double-tapping the green background in the timeline that represents the audio clip and adjusting the slider.

Sound Effects

Add these at relevant points by scrolling through the timeline so the playhead is where you want to add the sound effect. Tap the Audio button and then Sound effects. Preview a sound by tapping the Play button on the right. It will be shown as a blue bar in the timeline. Adjust the volume by double-tapping this and then moving the slider.

Backing Track

When you record the video, it might include all sorts of background noises or conversations. If the clip does have its own audio, iMovie will automatically lower the volume (known as audio ducking) of the background music.

Voiceover

Place the playhead where you want to start recording and then tap the microphone icon. Tap Record in the pop-up box and after a three-second countdown, start talking. Press the Stop button to finish recording. You then have the options to Review the voiceover, Retake, Cancel or Accept it.

Step 5: Set the volume of your background music by tapping the Waveform button and using the slider to change the volume until any red peaks disappear.

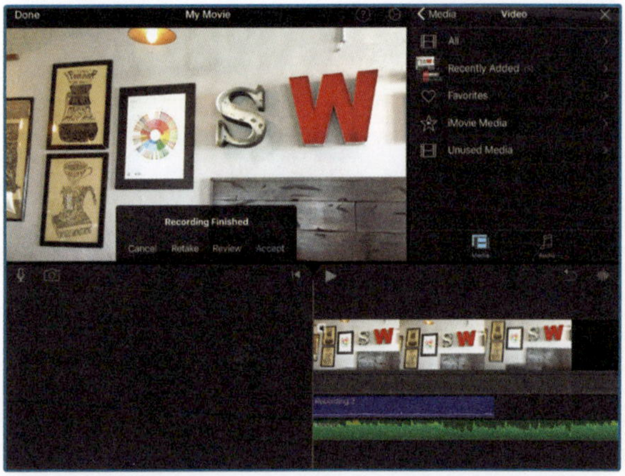

Above: After recording your voiceover you can choose whether to review it, retake it, cancel it or accept it.

SHARE YOUR VIDEOS

Once you have the perfect movie, the iPad makes it simple to share your video with friends, family or the wider world of the internet, via YouTube and Facebook.

Sharing from Photos

Go to the Videos folder in Photos, select the clip you want, tap the Share button and choose your preferred option.

- **Email**: There will be a slight delay while the video is compressed to reduce the size of the file that's sent. Because this also reduces the quality of the video, do not use email to send the video to your computer – it's better to sync them using iTunes.
- **Message**: The video is automatically attached, so you just have to add who it's going to and write your message.
- **Facebook and Twitter**: If you have the social media apps installed on your iPad, then these options will appear in the share menu too.

Sharing to YouTube

You'll need to do this from the YouTube app directly, but it's probably the best way to share your videos. Once you're logged into the YouTube app with a Google account, you can press the camera icon from the top right corner of the app to begin uploading. You'll be able to enter a title, tags and category for your video.

Sharing from iMovie

1. When you've finished, tap Done. If you haven't given the project a name, do so now. Tap My Project and enter the title. Tap the Share button and you'll see the options available.
2. Most links are to video-sharing sites, such as YouTube, Facebook and Vimeo. You will need to have an account for the site you select before you can upload your video.

3. The procedure is typically the same: enter your login details and then complete the form for your video. It should include a title, a description and a category for it.

4. Some sites also let you set who can see the video through the privacy settings. There may be some you want to share with close friends, but if you want your video to be seen, it's best to go public.

5. Alternatively, you can also send your video to iCloud Shared Albums or add it to iTunes, for syncing with your Mac or PC. Or save it to the Apple Files app.

Above: Tap the Share button in the iMovie Home screen to view and select how you want to share your video.

Clips App

Apple's video creation app Clips lets you share photos and videos. It's free in the App Store.

1. Download and open it to start, then select the camera and hold down the record button to record.

2. Before hitting record, use the options at the top of the screen to customize the clip: the speech bubble transcribes your speech on screen while recording; the filters button gives you a live view of various video effects; the Star icon lets you add a caption; and the T gives you access to title clips that can be placed at the start or end of the video.

3. Tap any clip within the timeline to trim it, delete it, mute the sound or amend the text. The result can be shared to social media (Twitter, Instagram etc.), or by Messages or email.

ENTERTAINMENT CENTRE

Whether it's a Hollywood blockbuster or must-see TV series, it can be bought or rented to view in glorious detail on your iPad – or to project onto your TV.

AIRPLAY

AirPlay lets you wirelessly transmit videos and other content from your iPad to the big screen – and show them on your TV.

Apple TV

As well as streaming what's on your iPad – music, photos and so on – Apple TV also lets you show content on the big screen from Netflix, YouTube and Vimeo, plus films and TV shows from the iTunes store and more.

Above: The Apple TV black box connects to your TV and wirelessly receives video streams from your iPad.

1. To mirror the screen of your iPad on the TV wirelessly, you will need the second generation Apple TV or later and an iPad 2 or later. This black box is physically connected to your TV by High Density Multimedia Interface (HDMI) cable and wirelessly receives the video stream from your iPad, using AirPlay mirroring.

2. Turn on AirPlay on your Apple TV. Using the remote supplied with it, navigate the on-screen display on your TV and select Settings, Airplay and turn it on. It's easier with the fourth- and fifth-generation Apple TVs and the Siri Remote, which has touch and voice control for the TV.

3. Swipe down from the top right of your iPad's screen (from the bottom on iOS 11 and earlier) to open the Control Center.

4. Select AirPlay and then tap the Apple TV you want to use to mirror the iPad. The first time you pair the device you may be asked to enter a code that appears on your TV screen.

Step 3: Open the Control Center, tap the AirPlay icon and then select Apple TV.

Physical Connection to Your TV

You can also connect your iPad screen to a TV or other display with a cable.

View Rented Movies through Apple TV

Once Apple TV is set up, you should see the iTunes Store, which lets you access the same video and TV shows available through the iPad.

1. Select Movies from the main Apple TV menu. Browse through the different options – top movies, new releases etc. You can also search by title if you have a film in mind.

2. Select the movie you would like to watch. Apple TV will offer you the HD option by default.

3. To change this preference go to Settings, Apps, iTunes Video and Purchases. Then select Limit Purchases and Rentals to SD. You can turn this on and off at your convenience. The newest Apple TV plays movies at the new 4K Ultra HD resolution, offering 4 times as much detail as HD.

4. Once you've purchased the movie you'll be asked to confirm. A message appears when it is ready to view. Press Play to start watching.

Buy and Rent Videos through the iTunes Store

1. Tap the iTunes store app and select Films at the bottom.

2. You can select from Featured movies, which shows you the most popular films to rent or buy, as well as recommendations from iTunes. Alternatively, select the Top Charts button and then the Films tab and you can see the most popular movies in each category.

Hot Tip

If you would like to watch your rented movie on the go, you can download it. After you tap the Rent button, tap Watch Later and find the title in the iTunes Store Rented tab. From here you can tap the cloud icon to download the movie.

3. By default, all types of movie are shown in both the Featured and Charts section. If you have a specific taste in film, such as horror, tap the Genres button and make your selection – then, just those movies will be shown.

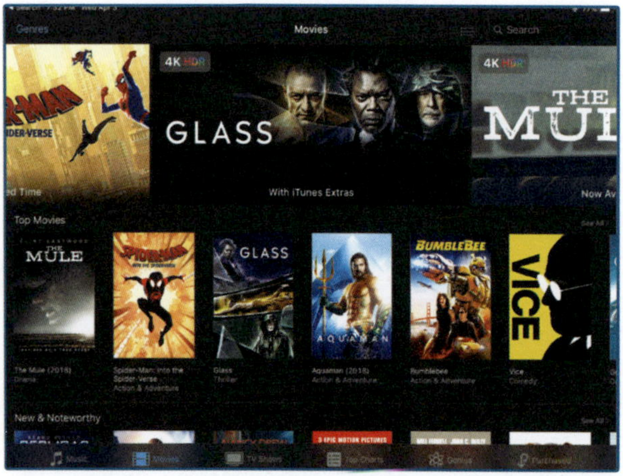

Above: Select the Film tab at the bottom of the iTunes app to view movies available for renting and purchase.

4. When you see a movie you want to rent, select it. You'll see Details of the film, including a trailer, synopsis and cast list. At the top is the overall rating from iTunes users and the price to buy or rent the movie.

5. To see more detailed opinions about the film – and add your own once you've seen it – tap the Reviews tab.

6. If it doesn't appeal, select Related and you'll see similar films that

customers who purchased the film you're looking at have also bought.

7. Tap the Rent button if you want to hire the movie and confirm payment with Touch ID or passcode. You'll have up to 30 days to view the film. But once you've started to watch it, you have 48 hours to complete it.

8. You can watch your rented movie on any device associated with your Apple ID, but you can't stream or download it to more than one device at a time.

9. To buy a film, select the relevant button. For the iPad 3 and later, the default is to download the HD (high-definition) version of the movie. For the iPad 1 and 2 it will be the SD (standard-definition) version.

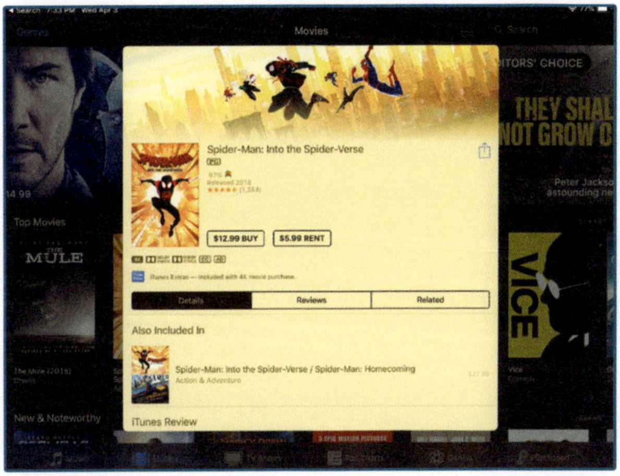

Above: Click on a movie you are interested in to see further details and the price to buy or rent.

Hot Tip

The HD version is more expensive and a much bigger file size, so will take longer to download.

Hot Tip

Don't worry if you accidentally delete a TV show or movie you have bought. Go to Purchased, select Films or TV Series and locate the programme you want to re-download.

TV Shows

TV shows operate in a similar way to the movies, except they are only available to buy. Tap TV Shows from within the iTunes Store app. You'll see a homepage of featured content. You can browse by Genre, Top Charts and Search Within each section you have the option to view single Episodes of a show or the collected Series.

PLAY VIDEOS

Whether it's for the latest movie, a music clip or a converted file of the children's school play, the iPad is an immensely powerful video player.

MASTER VIDEO PLAYER

All the video content downloaded from the iTunes store – whether it's a movie, TV show or music video – appears automatically in the TV app. You'll see Purchased content, have access to the iTunes Store and also some on-demand apps that enable you to link to the TV app.

Playback

1. Turn your iPad to switch between viewing your video in portrait or widescreen (landscape) mode.

2. Tap the Play button (forward-facing triangle) or the video itself to start playback. If you are streaming the video may take a moment to start. Press the centre button to pause playback.

Step 4: Navigate to your chosen point in a video by dragging your finger to move the playhead along the timeline at the top of the screen.

3. Touch and hold the Rewind or Fast Forward icon to speed backward and forward.

4. Alternatively, drag the playhead along the scrubber bar (as the video timeline is called) at the top to any point of the video you want.

5. To go right back to the beginning of the video, drag the playhead all the way to the left or simply tap the Rewind button.

6. Tap the speech bubble at the bottom of the screen for subtitle options.

7. Use the volume slider to raise or lower the soundtrack on the video.

8. To stop the video before it finishes playing, tap the Done button or press the Home button.

Hot Tip

Want to know what videos are available online? OVGuide (www.ovguide.com) is an independent guide that includes free full length movies, TV shows, trending viral videos and clips.

Multitasking with Video

A great new feature enables you to watch video while working within other apps. While watching video, you can click the home button to reduce it to a small portion of the screen. It will sit on top of any other apps you use.

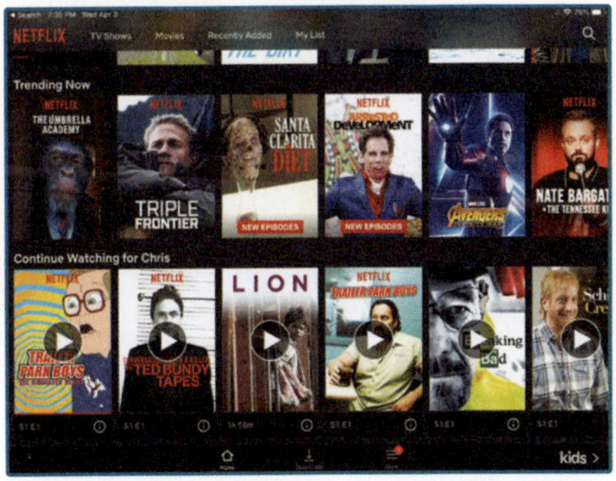

Above: Access the Netflix app to see what films and TV shows are available to stream.

- **Size:** You can alter the size of the player by pinching in and out with two or more fingers.
- **Move:** Press and hold the video app to reposition the window.
- **Full screen:** Make the video full screen again by pressing the box with the arrow in the corner.
- **Exit the app:** Close the video app by pressing the X.

OTHER VIDEO PLAYERS

In addition to the TV app, you can watch video on your iPad through the Safari web browser and third-party apps that connect directly to video sites.

Video Browsing

Browse the internet and you'll see that many websites, from personal blogs to international newspapers, music and entertainment sites, include video. Virtually any video in the standard MP4 format will play on the iPad through the Safari web browser. As with all Apple devices running iOS, no Flash videos can play on the iPad directly, but Flash video is sparse online these days.

Video Apps

There are several video sites that have their own apps for the iPad. Netflix and Amazon Video both have apps for subscribers to use their service, as does Hulu and a few others in the US. Typically, for a reasonable monthly subscription you can access any of the vast library of movies and TV shows these sites hold.

Video-sharing Sites

The popularity of YouTube was such that their app was built-in to the iPad's operating system in iOS 6, but if you have a later iOS you'll need to download it from the App Store. Another popular video-sharing site, Vimeo, has its own dedicated app for the iPad. Videos posted by your friends will also be available via apps like Instagram, Snapchat, Facebook and Twitter.

TV Sites

All the main TV companies – such as ESPN, ABC, Fox, Comedy Central – have developed apps that let you watch programmes on the iPad, sometimes live. They enable you to download and enjoy content on the go, away from your TV screen, whether you're on holiday or just in bed.

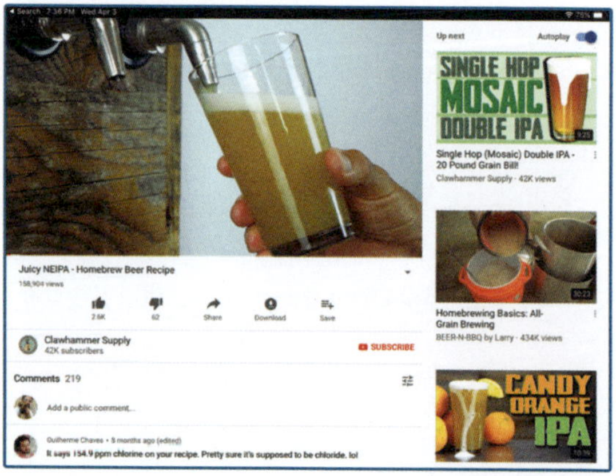

Above: YouTube is a popular video sharing site, which can be accessed through a dedicated iPad app.

STREAMING MEDIA/VIDEO

Most videos are streamed to your iPad via the internet, so you can start watching within a few minutes, rather than wait for it to download fully. Beware if you're streaming using a mobile data connection – it can use up your allowance quickly.

- **Streaming**: with streaming, just a small amount of data is downloaded to the iPad. This is a buffer against any interruption caused by any slowdown or delay on the internet connection that could affect your viewing.

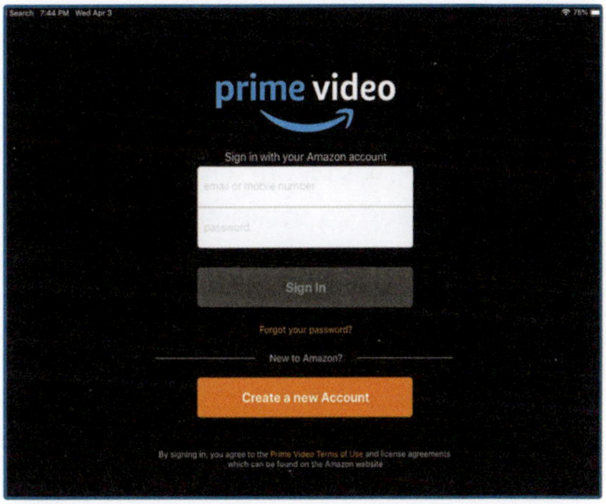

Above: If you're an Amazon Prime subscribers, you get access to a wide range of video content through the iPad's Prime Video app

- **Buffering**: while the movie is being buffered, you see a circular, revolving line. If the film is regularly halting and the buffering icon appears, it is because of a slow or problematic internet connection.

- **Bandwidth**: streaming video naturally takes up a lot of bandwidth. The higher the quality of the movie, the more bandwidth it needs. For example, Netflix uses 1 GB/hour for each stream of SD video, and up to 3 GB per hour for each stream of HD video. This shouldn't be a problem if you're using Wi-Fi only, but it will be for cellular data.

Hot Tip

If you are having problems viewing a streaming video, the first thing to do is choose a lower quality setting.

- **Viewing Problems**: in addition to how much bandwidth you have, streaming can be affected by other factors, such as the amount of other traffic, if you're sharing the connection, or interference from other wireless products.

SYNC VIDEOS

Having shot your video masterpiece or purchased the latest film release, you need to make sure it's available on the iPad in a format that will work.

iTUNES

Use iTunes to keep the videos on your computer and iPad in sync – or to share access to videos without having to transfer them first.

- Once you purchase a TV show or movie from iTunes, it will automatically download to your iPad. The next time you sync your iPad with your computer, it will be moved to your iTunes library on your computer.
- Through iCloud, it can also be automatically downloaded to other iOS devices that use the same iTunes account.

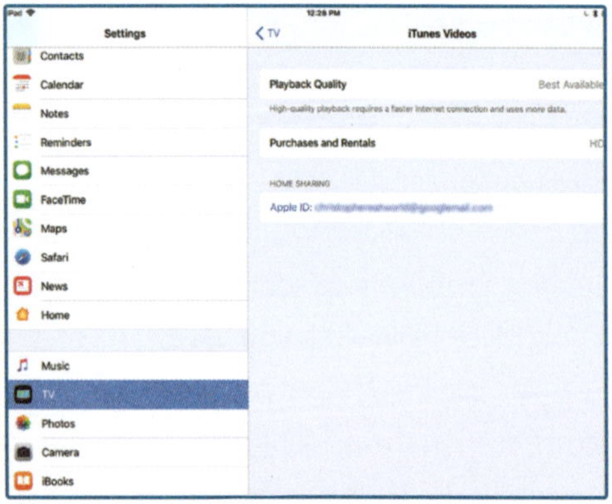

Step 3: Choose Videos (or TV depending on iOS version) from the iPad settings menu and enter your Apple ID and password under the Home Sharing title.

Home Sharing

Instead of transferring the movies to your iPad, you can play them from your Mac or PC over your Wi-Fi network.

1. To play videos from your iTunes library on Mac or PC to your iPad, you have to make sure they are both on the same home network.
2. Open iTunes on your computer and in the File menu choose Home Sharing and then Turn On Home Sharing. Enter your Apple ID and password and click Turn On Home Sharing.

3. Tap Settings on the iPad and choose TV; under Home sharing enter the same Apple ID.

4. Now launch the TV app and you'll see there's a new tab, Shared. Select a shared library; there may be several if you are sharing iTunes on different computers.

5. Tap the Library you want, select the type of video you want – Movies, TV Shows or Music Videos – and then choose the one you want to play.

iPAD-FRIENDLY VIDEO FORMAT

The iPad supports only a limited number of video formats. While movies and TV shows downloaded from the iTunes store and services such as Netflix will be iPad compatible, there are many that may not be, including your own home movies.

Convert Using iTunes

You can use iTunes on your computer to convert video into an iPad-friendly format. Add the video to iTunes by going to File, Add to Library and selecting the video file. After importing, select the video and in the File menu select Create New Version and then Create iPad or Apple TV version.

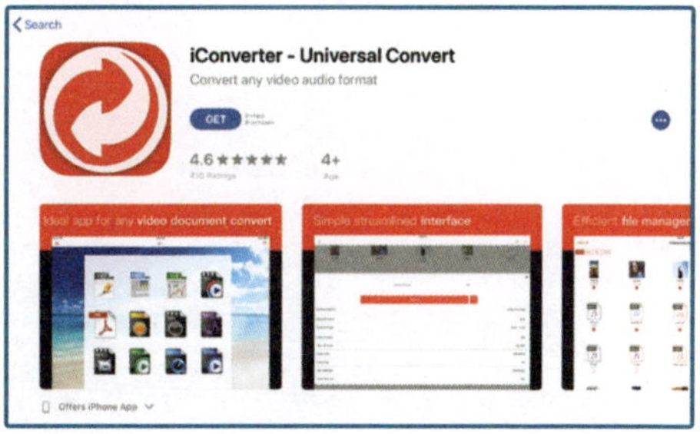

Above: The iConverter app can be found in the App Store.

Convert Using Third-party Apps

There are many third-party applications – free and paid for – that will make conversion quick and easy. Some, like iConverter or The Video Converter, will optimise your video for playback on the iPad and, once the conversion is done, automatically add it to your iTunes library for syncing with the iPad.

Hot Tip

You may have to be patient if you use iTunes to convert your home movie. The results are not always great and conversion can take a long time.

READING

BOOKS

Through this free reader, you can read books on the iPad, whether they're downloaded from Book Store, Apple's online bookshop, or elsewhere on the internet.

BUILDING UP YOUR BOOK COLLECTION

With thousands of free and paid-for books in Book Store, there's plenty of choice available.

Book Store

The Book Store is accessed from within the Books app, which is one of the iPad's built-in apps.

1. When the Books app opens for the first time, you'll see a set of empty 'bookshelves' ready to hold your books. Tap Featured in the bottom toolbar to browse Book Store.
2. Tapping the Book Store tab opens up an attractive and clean storefront. You can scroll down the page to see suggested titles, recommendations and tabs to access NY Times best sellers, the tap Top Charts and Top Authors. At the top of the screen there's a tab that allows you to switch to Audiobooks.

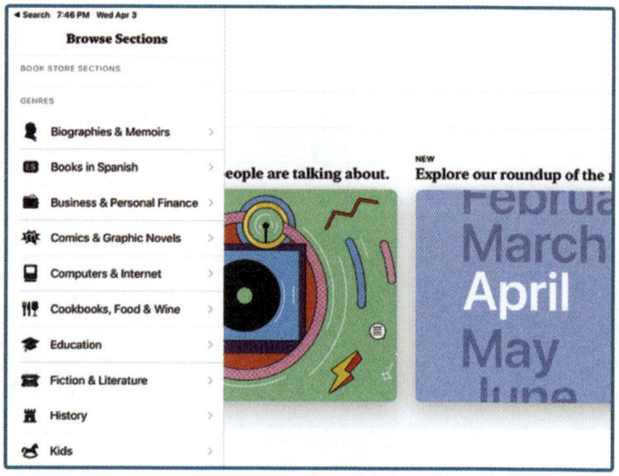

Above: Use the Browse Sections menu to find books from a particular genre.

3. To filter the list of available titles, tap the All Categories button at the top of the page and select which genre you are most interested in, such as Crime & Thrillers, Food & Drink, etc.

4. If you know what you're looking for use the Search box. You can also use the Browse Sections button at the top of the store page to narrow down genres, bestseller lists and special offers.

5. Tap the book cover and the information box opens with all the details to help you decide if it's one you want to read. As well as the standard book information about the publisher, author, price and so on, there is a Sample button, which lets you read a short extract from the book.

6. Below this is a more detailed description of the book, ratings and reviews by other iBookstore users and links to related titles.

DOWNLOAD BOOKS

Whether it's through Book Store or the web, there is a variety of ways you can build up your personal library on your iPad.

From the Bookstore

1. Once your choice is made, tap the price or Free button. You may be prompted to confirm your purchase by using Touch ID or entering your password for your Apple ID.

2. A circular progress bar shows the title being downloaded, which will appear on the top shelf.

3. Once the book is downloaded, tap the cover to open it and start reading (*see* page 135).

Internet

Books supports two of the most popular ebook formats, EPUB (electronic publication) and PDF (portable document format). You can find books in these formats all over the web; for example, from Project Gutenberg (www.gutenberg.org), epubBooks (www.epubbooks.com) or ManyBooks.net.

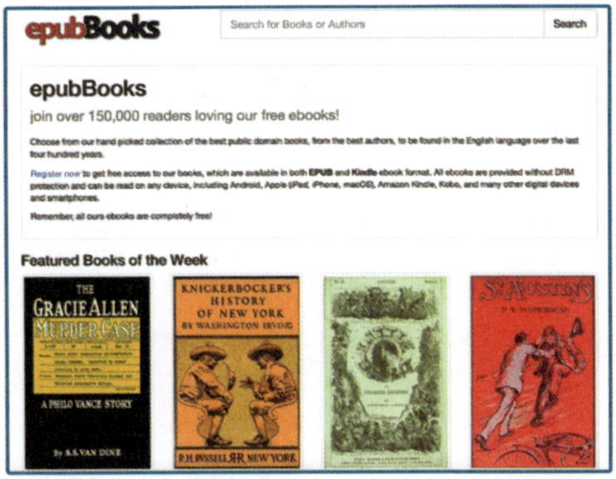

Above: Visit the epubbooks.com website to browse titles and download them to iBooks.

Step 1: Once downloaded you can choose to open your new book from your virtual bookshelf.

1. To download these books directly to Books, open Safari and go to the site. Select the book you want, choose one of the two formats above (if available) and tap the Download link. On sites such as ManyBooks.net you can then choose to Open in Books.

2. Similarly, if you receive an ebook or link to one in your email, tap it and it will be added to Books.

3. Alternatively, if you have already downloaded the ebooks to your computer, you can transfer them to Books on your iPad, via iTunes. Just drag the EPUB book file into your iTunes library on the computer (or select Add to Library from the File menu in iTunes and choose the file). When you sync your iPad with the computer, the ebook will be transferred to one of the shelves in Books.

Hot Tip

There is a third format that Books supports – interactive textbooks, where the text includes images, sounds, videos, animations and even 3D objects. These are made using a special Apple format and are available only in the Bookstore.

Automatic Downloading via iCloud

All the books you buy from Book Store will appear in your Books library but are actually stored in iCloud, Apple's online storage and backup service. This means that if you purchased a book on your computer or iPhone, you can download and read it on your iPad.

- **Purchased:** If it's a book you've already purchased, you can download it onto your bookshelf at any time. Tap the Cloud icon beside the book you want to download.
- **Sync Books:** In order to automatically sync books purchased across all your iDevices (iPhone, iPad etc.), tap Settings, Your Name, then iTunes & App Stores and turn on Books in the Automatic Downloads section.

Remove the Shelves

While the bookshelves appeal to some, others find them irritating. For a more traditional list view, tap the button with bullet points and three lines on the right of the toolbar. When you do this the lines will change to boxes, tap this to revert back to your virtual bookshelves.

Hot Tip

You can also sort books in list view using the buttons at the top, so that they are displayed by title, author or category.

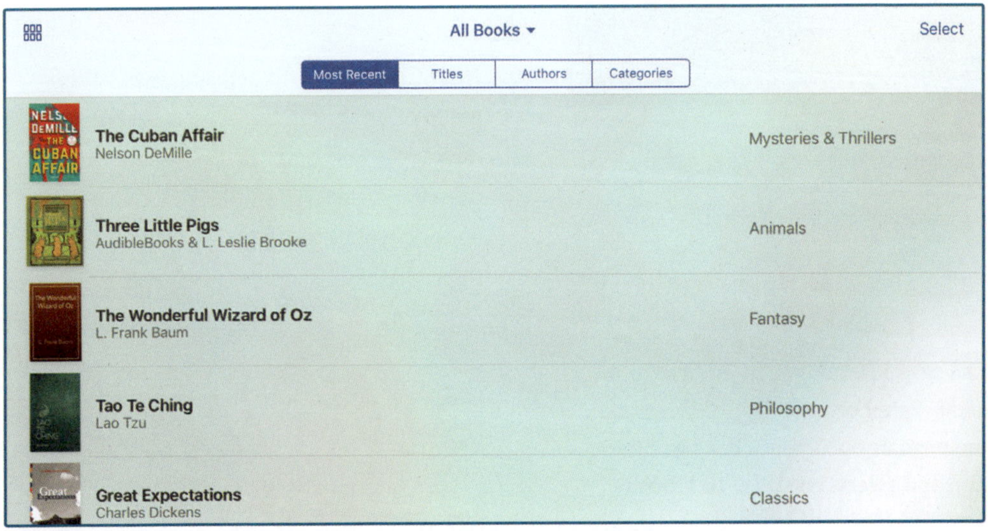

Above: You can remove the virtual bookshelves to display your books in a more traditional list view.

Delete Books

- **To delete a book**: Tap the Edit button from the bookshelf and choose one or more books. A white tick will appear on each one chosen. Tap the trash icon to remove the books, then Done.

Book Collections

If you've got a series of books on a particular subject, group them into a collection.

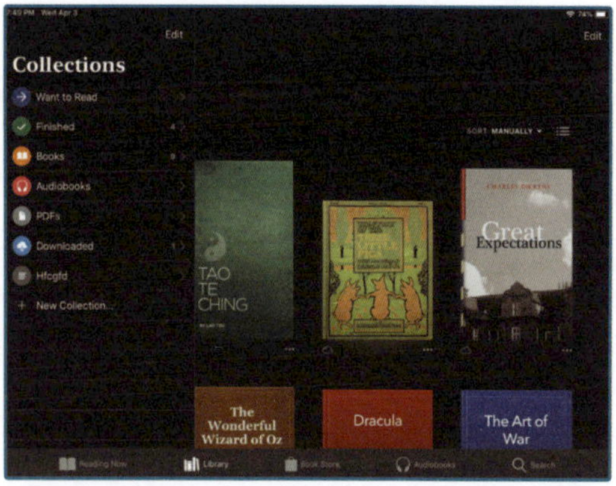

Above: All new downloads are assigned to a pre-set collection, but you can also create a New collection.

- **Pre-set Collections**: Tapping the Collections section on the library page shows a number of pre-set collections, which you can add to. You've got Want to Read (a Wishlist from the store), Finished, Books, Audiobooks, PDFs and downloaded. To move between them simply tap one of the items from the list.

- **New Collection**: To add your own group of books, tap Collections, and then New Collection, and write in a name. Then, from the main library, press Edit, select the books of your choosing, select Add To and then add the titles to the newly made collection.

- **Delete a Collection**: To delete a collection, tap the Collections button, select the one you want from the list, tap the Edit button and press delete.

Hot Tip

You can save PDFs direct to iBooks from your email, Safari or other apps. When you view the page or document click the Share button and select Save PDF to iBooks.

READERS

The lightness of the iPad, and the iPad mini in particular, gives it a natural advantage for reading books – especially when it can also hold most of your library.

eBOOK READERS

Most ebook readers work in a similar way. Apple Books, shown below, allows you to bookmark pages and write notes, and will remember where you last finished reading.

Reading on the iPad

1. Open Books and tap the cover of the book you want to read. If you have already started reading a book, Books will automatically open at the last page you read.

2. Generally, if you hold the iPad in portrait view, there'll be one page to a screen. In landscape view there will be two pages.

3. To turn a page, tap the screen on the right and flick left. To turn the page back, tap the left of the screen and flick to the right.

4. As you read, there's nothing on the page to distract your attention. To access the Reading controls at the top of the page and the Page Navigator at the bottom, touch the middle of the page. To close them, touch the page again.

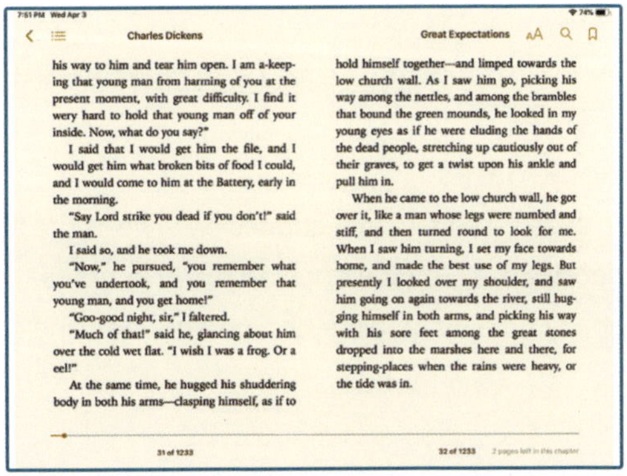

Step 4: When you read on an iPad there are no reading controls which may distract you. To access them, touch the middle of the page.

Navigating the Book

- **Library button**: The back facing arrow takes you back to the bookshelf or list view of your books.
- **Contents button**: Tap the list icon to jump to the Contents section. Scroll through the list of what's in the book and tap any of the headings to go direct to that page. Tap the button, now labelled Resume, to return to where you were.
- **Move to a page**: Drag the slider at the bottom of the page. As you move across, there's a text box with the Chapter heading and page numbers. When you let go, the book will open at that page. Alternatively, tap the magnifying glass icon and type the page number in the box.

Hot Tip

You can also turn a page by tapping the left or right margin. To activate this feature tap Settings, iBooks and turn on Both Margins Advance.

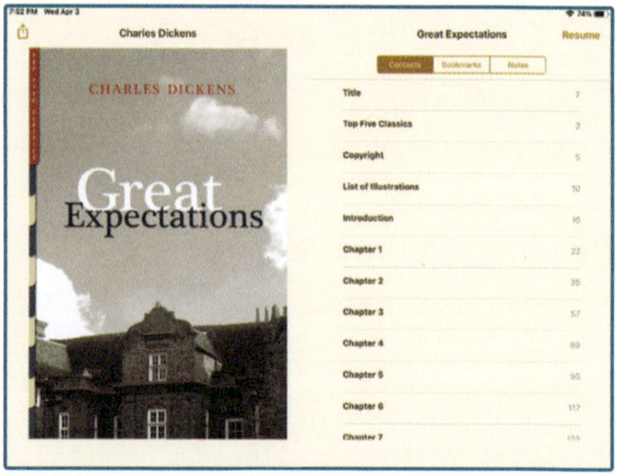

Above: Navigate through your iBooks by touching the screen to show control icons such as bookmarks, contents, and the slider at the bottom of the page. Here you can see the contents page.

- **Revisit a page**: Use the Go to Page XX link or Back to Page XX link at the bottom of the screen.

Bookmarks

If there's a particularly notable passage in the book that you know you'll want to revisit, bookmark it. Tap the bookmark icon in the far right corner. You can access all your bookmarks at any time by tapping the Contents icon and selecting Bookmarks.

Notes

Highlight a key passage or add a note by tapping and holding any word. Use the endpoints to choose the exact content you want. Then use the pop-up menu to do the following:

- **Copy**: Then paste into a document – handy if you want to add a reference to an essay or review.

- **Define**: Learn the word's meaning and how it's used.

- **Highlight**: This opens several other options, including a choice of highlight colour, adding a note or switching to underlining.

- **Note**: This opens the same yellow note box you can choose in the highlighting options. Add your comments using the on-screen keyboard. You can access all your notes by tapping the Contents button and selecting Notes. To delete a note, remove all the text in it.

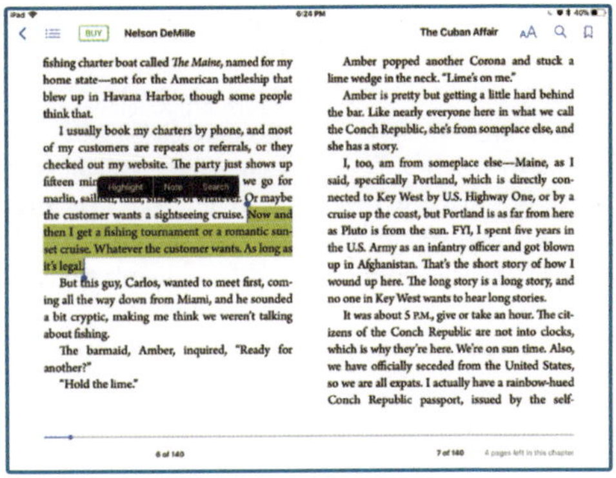

Above: Tap and hold to select a word or phrase, and choose from options to define, highlight and so on.

- **Search:** Lets you find where the same word or phrase is used, which is particularly useful in non-fiction books for searching for all references to a key topic.

- **Share:** For licensing reasons, this feature is not available everywhere. Where it is tap some highlighted text, then the Sharing button. It opens with options to add the highlighted quote to an email, text message, Tweet, Facebook update and Add to Notes, to open the Notes app.

Changing Appearance

In iBooks you can adjust the text and layout of your ebook to make it more comfortable for reading. Tap the letter A icon.

- **Screen brightness**: use the slider to adjust.

- **Font size**: Tap the smaller letter A to reduce the size of the text and the larger one to increase it.

> **Hot Tip**
>
> **Back up your bookmarks/notes, so you don't lose them and can also access them on any other iDevice you use. Tap Settings, iBooks and turn on Sync Bookmarks.**

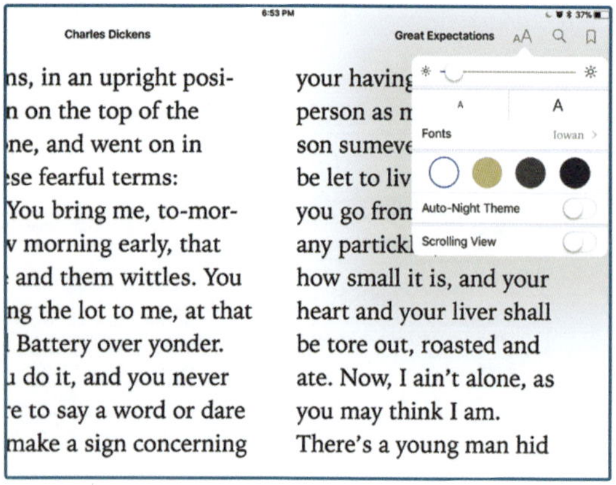

Above: Tap the AA button to improve readability by adjusting font choice and size.

- **Fonts**: Choose the font that offers the best readability.
- **Themes**: Change the background colour. Remove the virtual book imagery and read the book as one continuous page by turning on Scrolling View.
- **Justified text**: If you find it easier to read a book in which the text is evenly spaced across the line, go to Settings, iBooks and switch on Full Justification.

Searching Text

Tap the magnifying glass icon at the top of the page and type in the word or phrase you are looking for. All references to it that are found are displayed in the text box below. To widen your search to look on the Web or in Wikipedia, the online encyclopedia to which anyone can contribute, tap the relevant button.

Read Aloud

Save your energy when reading stories aloud and have the iPad narrate the tale for you. Books can read stories aloud using the VoiceOver screen reader that aids accessibility to the iPad for visually impaired users.

Find a Read Aloud Story

1. To find a Read aloud storybook, tap Featured in Books and then type 'read aloud' in the Search bar.

2. Tap the chosen book to open it and then the loudspeaker icon on the top menu. Under Read aloud select pages to turn Automatically and then tap Start Reading.

3. The storyteller starts and the text is highlighted word by word.

4. To move to any page, use the scrub bar at the bottom, which has tiny thumbnails showing where you are in the book. (If it's not visible, tap the middle of the page.) Slide your finger along the bar to the place you want and tap the word you want to start from, and the story will continue from there.

5. To pause reading at any point, tap the loudspeaker icon again and then Stop Reading.

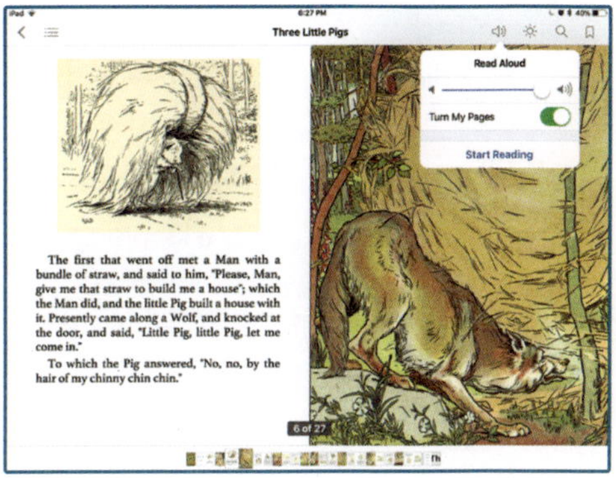

Above: After downloading a read aloud book tap the loudspeaker icon on the top menu. You can then select pages to turn automatically and tap Start Reading.

Audiobooks

Audiobooks have their own tab in the Books app, and even their own storefront. Tap the tab to access special offers, new and trending audiobooks, the current charts and custom-picked favourites. The books are purchased in the same way and you can also listen to a sample. All audiobooks purchased will sit in the main library and will exist inside their own collection.

OTHER BOOKSTORES

Google Play

This is Google's alternative to the iTunes store. Primarily aimed at those who use Android devices, its books can be read on the iPad through the Google Play Books app. Google claim their bookstore has the world's largest selection of ebooks, including millions of free titles, but because of Apple's policies you can't shop for new titles direct from the app. Instead, you have to access the store through Safari (on your iPad or your computer) and purchase the titles you want online. They will then automatically appear in the Google Play Books app, so you can read them. The book controls are similar to those in Books and you can download the books for reading offline, when you have no internet connection.

Kindle

Kindle for iPad is the free reading app from the Amazon bookstore. There are more than one million free and paid-for Kindle books available. As with Google Play Books, you have to get your titles online. Amazon's whispersync technology can then sync the book with any computers and iDevices that have the Kindle app. To save space on your iPad, you can store the bulk of your books in the Amazon cloud, only downloading the books that you want to read on the iPad.

As with Books, you can create Collections, which group your books into related areas of interest. Once you start reading the book, the last page read, bookmarks, notes and highlights will also all be synced, so wherever you are reading, you'll be able to start just where you left off.

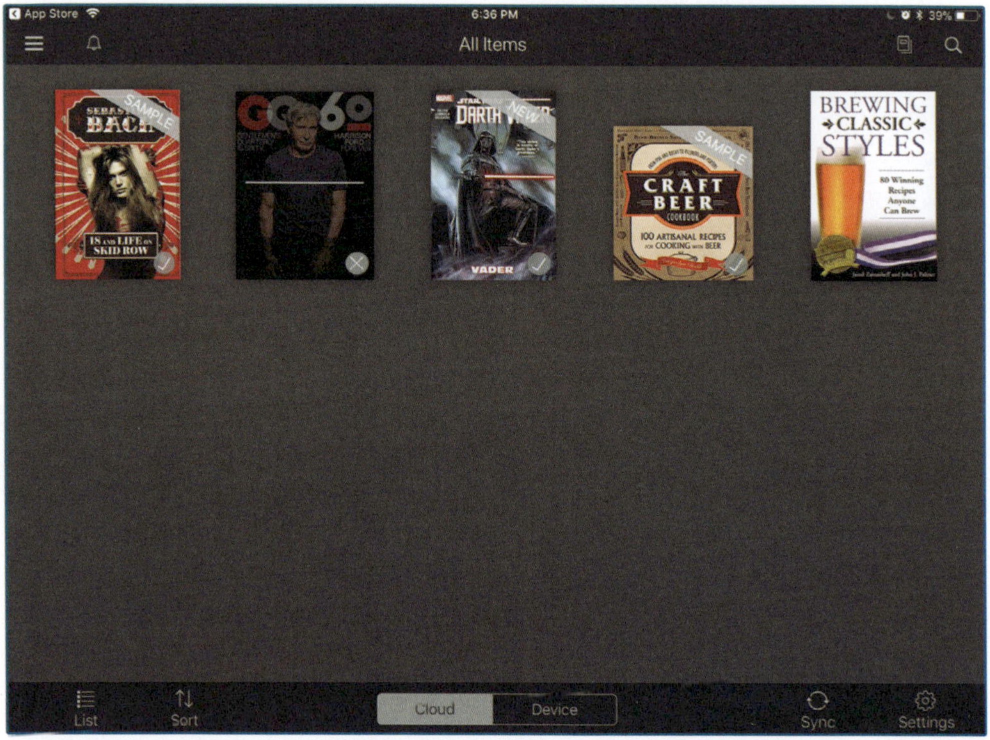

Above: If you're an Amazon Prime member you can download a range of books, comics and periodicals free of charge.

NEWS

No more drying out the paper that's got wet, or reading across a page that's torn or wrinkled: the iPad is the perfect paper boy.

NEWS APP

The News app, built into the iPad, is designed to be a one-stop shop for all your needs. It's a deeply personalized service that learns your favorite sources and subjects and keeps you posted on breaking news that matters most to you. It presents all of the information within a consistent design. It's a replacement for the Newsstand app that once held newspapers and magazines.

Getting the Publications

When you open the Apple News app for the first time you'll be asked to make some choices about what you're interested in. Siri may suggest some sources which are based on installed apps and web browsing activity (go to Settings, News, Siri & Search to enable this). The app is laid out in five major sections:

- **Today**: The Today section brings a curated look at trending stories from major news outlets. You'll also see a spotlight on a particular issue, and a For You section with recommendations based on topics and channels you read regularly.
- **Channels & Topics**: The sidebar in the News app shows all the news sources and topics you've decided to

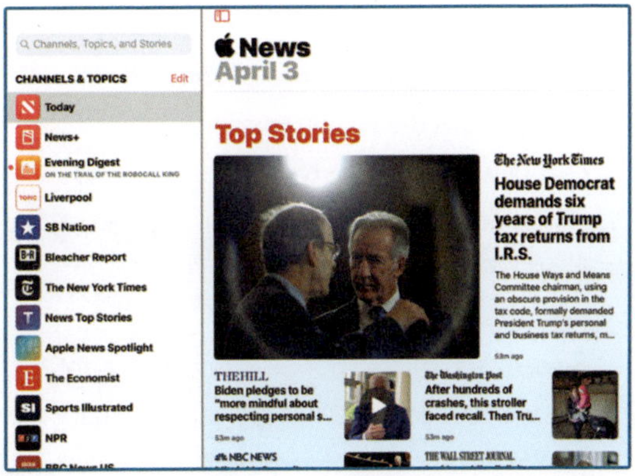

Above: The News app creates a personalized collection of stories for you to read.

follow. You can dive into any one to see the latest stories populating the main interface. To add or delete them select Edit. To hide the sidebar and view news in full screen, press the red page icon in the top left of the Today view.

- **News+**: This service offers access to thousands of magazines and paywalled news content for a single monthly fee of $9.99. If you're using iOS 12, you can see News+ as an option near the top of the Channels & Topics listing. Sign up for a trial to begin downloading magazines and to see articles from your favourites shows.

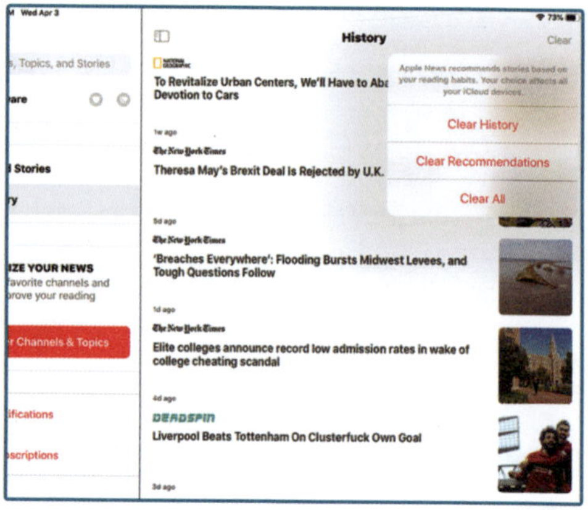

Above: To delete the History of stories you've read in the News app tap Clear History.

- **Following**: This tab lists the categories and channels you're following and allows you to select more. Tap the Browse button at the top of the screen to find additional sources and topics. Tap the heart next to any suggestion to begin receiving news.

- **Search**: At the top of the Channels & Topics tab is the option to search for channels, topics and stories. These results will be populated in the sidebar. Tap the heart to add to your favourite Topics.

Hot Tip

To receive push notifications from a particular source go to News, Following and tap the bell icon next to the source. It will turn blue and you will receive breaking news alerts.

- **Saved**: You might spot an article you want to save to read later. You can tap the Share menu in the top right corner of any story and hit the Save icon, which looks like a bookmark. Saved articles can be found at the bottom of the Channels & Topics sidebar, along with an option to view your reading history.

A Daily Briefing

If you'd like your daily news delivered directly to your inbox, Apple provides this service directly from News. This will be offered to you as an opt-in when you first set up news.

Your Digital Subscriptions

We've mentioned the new Apple News+ all-you-can-eat subscription service, but if you have an individual subscription to a publication, Apple News enables you to log in and access the content that's restricted for non-paying customers. When you access a story from the *Washington Post* or *New York Times*, or another site that keeps web content behind a paywall.

The subscription details will sit at the bottom of the screen when opening a story. Apple may encourage you to get this content by subscribing to Apple News+ here. If you have a subscription to that publication, for example The Wall Street Journal, you will see a prompt to log in. From here you will be redirected to use your login details.

Managing News Subscriptions

Most of the major news organisations have their own apps that exist outside of Apple News app. If there is paywalled content, you can sign up and be billed by iTunes. When you subscribe to a magazine or newspaper, it is made clear that this will auto renew. Therefore the onus is on you to remember to cancel your subscription if you no longer want it. Although it's not made clear, you can cancel auto renewal at any time. Subscriptions billed through your iTunes/Apple ID account can be modified directly from your iPad.

1. Go to Settings, Your Name and tap iTunes and App Store.

2. Tap the Apple ID address in blue at the top of the screen and you'll be asked to authenticate your account.

3. In the Account Settings screen you'll see Subscriptions. Here you'll see options to change your subscription, turn off auto renew or cancel it.

NEWSPAPERS

As well as providing news in the News app, the iPad makes it easy to enjoy the best content from your favourite newspapers. This might be through standalone apps or subscriptions to digital versions of the print edition.

Digitized Print Editions

If you love the format offered by the newspaper, boosted by some interactive digital elements then periodicals like *The Guardian* and *The Times* still offer special iPad editions of their apps. You can subscribe to the newspaper in the same was as you would from the News app.

Hot Tip

The best of the magazine and newspaper apps are customized to take advantage of the iPad, so will have a completely different look and feel from the newspaper, with unique navigation and interactive features such as video, music and live links on the page.

Newspaper Subscriptions

For publishers, the benefit of having a separate app for the newspaper is that it gives more freedom over pricing and content. Some offer a fixed version of their printed newspaper while others have standalone apps for the iPad that are linked to their website. There are various in-app subscriptions available with the benefit that you can update the content as often as you like, so you always have the latest news.

Above: Subscribing to the Guardian Daily Edition allows you to update content and stay up-to-date.

The Guardian Daily Edition

The Guardian isn't for everyone, but it's a great example of how a newspaper can be re-imagined for the digital format. You can swipe left and right to move between articles, share content online, quickly shuffle between sections. Stories are easy to access via large vivid imagery and you can even do the crossword. You get 14 days free when you download the app, but subscriptions start at $8.99 a month for The Observer on a Sunday or $15.99 for 7-day a week access. Subscriptions are handled by the App Store, but if you already subscribe to the print edition you can login for free.

Standalone News Apps

Every major news organization you can think of has an app for the iPad. Whether it's the BBC, a news agency like Reuters, a newspaper like the *New York Times* or a periodical like *The Economist*. These can be downloaded from the App Store. Some offer subscriptions for content.

RSS FEEDS

Subscribe to a news site's RSS feed and you can keep up with breaking news and get regular story updates. All you need is an RSS news feed reader (also known as a news reader) for the iPad.

Using a News Reader

There are several news readers available in the App Store, including Feeddler, Newsify and Feedly. Most websites today, whether it's a blog, news site, online magazine or entertainment site, will have an RSS feed. RSS stands for Really Simple Syndication and is the standard way for websites to publish the latest news and updates.

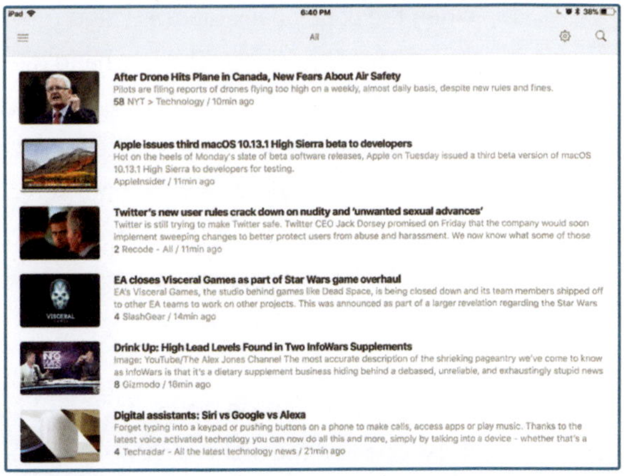

Above: Feedly is an RSS reader app that will deliver article updates from all of your favourite sources.

Adding a News Source

Feedly is shown here, but most readers work in a similar way.

1. Once you have downloaded and installed Feedly, tap to launch it. Tap the menu button to login or sign up.

2. For your convenience you can get personalized suggestions by logging in through your Google or Facebook account. Choose how you want to login, then Feedly will open the relevant app and ask you to sign in.

Above: Once you've opened the story in Feedly, press the Share button for different options.

3. Feedly allows you to assemble content from a vast array of sources in one place. These include publications like the *New York Times*, most blogs on the web, YouTube channels and many more. To find a source, type a name or topic, or copy and paste a website address in the search bar in the top corner.

4. When the page opens tap the + sign to add the RSS feed to Feedly. The left-hand menu opens with the option to add the new feed to an existing collection of sources or create a new one. Now when you tap your source in the left-hand menu a list of stories will appear in the main pane. Tap the headline, and the full article will be loaded.

Hot Tip

A news feed – RSS feed – includes a summary of new articles, links, and details of when they were published. The feed is read by news reader software, which can pull in feeds from thousands of sources.

5. Press the More button (three dots) and you have a number of options for sharing the story, opening the associated webpage or saving it to read later.

Mix in Your Social Life

Described as a Social News Magazine, Flipboard allows you to mix in your news feeds from Google Reader, newspapers, blogs and the like with information from your Facebook newsfeed, Twitter timeline, YouTube videos, Instagram photos and other social media.

As a result, you have a personalized magazine where your news and that of your friends, is scattered among national and international news, plus other feeds that match your interests.

Create Your Personalized Magazine

1. Go to the App Store and search for Flipboard. Press the Free button, and then Install App, and tap to launch.

2. You'll be asked to choose subjects that interest you. As well as the regulars, it also offers the chance to pick things like Big Ideas, Happiness and Self Improvement.

Hot Tip

Tap on the magnifying glass to discover more material to add to your Flipboard.

3. Hit Next and you'll be asked to sign up for a Flipboard account. This allows you to personalize your magazine, save stories for later and access them from any device. You can create a login or sign up using your Twitter, Facebook or Google accounts.

4. The tiles show different sources from which to create your personal Flipboard. Tap any tile to see more. Once in a section tap the story to see the original article and pictures.

5. Along the bottom are icons for sharing the story – adding a comment, tweeting it, marking it as a favourite or posting it online to read it later.

6. Tap the three line menu and then Following to see which sites and social networks make up your Flipboard. You can add more from the list or search through the different categories to see more potential sources. You can also search by keyword to find more sources that might interest you.

7. When you find a source you want to add to your board, tap the + button to add it to your Flipboard.

Step 5: When you open a story in Flipboard you can choose to add a comment or tweet it.

MAGAZINES

You need not be weighed down with a pile of glossy magazines. Carry the contents of several magazine racks with ease on your iPad.

Digital Magazine Viewer

When the iPad first came out publishers rushed to create brilliant interactive versions of magazines. However, some publishers prefer to make the digital version as close to the original print copy as possible.

Standalone Magazines

Some of the world's most popular magazines have great iPad Editions. Instead of waiting for your copy to go in the mail, iPad owners can download individual editions as soon as they become available. You can browse the available titles from the App Store.

Magazines in Apple News+

The Apple News+ service offers access to thousands of magazines for one low monthly fee. Apple reckons the $9.99 a month service gives you access to $8,000 in content each month. When you sign up for Apple News+ you can browse the catalogue to find and download new issues. You will even find individual articles from your favourite magazines in the For You section of the news app. Most of the magazines you see on your newsstand are present here.

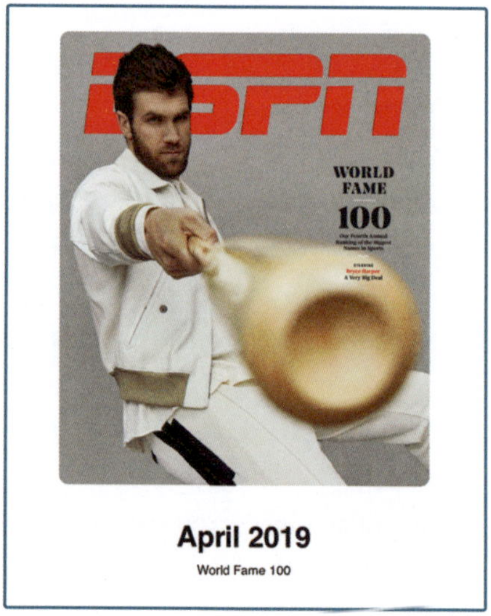

Above: Apple News+ will enabled you to download the latest issues of your favourite magazines, many of which in an iPad-friendly format.

Zinio

Zinio is the digital publisher for hundreds of magazines around the world. With Zinio you get an exact copy of the print edition in digital format, plus, sometimes, extra content in the form of video and audio. Download the app, then explore a series of free sample articles and browse to find the magazines you want. They are usually available to purchase as a single issue or on subscription. The magazines are turned into a standard format, so they can be read through the Zinio reader, which is available for desktop computers, as well as for the iPad.

Above: The Zinio app features exact copies of print magazine editions in digital format and a vast library to choose from.

COMICS

With its great display and reputation as the Superhero of the Tablets, the iPad is a natural medium for reading comics and comic books.

Comic Readers

There are many apps to choose from that enable you to access some of the great classic comics – from the Beano to Marvel and DC Comics. Like newspapers and magazines, the apps are free to download but there are in-app charges for purchasing a single issue of a comic or a longer-term subscription.

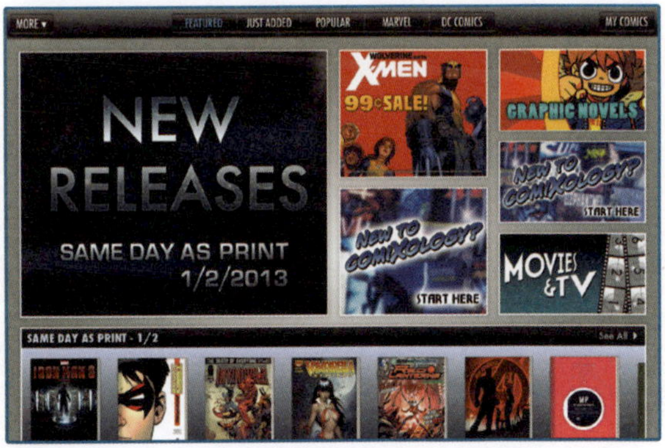

Above: Download the ComiXology app to buy and read comic books from major publishers.

Instead of downloading the apps separately, you can use apps like ComiXology, which are digital readers that let you buy and read comics and comic books from many of the major publishers. They publish many of the digital comics the same day as the print edition is published, so you don't miss out. You can search for titles according to popularity, genre, publisher and even creators. There are also free comics for you to try.

ENTERTAINMENT

ENTERTAINMENT MACHINE

The iPad is as good a music player as any, with the advantage of a bigger screen to browse through your collection. Apps including the iTunes Store, Apple Music streaming and Podcasts give you access to all the features and tunes you will ever need.

Hot Tip

You can play your music through the built-in speaker, attach headphones, use wireless headphones or play through your TV using AirPlay.

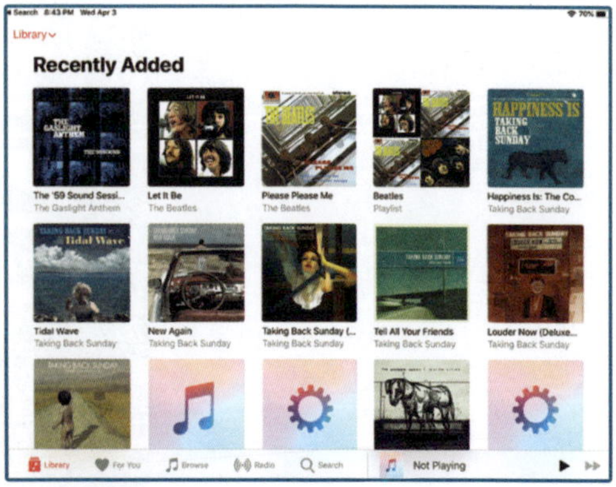

Above: Apple Music features your library, suggestions from the For You section and access to live radio stations.

USING THE MUSIC APP

This is the place to play much of your music content. It can store your digital music library from iTunes, purchased music from the iTunes Store and stream from the Apple Music service. You can also access a wealth of online radio stations.

Play Music

By default, Music is one of the buttons in the Dock that's accessible at the bottom of every Home screen.

1. Tap the Music icon to open it. In the splash screen that opens you'll have the choice to Join Apple Music, Apple's streaming service or, as here, Go to Library.

2. You'll see your music, with Recently Added songs and a grid of Artists and any music purchased from iTunes or synced from your computer's music library. Apple Music tracks you've saved to your library will also be here.

3. Select the artist, album or tile of the song you want and then tap the song to begin playback. For albums you'll also see options to shuffle the tunes.

4. From iOS 11, there's a Now Playing screen. It's a sidebar that slides out from the bottom-right corner of the screen whenever you hit play. You can access basic controls from here, but tap it to see more in an expanded view.

5. Here you'll see album art, the song title, a playhead scrubber, volume slider, the skip track buttons and the icon to send the audio to different speakers. You might also see a cloud icon with a downward facing arrow, which will allow you to download the content to your library.

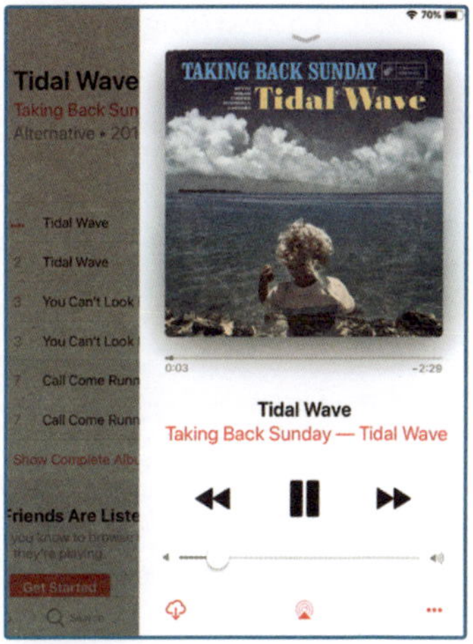

Above: The iPad music player displays the controls, scrubber bar and volume slider at the top.

6. Tap More to download the song (if it's stored in iTunes or Apple Music), delete it from the library, add to a playlist or share with another user. Tapping the Love or Dislike hearts will help generate recommendations in the For You section (Apple Music subscribers only).

The Music Queue

Hidden beneath the Now Playing screen is the queue of songs. This is called Up Next. Swipe all the way up and you'll see the Shuffle and Repeat options. Underneath that is the queue. If you're playing an album you'll see the remaining tracks in this list.

- **To add a song:** From anywhere in the Music app you can add a song to the queue. Tap the three dots menu next to the track and tap Play Next or Play Later to add it to the end of the current queue.

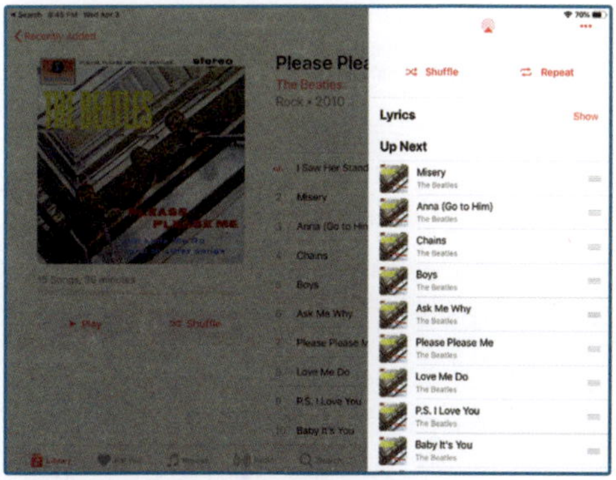

Above: The Up Next list shows what songs will follow. To change the order of the songs click the three line icon on the right of one of the tracks.

- **To rearrange a queue**: Tap the three lines next to the track and move them up and down the list.

- **To remove a song**: Swipe the track name from right to left.

Let Siri Be DJ

On the iPad 3 and later, take the stress out of changing track and let Siri control your music. Start by tapping and holding the Home button.

- **Play music**: say 'play music' or 'play'; 'pause' or 'stop' to halt the music; 'next song' or 'previous song' to change track.

- **Play a series of songs**: dictate 'Play album <name>', 'Play artist <name>' or 'Play playlist <name>' and all songs under that name are played.

- **Shuffle current playlist**: by saying 'Shuffle' while it's playing.

- **Get track information**: ask 'What's playing?' or 'Who sings this song?'

Hot Tip

To display the music controls quickly when you're in another app, swipe down from the top right corner of the screen to open the Control Center.

FIND YOUR MOOD MUSIC

The music you feel like listening to at any particular time will change. To make it easier to find the sound that suits your mood, try Apple's streaming music service.

Apple Music

People are moving away from buying digital music and towards streaming. For the price of one album a month you can get unlimited access to more than 40 million songs. With the Apple Music subscription service you'll also get unlimited radio, personalized and curated music lists, hand-selected by experts as well as your own music library saved for offline playback when you have no Wi-Fi. Tap For You to choose your plan.

The Cost of Apple Music

Apple offers all Apple ID holders a free three-month trial to Apple Music, giving you unlimited access. After that, it costs £9.99 /$9.99 a month, but you can cancel at any time via Settings, Your Name, iTunes & App Store, Apple ID, View Apple ID, Subscriptions. If you do this before the end of your trial you won't be charged.

ADDING MUSIC

You can add music directly to your iPad through the iTunes Store app or sync music gathered from other sources (as long as it isn't copy protected), through your computer.

iTunes Store

Access the online music store to download music.

1. Tap the app to go online to the iTunes store and select Music at the bottom.
2. If there's a particular type of music you like – from Pop to Hip-Hop – select it using the Genres button at the top of the screen.
3. Scroll down the page and you can see lots of different selections, such as new albums, themed collections, what's hot and what the Apple staff are listening to. There are also recommendations just for you. If you know what you want, use the Search box at the top.

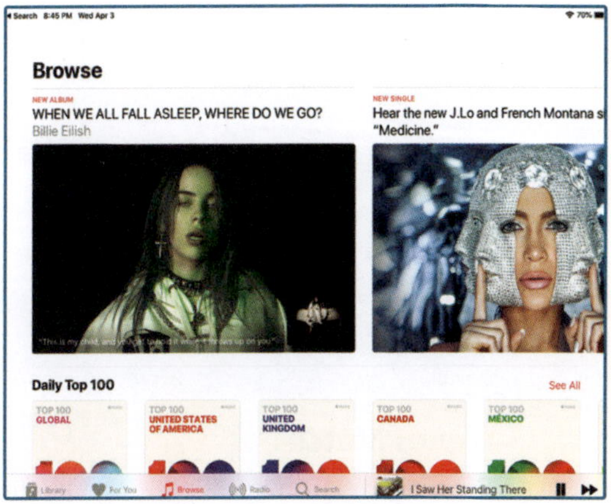

Above: Apple Music is a streaming service that puts hand-selected music, radio and your library, all in one place.

4. Once you have selected an album or song, tap to go through to the information page. This includes details of the artist, the release date and average rating by other iTunes users, plus the price button. Underneath is a listing of the track(s).

5. Tap the song title to listen to a 90-second sample of the track.

6. To buy an individual track, tap the price button to the right and then the Buy button. If it's the album on which the track features that you want to buy, tap the price button at the top of the page.

7. If you have a big collection, you may end up trying to buy a track you have already purchased. If this was bought in the iTunes store, Download appears instead of the price, so you won't be charged again.

8. When downloading, tap the More button (three dots) and then Downloads to see their progress. You can tap the square in the middle of the circle to stop the download at any time.

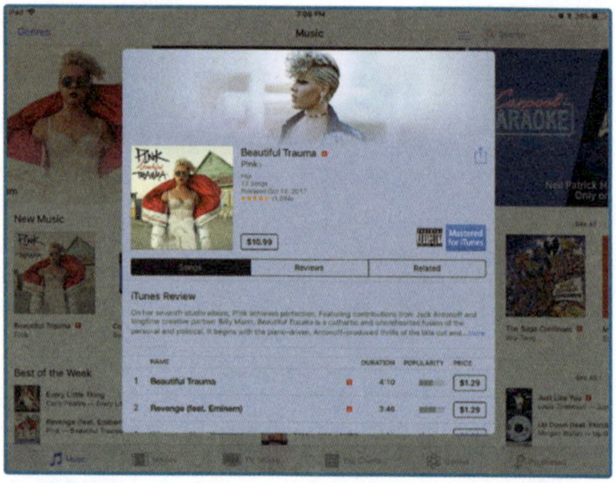

Step 6: Buy a track by tapping the price button to its right, and then the buy button. To buy the whole album, tap the price button at the top of the page.

> **Hot Tip**
>
> **With Apple Music you can improve your recommendations by tapping the Love and Dislike hearts within the playback screen. This will bring you more of what you enjoy to the For You screen.**

iTunes Match

Subscribe to iTunes Match for an annual fee and you can sync your music collection using Apple's iCloud. All your music, including music from CDs or other online stores, will sync with Apple's servers rather than iTunes on your personal computer. You will see your entire music collection on your iPad but it will be stored on iCloud. Learn more about iTunes Match and what it offers on page 171.

Apple Music and Other Options

We've explained many ways to get music on your iPad. None of them are 'the best,' it's all about what suits you.

- **Apple Music**: Costs £9.99/$9.99 a month, but offers more music than you'll ever listen to. Music can also be saved offline.

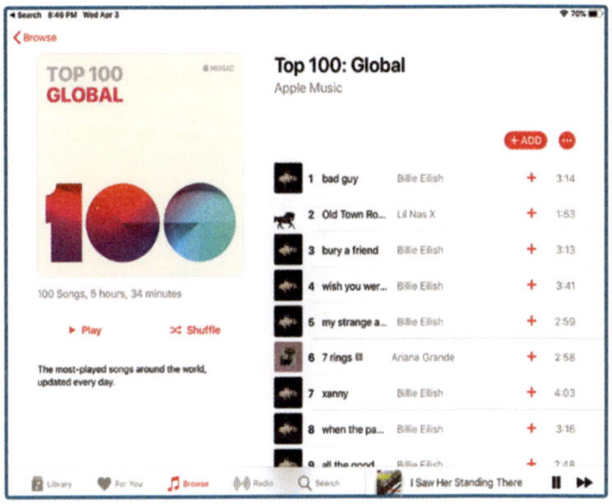

Above: Apple Music has over 30 million songs.

- **Syncing your music collection**: Adding your digital music collection from iTunes on your computer is cost free, it allows you to get more life out of your old CD collection, but it also takes up valuable space on your iPad's hard drive.

- **Buying from the iTunes Store**: The content is yours forever, but you get far less bang for your buck.

PODCASTS

There are thousands of hours of podcasts – audio and video shows – on a stunning range of topics that covers virtually everything from self-help to hobbies. Time to tune in.

Finding Podcasts

Apple's free Podcasts app is built into iOS. When you open the app, it will show your Library with podcasts you've already subscribed to.

Hot Tip

The Podcast app removes the podcasts and controls from the Music app. This means it's not possible to create playlists that include podcasts. Similarly, Audiobooks are now found in Books, when previously they were in the Music app.

You can choose to order them by Recently Updated, Alphabetical, Show order or an Episodes list.

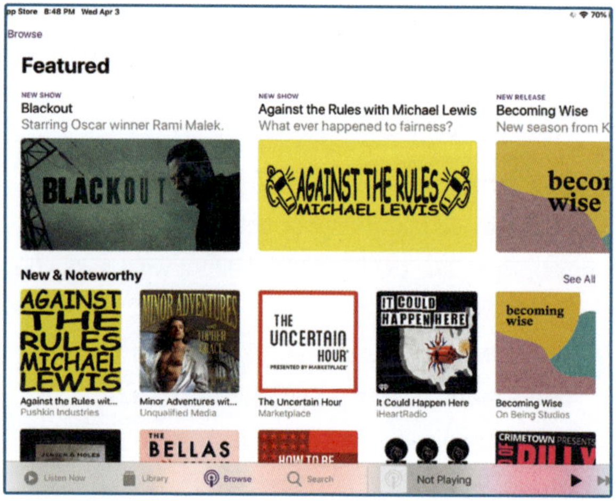

Above: Browse the Podcast store by category and tap any that interest you to find out more information and download.

1. To see all the available podcasts, tap the Browse button at the bottom of the screen. This shows you Featured podcasts. All Categories will bring you different genres, Top Charts gives you an idea of the most popular podcasts and Featured Providers has curated lists from Apple.

2. Tap any Podcast titles that interest you, and the information box gives you full details of the available episodes, how long they are, together with other users' ratings and reviews.

3. Tap on a single episode and a new Now Playing pane will load on the right side of the screen. Tap the plus button from the episode list, or tap More > Add to Library from the Now Playing pane to add it for later consumption.

4. Alternatively, you can tap the Subscribe button from the main podcast page, and the latest episode will be downloaded. You will also get future episodes downloaded automatically as they become available.

5. Press the Listen Now tab and you'll see available episodes and those waiting to be downloaded.

Play Your Podcasts

In Library you can view your podcasts as a series of tiles. There are two ways to play your podcasts:

- **Streaming**: tap any episode and it will start playing wihtout being fully downloaded first. To do this, you should be connected to Wi-Fi.

- **Download**: When viewing a podcast you're subscribed to in the library, you'll see a list of episodes with a download icon next to each one. To download episodes from podcasts you're not subscribed to, hit the + button to add into the library and then the download icon.

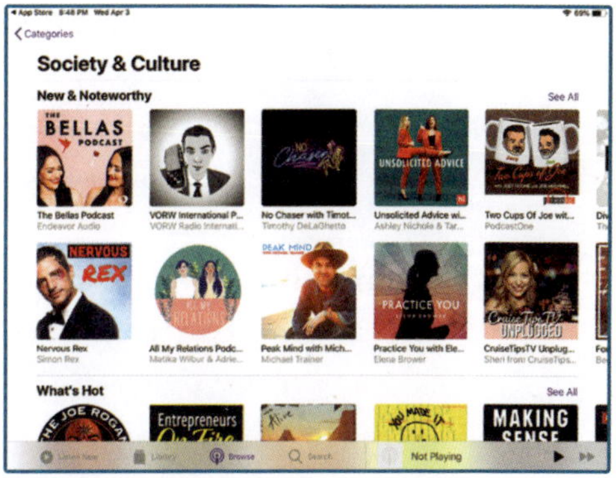

Above: Browse popular podcasts within a category by swiping through the options.

Control Playback

When you begin playback, the controls appear in a bar at the bottom right of the screen. Tap it to view the controls full-screen. Here are some of the most useful playback controls:

- **1x button**: lets you change the playback speed: 1x is normal, 1/2X plays at half speed, while 2x plays at double speed.

> **Hot Tip**
>
> **You can organize your podcasts into stations that update automatically on all devices. Tap Library and then the Edit button in the top left. Tap New Station, name your station, tap Save and add your podcasts.**

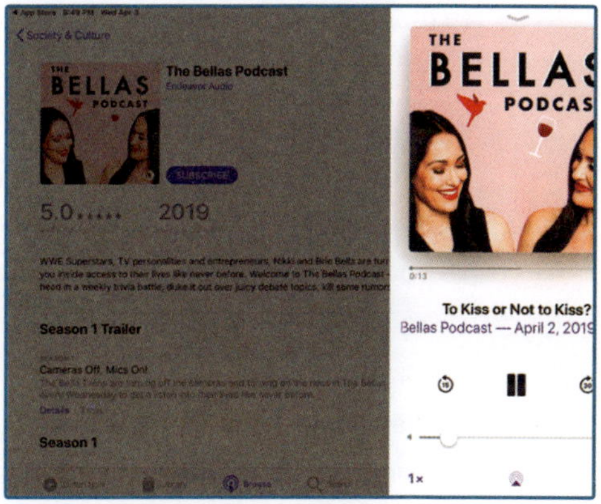

Above: Starting Podcast playback displays playback controls in the bottom right.

- **Replay button**: with the number 15 inside a left-pointing loop: tap this to go back 15 seconds in the podcast.
- **Play/Pause button**: toggle this to start playing the podcast or pause it.
- **Skip Forward button**: with the number 30 inside a right-pointing loop – this moves the podcast forward 30 seconds.
- **Volume slider**: move left or right to set the volume. You can also use the buttons on the side of the iPad to adjust the volume.
- **Playhead**: tap, hold and drag this to move to another part of the podcast. Move your finger to the top as you drag and you can skip backwards and forwards more accurately.
- **Switch Audio**: the triangle icon with the circle switches to different speakers.

Beneath the Fold

Swipe up on the Now Playing Screen to access more options. These include:

- **Share button**: the box with an arrow coming out opens the Share box so you can send a link to the podcast by mail or text, or post it as an update to Twitter and Facebook.
- **Sleep timer**: this is handy if you want to be lulled to sleep by music or someone reading a story. Choose a stop point for the podcast.

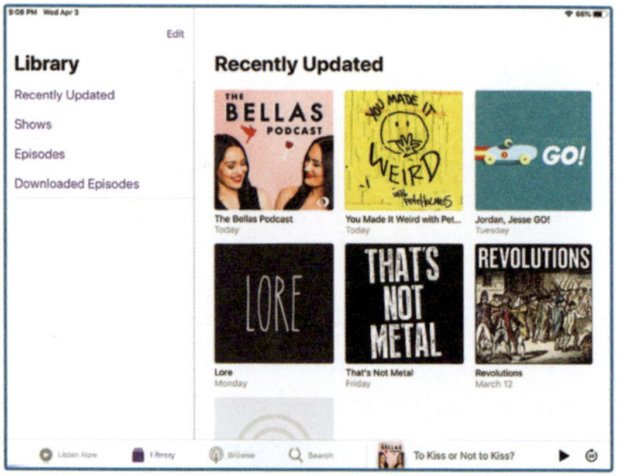

Above: Your podcast library shows the latest episodes from your favourite shows.

- **Episode Notes**: Tap Show to see what the producers have to say about the episode.

- **Up Next**: Like the music app, you'll see a queue of episodes you have upcoming.

Video Playback Controls

There are similar buttons to control viewing of your video podcast. To access them, simply tap the screen while watching the video.

Delete Podcasts

In the Listen Now tab swipe to the left over the chosen podcast and press the red Delete button. In the Library tab you'll see an Edit button in the top right corner; tap the red dot. You can re-subscribe to any shows or download individual episodes again if you change your mind.

SYNCING MUSIC

While the iPad is a great entertainment centre, it may not have as much space as your computer for holding all your songs, etc. So when it comes to syncing with iTunes, it pays to be selective.

iTunes Sync

Connect the iPad to iTunes using a USB connector to your computer. The icon for your iPad will appear in the menu.

1. Click Music in the sidebar. If you're using iCloud Music Library to hold all your music in one place you don't need to sync your music with iTunes. If you don't you can choose to Sync Music with your Entire Music Library. However, as you are likely to have more music than will fit on your iPad, the safer option is Selected playlists, artists, albums and genres.

Hot Tip

You can make sure episodes only download via Wi-Fi by going to Settings, then Podcasts and turning on 'Only Download on Wi-Fi. On this page you can also choose how often the Podcasts app refreshes to find new episodes.

Above: When using iTunes to sync music from your laptop to your iPad, select the option to sync Selected playlists, artists, albums and genres. You can then go through these different categories and tick those which you would like to copy over to your iPad.

2. You can also choose to add music videos – although be careful if you have a lot, as these tend to be very large files and will quickly eat up your free space – and voice memos.

3. Now go through your playlists and select those you want on your iPad.

4. Do the same for artists, albums and genres. Don't worry about duplication. Even if you choose an artist whose songs are on the playlists or genres you've also selected, only one copy of the actual song will be copied over – although you'll still see it referenced in each list.

5. An alternative option is to create your own special playlist that has all the songs you want to copy over to your iPad. Then select only this playlist to sync.

6. Click Sync at the bottom of the screen when done and your music will begin transferring.

ORGANIZING YOUR MUSIC

The bigger your music collection the more difficult it is to keep under control. Fortunately, playlists make it easy to organize your sounds to suit your mood, while features like Home Sharing and music streaming make it possible to listen to your music without overloading your iPad.

MUSIC SETTINGS

When it comes to playing your music, there are several features you can change to suit your personal preferences. Tap the Settings icon, then Music, to get started.

Changing Sound Levels

- **Sound Check**: turn this on to play all songs at roughly the same volume, even if an individual track is louder or softer.

- **Equalization (EQ)**: changes the quality of the sound to suit the type of music you are listening to. There are 23 different effects, ranging from Bass reducer to Spoken word. Generally, these settings apply only to music played through the Music app, except for Late Night, which applies to video as well. It reduces volume in loud parts and increases it in quiet sections.

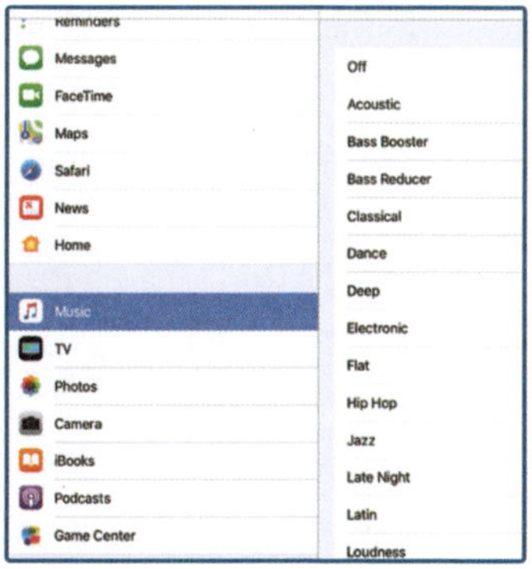

Above: Choose from Equalization effects to adjust sound settings to suit certain types of music.

- **Set a Volume Limit**: for when the children have grabbed the iPad to play their music. Tap Volume Limit, and then adjust the volume slider.

- **Use Listening History**: If you're an Apple Music subscriber you can choose whether you want your listening history to inform recommendations in the For You section.

PLAYLISTS

These are mini-collections – lists – of songs based on a theme, which can be as personal or as general as you wish. For example, you could have a playlist of the songs played at your wedding, all 1990s songs in your Library or your Adele collection.

Create Playlists: Step-by-step

Playlists that you create on your iPad can be synced with iTunes on your PC or Mac.

1. Tap the Music app to open and then Library in the top left. There you'll see any existing playlists. To start a new one, tap the New button.

2. In the box that opens give the playlist a name that describes its content, for example 'Easy Listening'.

3. Tap the Add Music button. Here you can select from music folders in your library or use the search bar to find specifics.

4. If you hit Songs, for example, the full library of tracks stored on your iPad opens. Tap the + button beside those you want to add to the playlist.

5. When you have added all the songs you would like to your playlist, just tap the Done button. You can change it later if you want (see opposite).

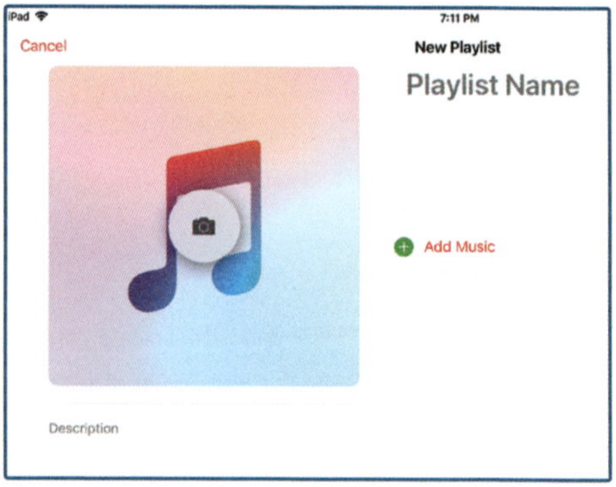

Step 2: Enter a name for your new playlist.

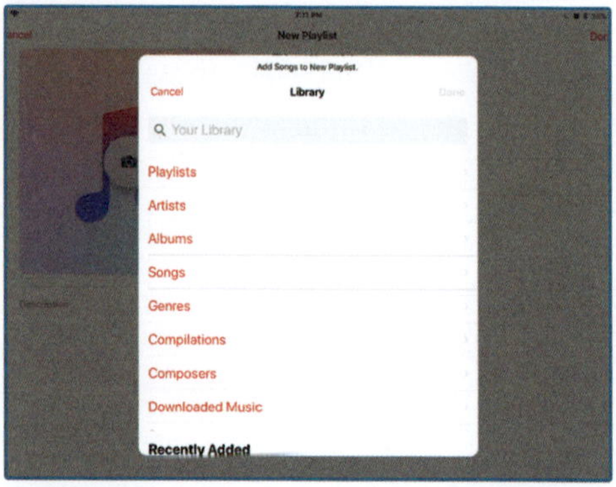

Step 3: Tap the Add Music button to start selecting music by Artists, Albums etc., that you want to include on your playlist.

6. Your new playlist will be copied to the iTunes library on your computer next time you sync your iPad.

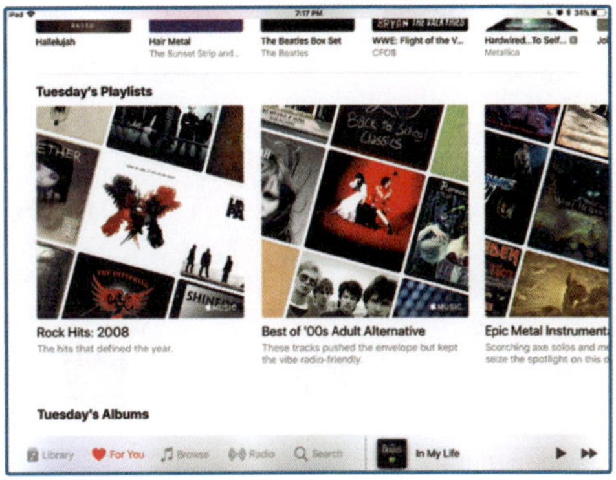

Above: Apple Music subscribers can find pre-made playlists rather than slaving over creating their own.

Edit Playlists

Rather than create a new playlist, you can change an existing one. If you're playing a song you'd like to add to a playlist just select the More button from the playback screen and select Add to a Playlist. Or:

1. Tap Playlists, select the playlist to modify and press the Edit button.

2. Tap Add songs to add more tracks to the playlist in exactly the same way as creating a playlist. Tracks from your library or Apple Music can be added to a playlist and you'll see tabs for each while adding tracks.

3. To delete a song, tap the red button and then press the Delete button that appears on the right-hand side.

4. To change the song order, tap the Drag handle on the right and move it up or down.

5. To delete a playlist altogether, press the Playlists button, tap and open the playlist then tap the More button and select Delete from Library.

Hot Tip

Once you've set the volume limit, stop someone else changing it back. Tap Settings, General, then Enable Restrictions. Enter a four figure Restrictions Passcode and re-enter it for security. Under Allow Changes, select Volume Limit, and then tap Don't Allow Changes.

Find Playlists

Making the perfect playlist is a labour of love, but sometimes you just want to dive right in. If you subscribe to Apple Music you get access to a host of playlists created just for you, based on your

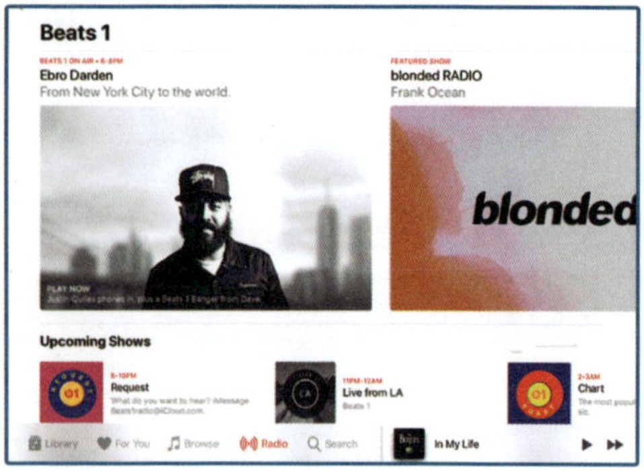

Above: Beats 1 is a free, always on radio station that's available through the Music app.

Hot Tip

In the For You tab, tap on your profile icon and then Find More Artists & Curators to see who you're following.

Above: The Artist home page in Apple Music features top songs, featured releases and more.

listening habits and previously expressed interests. You'll see these in the For You section.

Deleting Songs

To delete a song from the iPad, press the More button (three dots) next to the song, then tap Delete in the pop-up box. This will remove the song from your iPad, but it will remain in your iTunes library on your Mac or PC, or on iCloud.

Artist Pages

In Apple Music, the artist page is your hub for all the content from your favourite bands and groups. Tap the name of the group at any time to visit their hub page. Here you'll be able to access the latest releases, most popular tracks, albums, music videos, artist playlists, a biography and similar artists.

Radio

There are two types of playback available within the music app. Broadcast radio that's available for free and custom radio stations you'll need an Apple Music subscription to access.

- **Beats 1 and Web Radio**: In Music tap the Radio button and you can access Beats 1. Always On, it features top DJs and curated playlists that let you explore new music in a variety of genres. You don't need an Apple Music subscription either.

- **Custom Radio:** If you have an Apple Music subscription you can create your own custom stations – which is more like a playlist – based around your pick of artist or song. Find the music you want and tap More button (three dots) hit Create Station.

HOME SHARING

Play music on your iPad from the iTunes library on your computer – without having to download the music files.

Setting up Home Sharing

For Home Sharing to work, your iPad and computer must be on the same Wi-Fi network.

1. Open iTunes on your Mac or PC, go to the File Menu, Home Sharing and choose Turn On Home Sharing.

2. You'll be prompted for your Apple ID and password. Enter these and then click Create Home Share.

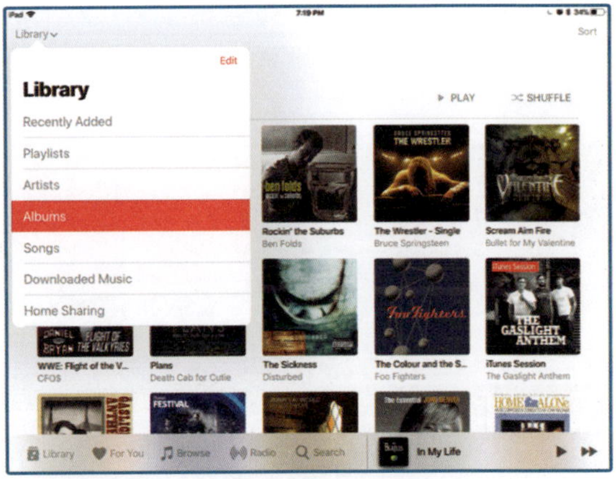

Above: Enabling Home Sharing lets you see music you have stored in iTunes on your computer.

3. On the iPad go to Settings, Music and under Home Sharing enter the same Apple ID and password.

4. Open the Music app and tap Library. In the dropdown menu you'll see Home Sharing near the bottom.

5. Choose this option and you can see and play the music from your computer.

Hot Tip

Only want to keep music on one computer? Home Sharing can make an iTunes library available on up to five different computers running iTunes, as well as Apple TV and iOS devices.

STREAMING MUSIC

Instead of storing and playing your own music, you can get songs, radio shows, concerts and more streamed, on demand, to your iPad.

Streaming Music Apps

As well as Apple Music, there are several other on-demand music services that allow you take your pick from millions of songs and discover new artists.

- Typically, these services offer the wide spectrum of music – from rock, pop and funk to the classics. Some include talk radio, covering sport and comedy.

Above: Spotify is the world's most popular music streaming service. You can access it on the iPad.

- While several sites offer a free service with upgrade to **premium** paid features, such as removal of ads or listening offline, you usually have to pay a **monthly subscription** to get the most benefit from the iPad app.
- Among the services with iPad specific apps are **Spotify** (spotify.com) and **TuneIn Radio** (tunein.com) both of which have extension apps for the Apple Watch. **Slacker Radio** (slacker.com) is only currently available in the US.

Concerts

Get the best of the bands playing for you on your iPad. The Qello app streams HD concert film to your tablet. Subscribe and you get unlimited access to their concerts and can create your own set lists.

AIRPLAY

For great sounds around the home, you can use Airplay to play music from your iPad through your Hi-Fi speakers, wherever they are. All you need are AirPlay-enabled speakers, which are available from well-known manufacturers like Denon, B&W, JBL and so on in the Apple Store. And in late 2017 Apple released its own Siri-enabled HomePod speaker.

Above: Use Airplay to play music from your iPad through Airplay capable devices with Hi-Fi speakers. You can also send it to Apple TV.

As well as the music, all the information about it, such as the song title, artist's name, playing time and so on, are also streamed across your Wi-Fi network.

Using AirPlay

You can stream music to AirPlay speakers with a couple of taps. First though, you must make sure your iPad and the AirPlay speaker are connected to the same Wi-Fi network. See the manufacturers instructions if you need help with this.

1. Once you're playing music you can access the AirPlay settings in a couple of ways:

- **From within the Music app** tap the broadcast icon (triangle with three circles) to choose from available AirPlay devices. If you have an iPad running iOS 11 and up and a compatible speaker you can broadcast to more than one speaker at a time through the AirPlay 2 update.

- **When on the lock screen** you'll see the broadcast icon on a special playback controls menu. Again, press it to see available options.

Hot Tip

If you have more than one Apple TV in the house, you can rename it to make it easier when you stream from your iPad via AirPlay. Go to Settings, General, About, Name on the Apple TV. You can even choose a custom name.

- **When outside the Music app**, swipe swipe down from the top right corner to access the Control Centre. You'll see the music shortcut. Press and hold this card then select the broadcast icon to see available speakers.

2. Select the receiver you want to use and a tick appears beside it. Now you can play and control music from your iPad and it'll play back on the speaker you've chosen rather than the iPad's built in speakers.

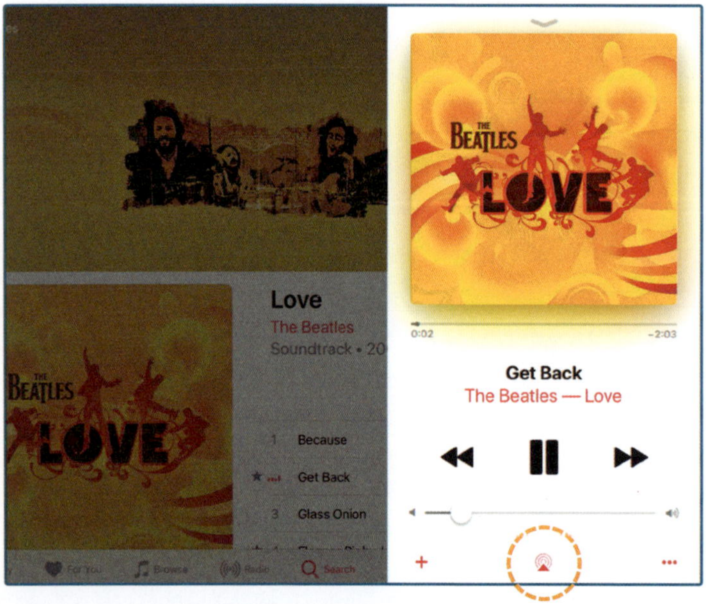

3. Control the sound from your iPad, using Music's audio controls to play or pause a song, skip a track or change the volume.

4. To return playback to the iPad, tap the Airplay icon again and select iPad from the list.

Left: Tap the broadcast icon (a triangle with three circles) to use Airplay to play music from your iPad through Airplay capable devices with Hi-Fi speakers.

STORING MUSIC

Despite the limited space on the iPad, it's possible to have access to your music any time, anywhere by using online storage services.

iTUNES MATCH

With iTunes Match you can access your entire music collection, even songs imported from CDs or bought online, from your iPad.

Music Match-maker

iTunes Match is a paid subscription service that lets you store your music library in iCloud – that is on Apple's servers – rather than your own computer. It means you can access and play your music from your iPad virtually wherever you are.

You can sign up for iTunes Match on your computer. Open iTunes, go to Store menu and select iTunes Match from the Features section at the very bottom of the page. Below the brief overview of iTunes Match click the button to subscribe and enter your details. Your subscription is tied to your Apple ID and it costs $24.99 per year.

Above: Use iTunes to activate iTunes Match. You will be asked to enter your Apple ID.

Matching Tracks

Once you're subscribed, iTunes Match looks through your music library, matching any tracks you have against the 30 million plus songs in the iTunes store. These are added to your music library in iCloud. The matched tracks play back at high quality – 256-KBps AAC DRM-free – regardless of the quality of your original track.

Hot Tip

You can store up to 100,000 songs in iCloud, big enough for most music collections.

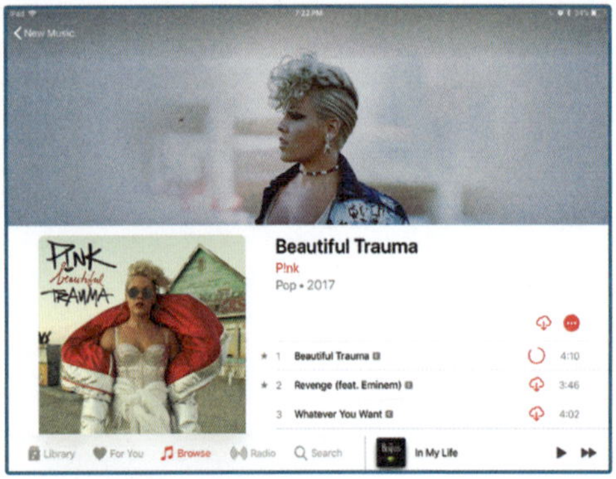

Step 5: Download tracks for offline listening by tapping the iCloud symbol.

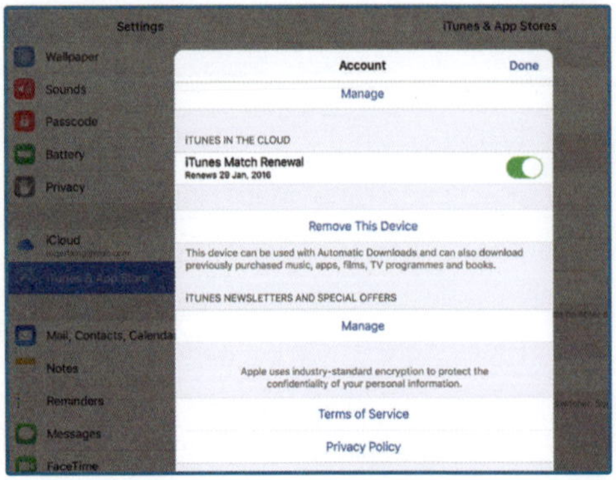

Step 8: You can turn off automatic renewal of iTunes Match in Settings, iTunes & App Store.

Any songs that can't be matched are uploaded to iCloud. How long this will take depends on the number of songs and the speed of your connection.

Listen to Your Matched Music

1. iTunes will scan, match and upload any unmatched tunes from your library, so make sure you import all of your music collection into iTunes on your computer before you start (iTunes, File, Add To Library). A status indicator lets you track progress.

2. iTunes Match will be available alongside any existing music or playlists on your iPad, with full details of your iCloud library.

3. The download icon – of a cloud with downward-pointing arrow – is shown next to items available for download from iCloud. If it's not shown the item is already in your local iTunes library.

4. Tap the song title and it will be streamed from iCloud, via your Wi-Fi connection, and downloaded fully as it plays.

5. Tap the cloud to download tracks so you can play them when you don't have an internet connection.

6. Once you play a track on a playlist, playback continues automatically down the list, whether the song is already downloaded or is still in iCloud.

7. The iCloud status of individual songs shows if it was purchased from iTunes, added from Apple Music or matched with iTunes Match. Go to iTunes on your computer, click my Music, then Songs in the right-hand corner. In the same menu, click Show Columns, then iCloud Status.

Hot Tip

Song files larger than 200MB or longer than two hours in length won't be uploaded to iCloud.

8. By default iTunes Match will automatically renew the annual subscription. To change it, choose Settings on the iPad, then iTunes & App Store, sign in if necessary and tap View Apple ID. Scroll down to iTunes in the Cloud section and turn off iTunes Match renewal.

iTunes Match vs iTunes in iCloud

iTunes Match is a paid-for song-matching and storage service. iTunes in iCloud is a free service which means that any music you've bought from the iTunes store, can be automatically downloaded to your iPad. While iTunes Match tracks are downloaded DRM-free, Apple Music files downloaded for offline listening do have restrictions. If you want to play tracks on non-Apple devices, keep a back-up of your DRM-free tracks, because Apple Music downloads cannot be transferred to these devices.

Other Cloud Services

There are several other online services that will let you store and play your music – either streaming it from the cloud or downloading to play on your iPad. Amazon Music with Prime Music app lets subscribers stream over a million songs, download them to play offline and access songs in their collection that they have bought from Amazon. Google Play Music is another option.

Above: The Amazon Music with Prime Music app also lets you play songs from the cloud.

MAKE YOUR OWN MUSIC

Several popstars, including Justin Bieber and Adele, have been discovered after recording their songs at home and posting them online. Try for yourself, using the iPad to make your own music.

TUNE UP YOUR LIFE

Whether you are a professional musician or have no musical knowledge at all, GarageBand for iPad will get you hitting the right notes.

GarageBand

Apple's GarageBand is a sophisticated program, which lets you record backing tracks for your songs or just for amusement. There are three types of instruments used to record sounds.

- **Smart instruments**: great if you have no musical know-how. They cover guitars, keyboards, bass and drums and ensure all the notes and chords you play are in tune with each other.

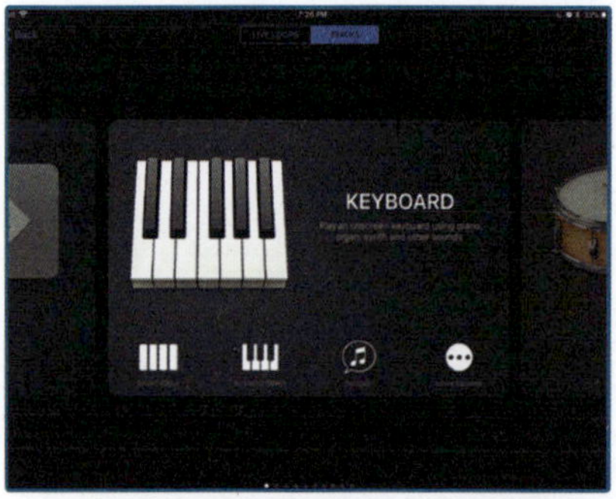

Above: You can use GarageBand's touch keyboard to play and record songs, no matter your musical talent.

- **Touch instruments**: best if you play guitar, bass, keyboards or drums for real. Tap the virtual instruments on screen to create your sound, but beware: they are pressure sensitive. The harder you press, the greater the volume.

- **Real instruments**: give the most authentic sound. You'll need to connect your guitar, keyboard or drum pads to the iPad directly. For example, you can connect a USB keyboard to the USB port using Apple's Camera Connection Kit. There are also special guitar cables that enable it to plug directly into the iPad's headphone jack.

RECORD YOUR SONG

GarageBand for the iPad is a paid-for app available from the App Store (or it may be pre-installed on your iPad). Download and install, then tap to open.

1. Choose your instrument. Swipe left or right to see what's available. In this example, the keyboard is selected.

2. The keyboard opens. Tap the image of the Grand Piano and select the type of keyboard, from Electric Piano to Classic Rock Organ.

3. If you don't like the keyboard layout, press the keyboard button on the right and you have two rows of keys for left and right hands.

4. Tap the keys to play your notes. The spot where you tap and the force of your tap dictate the precise sound and volume.

Step 2: Tap the Grand Piano image and select a keyboard type, such as Electric Piano.

5. Tap the button in the middle to change how the keyboard moves when you swipe it. Glissando is more like a piano, whereas swiping plays the notes smoothly. Switch to scroll and swiping moves you left or right on the keyboard.

6. When you're ready to record, tap the red Record button in the top bar. The metronome starts and counts through one measure before recording begins and the Play button turns blue. Tap this to stop recording.

7. If you fluff the notes, tap the Undo button and start again. Press the View button to change to Tracks view, where you can see the music you recorded. Tap once to select it and press the Play button to listen to it.

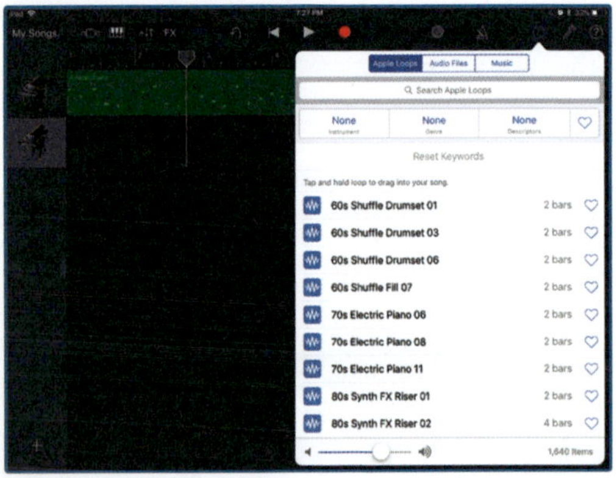

Step 8: Tap the loop icon and drag a clip from the list onto the mixing deck.

8. Once you have finished recording that element of the track, you can select My Songs to add it to a new song.

9. To save your song, tap My Songs in the control bar.

Build a Song

To create a song in GarageBand, you record the Touch instruments and then arrange the recordings in Tracks view. You can have up to eight tracks.

1. Select Tracks view in the top control bar. You'll see each row is a track, which has the recording of one Touch instrument, shown as a rectangular block. The icon beside the recording shows which instrument it is.

2. Swipe this icon to the right to reveal the track controls where you can control the relative volume of the track within the song.

3. Move blocks of music around by tapping-and-dragging them to new positions in the song. To trim the clip, push the edges in.

> **Hot Tip**
>
> **Double-tap on a track – or region as it's called – and you get the editing controls: Cut, Copy, Delete, Loop and Split.**

Sharing a Song

Once you're happy with your song, you can share it to the normal places. Tap My Songs, then press and hold the song in question. Tap the share button from the pop-up menu. You'll see there are options to share as a song, ringtone or as a project, which contains all your multitrack recordings.

GAMES

When it comes to gameplay, the iPad's large screen gives it a natural advantage over its smaller screen rivals, particularly if you have a Retina display to display the high-quality graphics.

STANDALONE GAMES

Whether you're a casual or serious gamer there's plenty to keep you entertained with apps specially made to take advantage of the iPad's increasing processing power.

Games Store

Download games direct to the iPad from the App Store. Simply tap the App Store icon to open and select the Games tab at the bottom. It's a brand new page based around what games Apple wants to show you. There's featured games, featured categories, new games, top free and paid games and a chance to select from all categories. Everything is there, from action to adventure to puzzle games.

Popular Games

There are thousands of games available in the App Store, so it's good to get personal recommendations. To see what others are playing, select the App Store, tap Games and then scroll down to the charts to see what people are downloading.

Hot Tip

Playing with touchscreen controls takes a little getting used to compared with physical controllers, so it might be as well to practice before challenging friends.

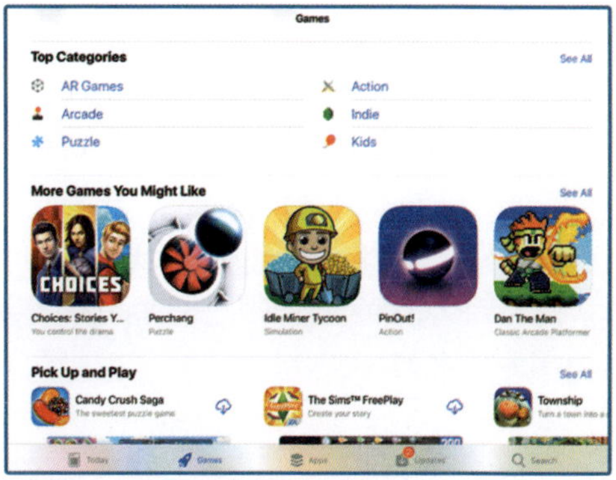

Above: Download games from the App Store by selecting Games. Scroll down to Top Categories and hit See All to narrow down the genres.

Here you can see the most popular free and paid-for games. If there's a particular type of game you're looking for, such as Arcade or Kids, tap the All Categories button in the top-left, select Games and make your choice.

Below are five of the most addictive games that also show why the iPad is great for gaming.

- **Angry Birds Star Wars**: who wouldn't be angry when you're blasted through space. Amazingly popular and compulsive to play, Angry Birds are now the rebels having to battle Darth Vader in a Star Wars adventure. If you get tired with that fantasy, don't forget there are Angry Birds Space, Rio, Seasons and so on.

Above: Angry Birds is one of the most popular games in the App Store. There are many different versions to try.

- **Minecraft**: A modern phenomenon, Minecraft is an open world building game that enables players to fashion tools and building materials to create giant structures for others to admire. You'll even have to defend them from would-be attackers. It has become exceedingly popular so give it a try!
- **Super Mario Run**: Nintendo's most loved character is finally available on iOS. With this endless runner game,

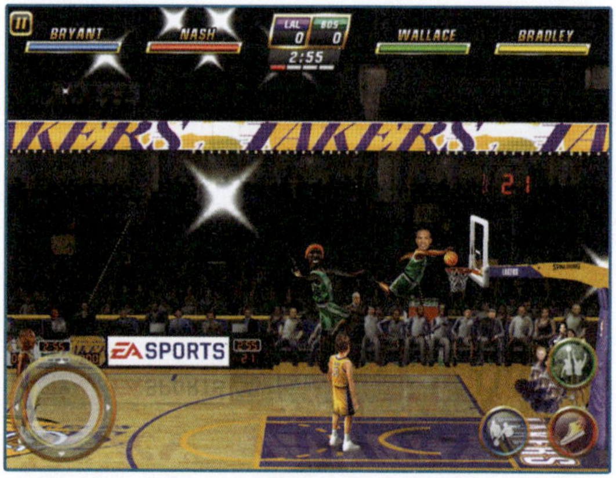

Above: Hit outrageous Slam Dunks in EA Sports classic arcade basketball game NBA Jam.

you can guide Mario through levels as he attempts to rescue Princess Peach from the clutches of Bowser.

- **Scrabble**: the traditional word game has had a makeover and comes with exclusive features for the iPad. There are HD Graphics to take advantage of the iPad screen, sound effects and animations plus up-to-date dictionaries to help put a stop to the arguments about what words are allowed.

- **Clash of Clans**: Have you ever wanted to build up your own civilization, create weapons and warriors, conquer lands and fight-off would be invaders? The real-time strategy game Clash of Clans offers hours of fun. Beware, it's requires online connectivity and is hard to put down.

Above: Super Mario Run is a fun little platform game featuring Nintendo's most famous character.

- **NBA Jam**: EA Sports NBA Jam is among the best sports games. It's fast-paced arcade-style 2-on-2 basketball games with plenty of outlandish slam dunks for you to practice.

GAME CENTER

Many games that offer online leaderboards, save your achievements or allow you to challenge friends or strangers use Game Center. This is Apple's back-end online gaming service, but you won't be able to find it on your Home screen. Game Center has changed a lot in recent years and is no longer a standalone app. Instead it is associated with your Apple ID and can be accessed in the Settings menu.

Using Game Center

Game Center isn't something you'll particularly notice and is generally aimed at developers these days. When you open a game that's compatible, you'll see a message that says 'welcome back', meaning there are possibilities for leaderboards and online multiplayer features. The way to access them will vary depending on the game.

Above: When you open a game you will see a 'Welcome back' message from Game Center at the top of the screen.

- **Leaderboards:** If you see a leaderboard in your game, there's a chance the developer is using Game Center to compare your stores with other gamers.
- **Achievements:** If your game has a trophies system, Game Center will keep track of the ones you've earned.
- **Invites:** If your game has an online element you may be able to use the Invite system to play with or against each other. Search for invites within a game and then you can send it through iMessage.
- **Challenges:** To challenge someone find the Invite button within the game (if it exists) and tap it.

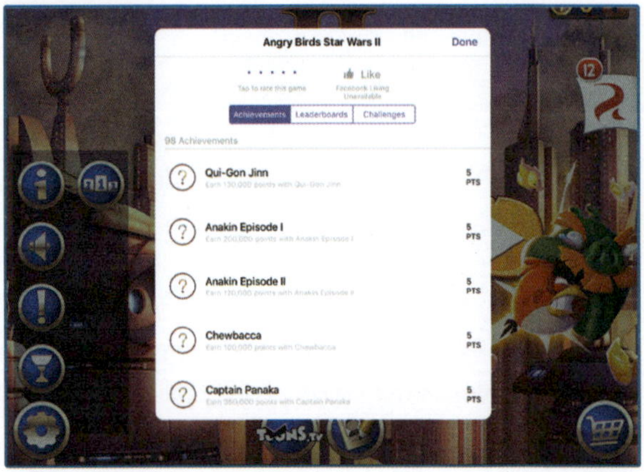

Above: Game Centre looks after the in-game achievements and leaderboards, like here in Angry Birds Star Wars.

You can send the invite via iMessage to a friend. The Nearby Players feature will help to pair you with people on the same Wi-Fi network or in Bluetooth range.

Playing with Friends

While many games handle multiplayer differently, EA Sports NBA Jam enables local multiplayer between up to four friends on the same Wi-Fi network. Here's how it works:

1. Open the NBA Jam app and select Multiplayer from the menu.
2. Next, select Create and enter your initials. The next screen will show positions for four players.
3. On the other iPad, your friend should open NBA Jam, select Multiplayer and tap Join. They can tap P2 to play on the same team or P3/P4 to play against you. Up to four players can join the game.
4. Once everyone has joined the game, the player who initiated the game can press the tick to advance to the game itself.
5. Enjoy the two-on-two arcade basketball action.

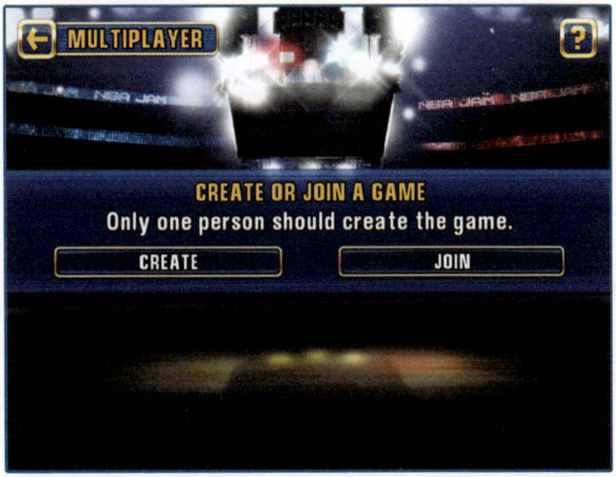

Above: The Game Center infrastructure lets you play games against other people and shows leaderboards of scores. Find a specific game's multiplayer feature to find a matchup.

Hot Tip

Head to Settings, Game Center to turn Game Center on or off and to amend your profile. You can also decide if nearby players can invite you to multiplayer games.

LIFESTYLE

Whether it's an essential life skill, such as cooking, or life enhancing, such as a Vogue Cropped T-Shirt, it will be covered in one of the thousands of lifestyle apps available for the iPad.

SHOPPING

From online exclusive retailers like Amazon and eBay or apps for your favourite high-street stores to big box retailers, you'll be able to buy absolutely everything on the iPad.

If you're looking for great local deals, then try Groupon. Or if you're looking for unique arts and crafts items or handmade products then give Etsy a spin. You'll be surprised at how many unique things you can find. Many apps even include compatibility with Apple Pay that simplifies payments and means you don't have to enter your card details.

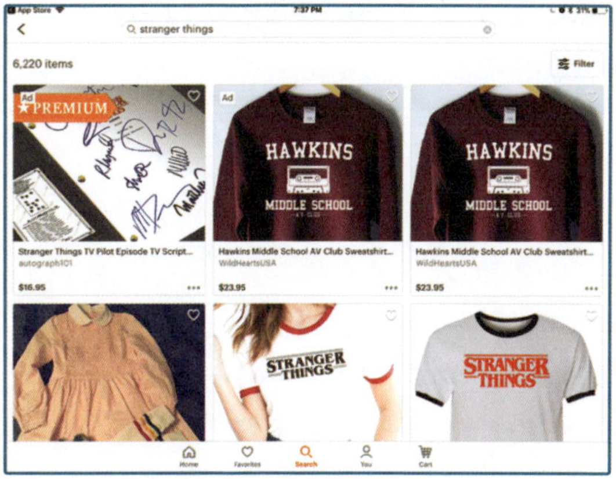

Above: The Etsy app helps you find unique arts and crafts supplies and vintage items online.

FOOD AND DRINK

Jamie Oliver's Ultimate Recipes is a great digital cookbook app, while the Food Network app provides all there recipes you'll ever need. Open Table helps you find a seat at a local restaurant if you don't feel like cooking, while Uber Eats or Post Mates help you to order food from local restaurants that can be delivered directly to your door. Foodies in need of a recipe can try Epicurious, which also creates shopping lists based on the dish you choose. To wash it all down, mix your own drinks with Cocktail Flow.

SPORTS

The sporting life is covered, with everything from the Yahoo Fantasy Football to help you manage your team, to ESPN and BBC Sport covering results and news from sports around the world. There's also a variety of apps that enable you to watch sports online, if you have the subscriptions and apps like Stub Hub that help you acquire tickets for the game.

HEALTH AND FITNESS

Wearable technology is exploding and, whether it's Fitbit or Misfit, there's an app to accompany every fitness tracker. Apps like Couch to 5K and 7 Minute Workout do what they say on the tin. Headpsace and Aura help you be more mindful, while Glo provides an abundance of online yoga classes.

TRAVEL

Wherever you're planning your trip, there's an app to help. TripAdvisor lets you check out hotels, flights and restaurants in your destination with reviews and ratings by other users. Airbnb has also taken off and gives you an easy way to book places to stay. If you prefer to travel in spirit rather than the flesh, fly around the planet with Google Earth or explore the universe with NASA.

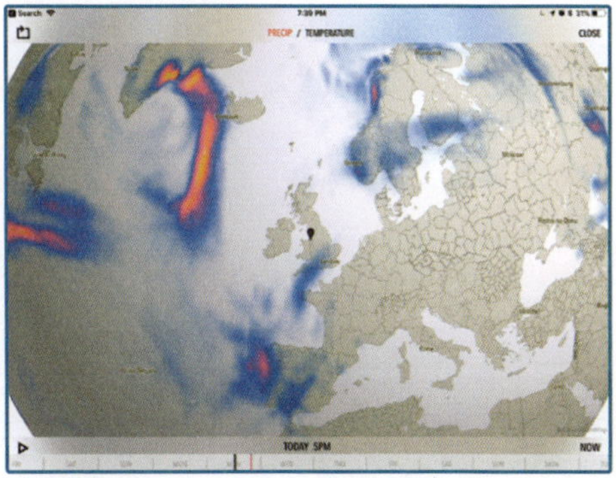

Above: There are many weather apps, which can be adjusted to your location. Here you can see Dark Sky.

REFERENCE

Previously, when there was a lively discussion in the pub or elsewhere, it was difficult, if not impossible, to prove who was right. Now it takes a moment's research on the iPad. What causes a plane's vapour trail? Look it up in Wikipedia, through one of the companion apps like Wikipanion. Test your romantic streak with a look at the sonnets in the app that covers the complete works of Shakespeare or find out what the prospects of rain are for school sports day.

WORKING

NOTES

One of the key ways of staying organized is to jot down a note when something occurs to you. With the Notes app you can sync with other iDevices and your computer, so you're always on top of what you have to do.

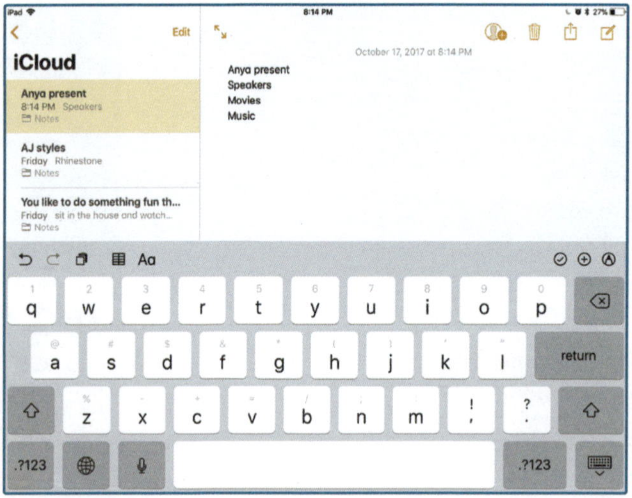

Above: The note that is currently open is highlighted in yellow in the left-hand pane.

TAKE NOTES

Notes isn't designed for writing your novel or essay, as it doesn't have the rich formatting features of programs such as Word, but is perfect for mapping out your ideas, making lists, doodling and adding photos. From iOS 11 up, you can even scan documents and add your signature.

Add a Note

In landscape mode, you'll see folders offering access to any previous notes on the left and a blank canvas on the right. In Portrait you'll see a clean page. You can just tap the screen to summon the keyboard. To start a new note, tap the pen and paper icon in the top-right corner.

Navigating Notes

1. In portrait mode, tap Folders and a pop-up window lists all your Notes accounts (iCloud, Gmail etc.).

2. Tap the account you want and the notes are listed with the date they were written or updated, from the most recent to the oldest.

3. The note that's currently open is highlighted in yellow. Simply tap the note you want, and it opens in the main window.

4. When the iPad is in landscape mode, the list of accounts and their notes is permanently shown.

5. To search the text of your Notes scroll to the top of a list of notes to reveal the Search box, then type in the word or phrase you are looking for.

6. You can also search for a specific attachment by selecting the four squares icon in the lower-left corner.

Delete Notes

Tap the dustbin icon at the top of the screen to remove a note. In list view swipe left or right across the note title and then tap the Delete button. This will delete the note from iCloud and all other devices.

> **Hot Tip**
>
> **The title of your note is the first line of text, which means you can end up with some odd headings. It's a good idea to put the title you want as the first line of text.**

SYNCING NOTES

So you can always be up-to-date with your jottings, you can sync notes between your iPad, your PC and other iDevices, as well as share them directly with others.

Sync with iCloud

Use iCloud to keep any notes made in the Notes app on the iPad in sync with your computer and other devices, such as the iPhone, Mac and iPod Touch.

If you're using an Apple email address with iCloud (such as yourname@me.com or yourname @mac.com), tap Settings then iCloud and switch Notes to On.

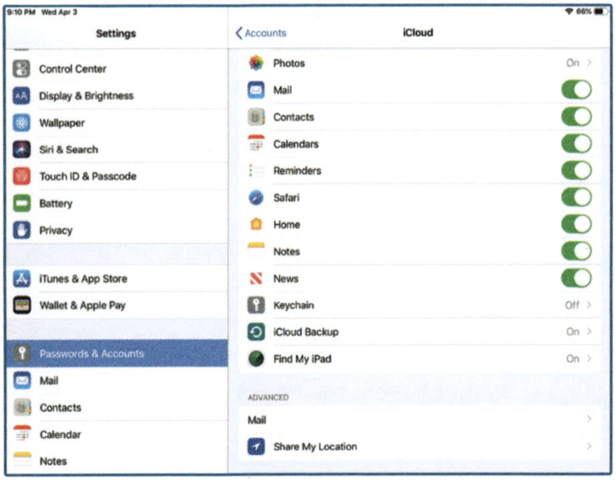

Above: If you have an Apple email address you can sync your Notes through iCloud by toggling Notes to On in the iCloud settings menu.

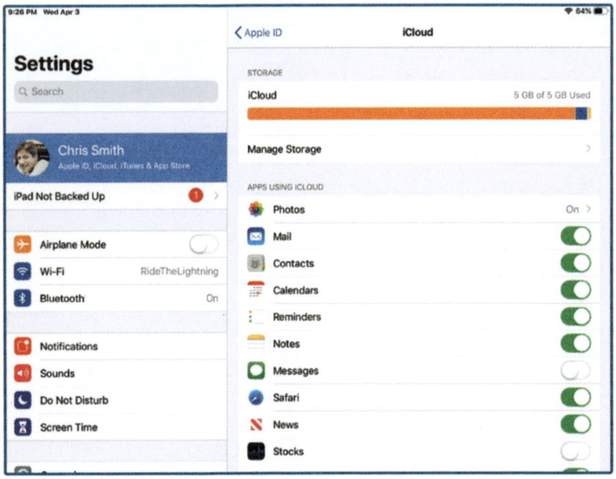

Above: When you create a note using Siri it will be attached to an email address. You can change this address through Settings, Notes.

Alternatively, if you're using Gmail or a similar email account like Yahoo or Hotmail with iCloud, then go to Settings, Accounts & Passwords, Gmail (or Hotmail etc.) and turn on Notes for the account.

Share Notes

While reading the note, tap the Share button (a box with an arrow) at the top of the screen. You can then choose to email the note, send it as a message or print it, using AirPrint. However, you can also collaborate with contacts on the same note. This will let two or more people contribute to the plan. The Note will be synced in the cloud and everyone will see the latest changes.

1. Tap the Add People icon in the top-right corner and a new pop-up window will open.

2. Here you can choose how to invite someone to view and edit the Note. All of the usual suspects are there, while you can also copy the link and paste it into any app.

3. If you pick an app to Share with, a copy of the note will be attached to a new message, email, post, etc.

4. The recipient will be notified, allowing them to open the note to view or edit.

MORE THAN TEXT

Notes doesn't just have to be a typed list of what you have to do. You can also sketch an idea or plan, add photos and videos, scan documents and much more. All media types can be placed in the same document too. The options to add different media types sit in the top right of the keyboard or the bottom right of the notes page itself.

Finger Art

1. To get started tap the pen icon and use your finger (or Apple Pencil) to sketch. You can select the type of sketch tool you'd like to use. There's pencil, marker and pen options.

2. Next to the pens you'll also see a colour palette, enabling you to sketch in black, blue, green, yellow and red.

3. If you want to close in on the details, pinch open your fingers to zoom in or pinch closed to zoom back out. Drag two fingers moves the sketch around.

4. There's an eraser tool to remove things and undo/redo arrows in the bottom left corner to amend your last actions.

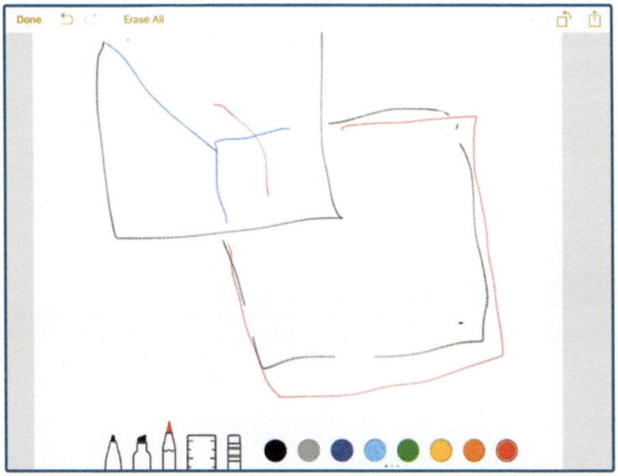

Above: Draw your idea or plans using your finger and the sketch tools in Notes.

Above: Summon Siri, request 'Take a Note' and start dictating.

Add Photos and Videos

1. Tap the + button at the bottom of a note.
2. Here you'll see the option to access the photo library, take a photo/video or scan a document using the built-in camera.
3. Take the photo/video or choose one from your gallery and add it to the note.
4. Tap the pen icon to doodle on the photo.

Drag and Drop

If you've attached media to a note, the iPad's drag and drop rules apply. You can place your finger on a photo and drag it to a different note on the photos. Or you can select Attachments from the search menu and drag that into your notes. The Slide Over, Split View tools also work extremely well here. For example you can drag a picture from the Photos app or from a URL from Safari website directly into a note. This is great for an ideas board.

DICTATE YOUR NOTES

As a virtual personal assistant, Siri is just what you need when it comes to finding, dictating and updating your notes. Unfortunately, he only works with an iPad 3 or later.

Summon Siri by tapping and holding the Home button. Ask to 'Show all my notes' or notes with the keyword you are looking for, such as 'Show my note about birthday presents.' If it's some time since you wrote the original note you'll first have to find it. Tell Siri, 'Update Note' and select the one you want from the list. It will open in the Notes app. Get right to the point and tell Siri to 'Take a note' and then dictate your message.

DOCUMENTS

The iPad lets you create, view and edit documents just as if you were at your desktop computer, and has built-in sharing and syncing too.

CREATE DOCS

While a touchscreen keyboard may not be as practical as the one on your computer for creating long or complex documents, it is still possible to produce some great-looking work.

Writing on iPad

Given that it is a mobile app, Pages is an amazingly powerful word processor. It is available as a free download from the App Store, but may also be included in your iOS.

1. Once downloaded, tap Pages to open it. On the Documents screen tap the + button in the top right corner to start from scratch.

2. In the Choose a Template section you'll see options for documents, reports, letters and more. To create your own, select Blank.

3. When you open a template, it will include dummy text and images. To edit these elements tap them on the screen and just overtype or hit the delete button.

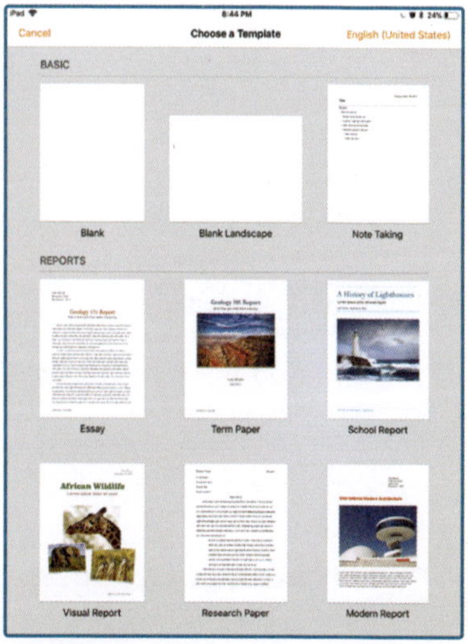

Above: Pages allows you to choose a template from existing formats.

Locating a Document

If you already have documents created in Pages on your Mac or elsewhere, you'll see Recent documents when you open the app. Or hit the browse button to access everything stored in the new Files app (*see* page 53). In the Files app you'll see everything you have stored in various cloud accounts you've added (Google Drive, iCloud Drive, etc.) providing you've allowed Files to access those platforms.

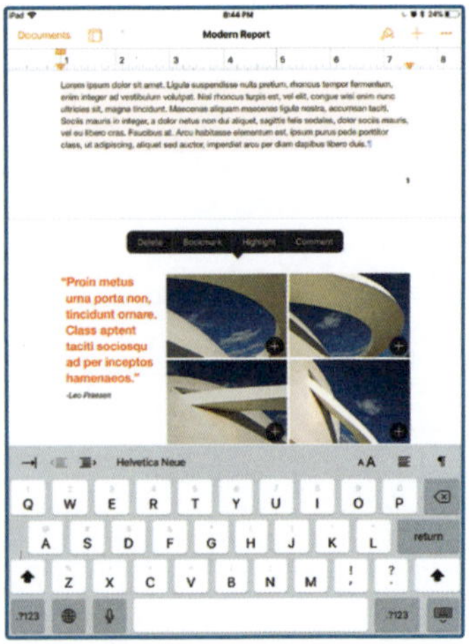

Above: When editing a document you can change the preset template text. Start by highlighting the passage.

1. Once you've found the document, tap it.
2. Depending on the file format of the document, the iPad will try to convert it to work with Pages. If you have an app like Microsoft Word on the iPad it'll open in its native app.

Editing a Document

- **Format text:** highlight the part you want to alter and use the settings at the top of the keyboard to change the font, font size etc.
- **Edit styles:** for paragraphs, headings, etc. select the text and tap the Paintbrush icon in the top bar. Tap the Layout tab to change the number of Columns and Line Spacing.
- **Add Photos, Tables, Charts or Shapes:** just tap the + button in the top-right and choose.
- **Resize a graphic:** tap it and push one of the blue anchor points to amend.
- **Settings:** press the spanner in the top-right corner and Document Setup to alter paper size, margins and so on.

Working with iWork

Pages is part of the iWork suite of programs, which also includes Numbers for spreadsheets and Keynote for presentations. There is now a single format for the apps on iOS and the Mac that enables Handoff. So you can stop working on Pages on the iPad and pick up where you were on the Mac and all the latest edits will be there. If you have iCloud set up on your iPad, the three iWork apps will automatically back up your documents to your iCloud Drive on Apple's servers. The changes are then synced to your Mac and iDevices, so any alterations made to your documents on the go are immediately available when you're back in the office.

Sharing iWork Files and Collaborating

iCloud makes it simple to move your iWork documents between your Mac or PC and different iDevices, but there are other ways to share your files. Just like with Notes you can collaborate on documents with other people, with all changes synced back to a single document. Tap this option to invite people. Tap the person icon with the + button to start inviting people. Changes they make will be synced on versions of the document in real time.

Above: Share your documents by selecting from the options in the Share box.

Sharing Documents

When the document is open in Pages, Numbers or Keynote, tap the More button (three dots) to see options for printing, sharing, collaborating and more.

- **Share**: Access all of the usual sharing options.
- **Print**: Send the document to any available network AirPrint printer (see page 32 for more on printing).
- **Export**: Here you can choose to export your document in a format that plays nicely with other apps (Word, PDF, ePub, etc.). Next you'll need to choose how to share it.

Dealing with Numbers

Numbers for iPad lets you access, create and edit your spreadsheets on the go. Even if you're sent a spreadsheet that wasn't created with Numbers, you can work on it, as the program can open Excel documents or spreadsheets saved as comma-separated value (.csv) files. This can be extremely helpful.

Getting Started with Numbers

Open Numbers and you have a choice of templates, from expense reports to a loan comparison, savings sheet or invoice. To set up your own, select Blank. Choose one to get started and tap to open.

> **Hot Tip**
>
> **Although there is no PC version of the iWork suite, the files can be saved and transferred in a format that can be used by Office-compatible programs or viewed as PDFs.**

- **Edit text**: to change the text in a cell, double-tap, then tap to select the text entry box that appears and type in your changes. The Text icon (abc) on the keyboard should also be selected.

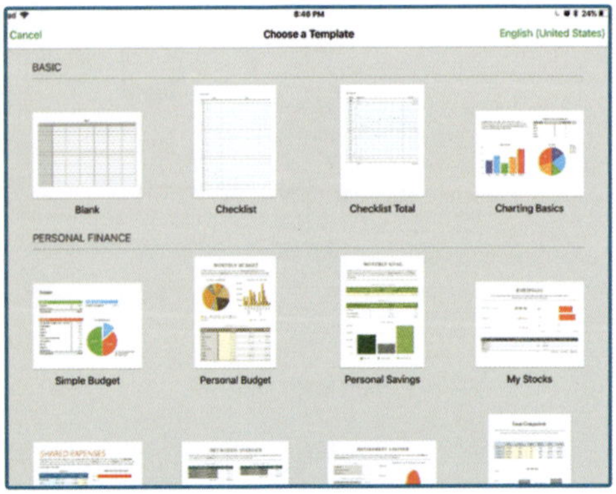

Above: Numbers provides you with a variety of template options to use as the basis for your document by entering your own data and words.

- **Edit numbers**: double-tap the cell where you want to change the figures and select the Numbers icon (123) to open the calculator.
- **Equations**: for more complicated spreadsheets. Tap the = icon on the keyboard and you have access to a calculator with a wide range of functions, from the financial to the statistical.
- **Cell**: Tapping the green Cell button at the bottom of the screen enables shortcuts to add today's date, the current time, a comment, a stock quote and quick formulas.

Change Styles

To alter the appearance of your spreadsheet, tap a cell and then press the paintbrush icon on the top bar. Choose the relevant tab to alter:

- **Table Styles**: select the Table tab and choose the layout you prefer or set them manually by tapping Table Options.

- **Headers**: extend the size of header rows and columns and add a footer if required.

- **Cell**: tap Text Options to change the font, size and colour. Use the other buttons to alter alignment and the Border Style or the Fill Colour of the cell.

- **Format**: you can change the cell format so that, instead of a number, it contains a percentage, date, text or checkbox, etc.

Creating Presentations

Could business life survive without the presentation? Certainly not at the moment, so if a presentation is needed quickly or there are some last minute changes to your slides, Keynote on the iPad is your answer.

- **Start a New Presentation**: open Keynote and then tap Create Presentation. To get started, choose one of the stylish templates available as your theme for the slides.

- **Edit the Presentation**: the theme is a single page at the moment. To add more, tap the + icon in the bottom-left. To edit the current slide, just double-tap on the text and type in your changes using the keyboard that appears or press the microphone and dictate to Siri (iPad 3 and later).

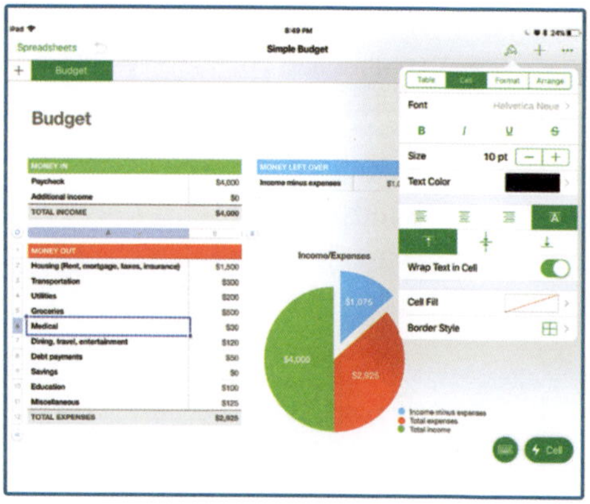

Above: Cell text options allows you to adjust font characteristics and styles so that any headings or labels appear as you would like them to.

Hot Tip

The easiest way to see changes in your data is to add a chart. Tap the + button on the Numbers toolbar, select the Charts tab and choose the type of chart to add. Tap the blue box to select the cells on which the chart is based.

- **Change Styles:** tap the paintbrush icon and you can change font sizes and styles, the appearance of lists and the layout.

- **Resizing Images:** double-tap the picture and use the blue anchor points to adjust the size. Tap the paintbrush icon on the toolbar and you can style the borders and flip the image.

- **Build Your Presentation:** Press the more menu and you have access to settings like transitions, allow for remote control, change the document set-up, add a soundtrack, broadcast it online or access a range of settings.

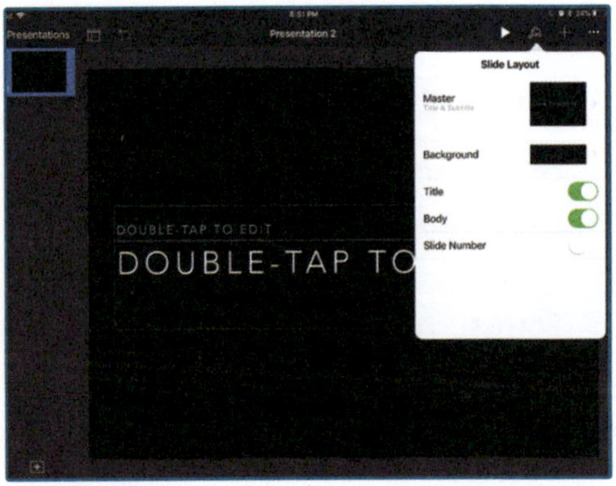

Above: When using Keynote for presentations you can change styles by tapping the paintbrush icon and selecting from the options displayed.

Journaling and blogging on iPad

If you like to keep an online journal, Day One Journal is a great option. Similar to the Notes app, it's easy to write, create reminders, insert photos from your day, sketch using built-in tools and even add audio recordings.

If you're looking for a distraction-free writing app that'll allow you to keep focus iA writing is brilliant, especially if you have a Bluetooth keyboard to connect to.
If you like to blog online then are are dedicated apps for the Word Press blogging platform that'll enable you to craft and post to your blog, likewise for the Twitter-owned blogging platform called Medium.

Drawing on iPad

Celebrated British artist David Hockney pays testament to the brilliance of the iPad as a drawing tool. He has used the Brushes app to create more than 400 works, first on the iPhone and then on the iPad. Several of the works were displayed, on the iPad, naturally, at the exhibition Me Draw on iPad in Denmark's Louisiana Museum of Modern Art. If you have an iPad compatible with the Apple Pencil stylus, you can create masterpieces in apps such as Adobe Photoshop Sketch, Lake Coloring Books and Sketch Club.

Above: The iPad can be a very effective drawing tool, as demonstrated by David Hockney using the brushes app.

EDIT DOCS

As many businesses use Microsoft Office for their word processing, spreadsheets and presentations, there are apps that let you work with these on your iPad.

Office on the Move

In late 2018, Microsoft finally added support for its Office 365 subscription platform for iPad and made individual apps available for the App Store. If you have a subscription you can use Word, PowerPoint and Excel apps on your iPad to create and edit documents. If not, you'll be able to access read-only versions of documents, spreadsheets and presentations.

Getting Your Office Files

You can sync your Office files through Microsoft's OneDrive cloud storage so any changes you make to the files are automatically updated. They can be accessed via the Apple Files app. You can also open documents sent as email attachments in Word, Excel or PowerPoint.

Google Docs

Online storage services let you access your files and in some cases edit them from anywhere. Among the most popular services for business is Google Docs. With this free service, the documents you create are stored on Google Drive. You can download Google Docs from the App Store for free.

Above: Use the Google Docs app to access and organize documents stored on Google Drive.

1. Use the Google Drive app, available from the App Store, to access your documents.

2. Tap the document to open it and then Google will open it in Google Docs to edit. If you don't have it, you'll be prompted to download it.

3. To share your document in Google Drive, tap the More button (three vertical dots) and click Add people. You can now add the names of those you want to invite to edit, comment or view it.

Hot Tip

To access your Mac documents on an iPad, go to System Preferences > iCloud on your Mac and make sure iCloud Drive is switched on.

SYNC DOCS

If you have a Mac, it's easy to sync all your documents to your iPad by using the iCloud Drive platform. Once set up, those documents will appear in the iCloud Drive section of the Files app.

1. First, set up iCloud Drive on your Mac. Go to System Preferences > iCloud and ensure iCloud Drive is ticked.

2. Select Options to control which folders and files are synced to iCloud Drive. If those folders contain more than your available iCloud storage, you may be asked to purchase more.

3. Once syncing is complete, you'll be able to open the Files app on your iPad and select iCloud Drive from locations. Here you'll see all of the available documents. Tap to download or open them.

PRINT DOCUMENTS

While we increasingly view documents on a screen of some size, there are times when we do need to print out a hard copy.

AirPrint

AirPrint is Apple technology that's built into the iPad's operating system, so you can print directly to a printer. Unfortunately, it's not quite that simple. The printer itself has to be AirPrint-enabled and on the same wireless network as your iPad.

Hot Tip

There's a growing list of manufacturers, available on Apple's website, who have added AirPrint support to their printers.

Print through Your Computer

With this method you install a program on your Mac or PC that receives your print job from the iPad and sends it to the printers your computer uses. Printopia (www.decisivetactics.com/products/printopia) is among the programs available for this.

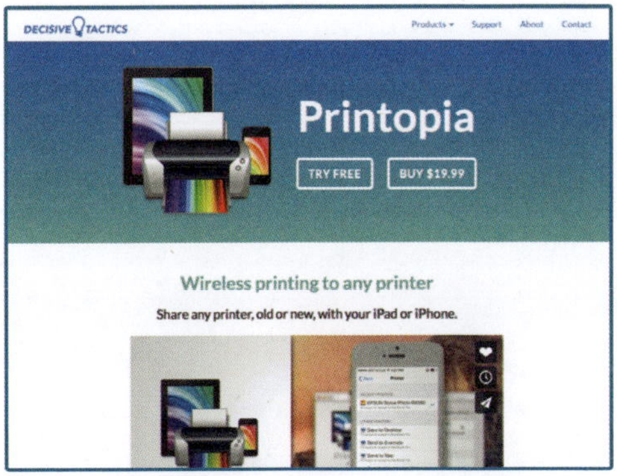

Above: You can install programs like Printopia on your Mac or PC and use it as a means of wirelessly printing your iPad documents.

Print Wirelessly

Provided the printer is on the same wireless network as the iPad, there are apps that will print directly to Wi-Fi printers. Alternatively, if your printer is physically connected to your computer, by the USB port, for example, several apps have a desktop helper application for your computer, so you can wirelessly send your document to your Mac or PC to process for printing. Apps available for this include PrintCentral and Printer Pro.

CALENDAR

The hectic pace of modern life makes it more important than ever to get organized. With your iPad digital assistant you can keep up-to-date with all your calendars – at work and play.

MANAGE YOUR SCHEDULE

The Calendar is a core app that's already on your iPad. Use it to set up your events and set alerts, so you don't miss anything.

Calendar Views

Select the view you want – by day, week, month or year – by tapping the tabs at the top. Each calendar uses a different colour to mark its events, so you can see at a glance when there are busy work periods, for example.

Creating Events

1. In any view, tap the + button, and a new event box appears.
2. Enter a name and location for the event.
3. Tap the Starts section to bring up the date and time controls, and enter the details.
4. Select Repeat and choose how frequently it reoccurs, then select the calendar to add it to. When finished, tap Done.

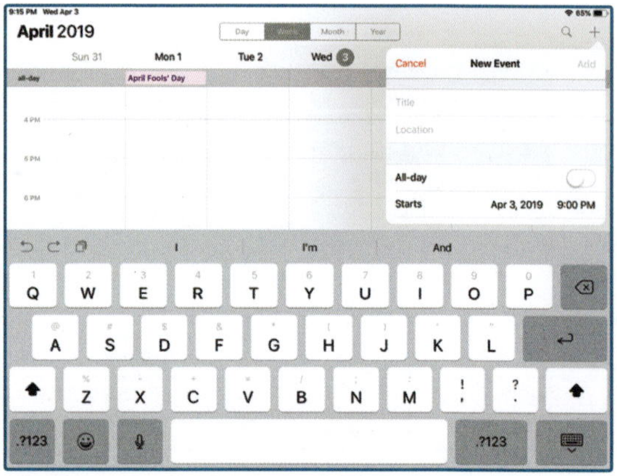

Above: Tap the + button to add a new event to your calendar by entering the name, location, time and details.

Use Siri

Even if you're not in the Calendar app, you can get Siri to add an event or check what you've got coming up if you have iPad 3 or later.

1. Press and hold the Home button, and when Siri responds, give the event details, e.g. 'Schedule haircut 3pm next Tuesday.'
2. Siri will check to see if there's a conflicting event. If there is, he will give the details and ask if you want to proceed.
3. To see what's coming up, ask Siri: 'What appointments do I have today?' or 'What's happening on Thursday?'

Hot Tip

In all but the year view, you can also tap-and-hold until the new event box appears and then release to open the Add Event box.

Edit Events

Tap the event and then tap the Edit button. In week or month view, if you've got the wrong day, just drag the event to a new date.

Search Events

If you know there's something you've been invited to but can't remember the date, search events. Tap the Search icon on the top menu bar and then enter the keywords you're looking for – such as Jeff's presentation – in the Search box.

Setting Alerts

Adding an event to your calendar is one thing, but many of us need a reminder when it's about to happen. Alerts are set in the Add Event box.

1. Tap the Alert button and select how long before the event you want to be reminded. The options vary from a week before to the actual time of the event.

2. For events such as birthdays, you probably want an earlier alert, so you have time to get a card or present. You can set the default alert period in Settings, Calendars and Default Alert Times. Scroll down to the Calendars section and select Default Alert Times. You can change these for timed events, birthdays and all day events.

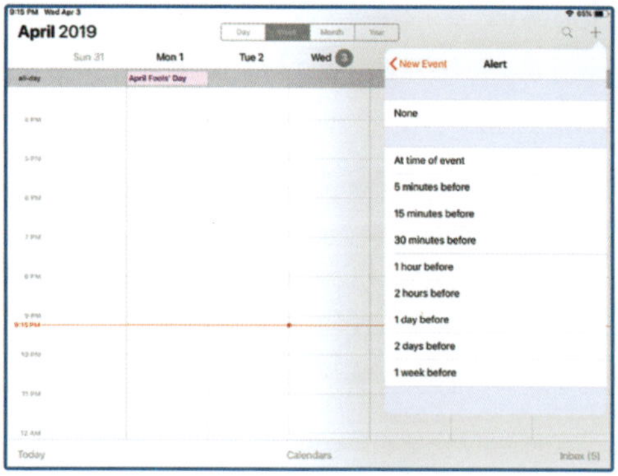

Above: You can set specific timed alerts for different events.

SHARING CALENDARS

In one calendar you can view lots of different calendars at once, including web-based calendars. You can also choose to share individual calendars with others.

Subscribing to Calendars

1. If you use an online calendar, such as Google or Yahoo!, add this by going to Settings, Passwords & Accounts, and then tapping Add Account. Select from the list or tap Other if your calendar service isn't named.

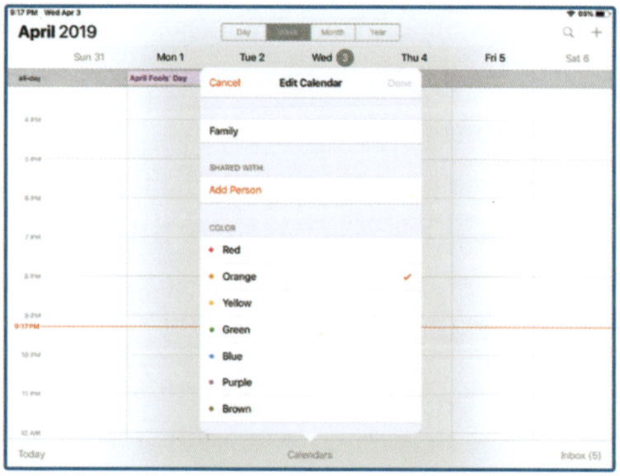

Above: You can switch oil access to the calendar in the Passwords & Accounts section of the Settings.

2. Once your account is added (you can also choose an existing one), you can toggle the Calendar button to on.

3. To select which calendars to view, open the Calendar app and tap the Calendars button. You'll see they are separated in the different accounts. Tap those you want visible.

Sharing Events

1. The calendar system is linked to your email. On certain email systems, such as iCloud or Microsoft Exchange, you can send and reply to meeting invitations.

2. To invite others, tap an event, and then the Edit button. Tap Invitees and select them from your Contacts by clicking the + symbol.

3. To reply to an invitation tap it in the calendar. You can see who's organizing it, who else is invited, as well as who has accepted. If you add comments, only the organizer will see them.

Sharing iCloud Calendars

Instead of individual events, you can share complete calendars you have on iCloud, such as for a work project, with others. They will need an iCloud account. Tap the Calendars button and choose the i button next to the iCloud calendar. Under Shared with, tap Add Person and tap the + button to choose from Contacts. An invitation is emailed to them to join the calendar.

Make Your iCloud Calendar Public

You can make your iCloud calendar viewable by anyone, although they can't change anything. Follow the steps above and turn on Public Calendar. Tap Share Link and email or text the URL to anyone.

Handy Calendar Features

- **Found events:** If Siri spots an upcoming event in your email, messages or the Safari web browser it'll give you an easy option to add it to the Calendar.

- **Time to leave:** Calendar now plays nice with the Apple Maps app. It'll look up locations, traffic conditions and public transport options to tell you when it's time to leave.

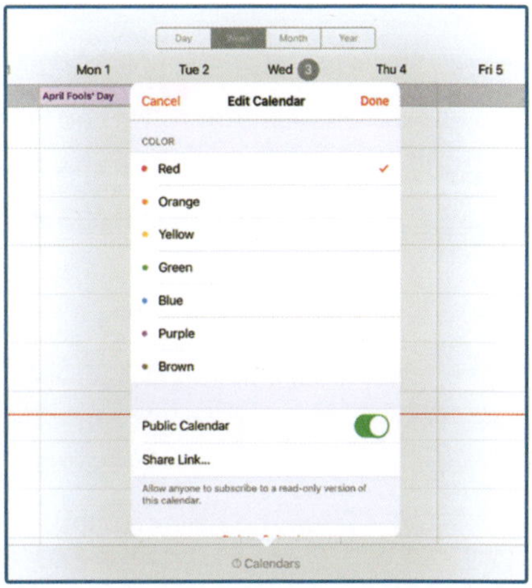

Above: You can share your iCloud calendar by adding contacts to the Shared with box, and make it public by toggling Public Calendar to On.

- **Location suggestions**: When setting a meeting, Calendar will consider past events to make suggestions.

Hot Tip

Making your project calendar on iCloud public is a good way of sharing important milestones with a project team.

Sharing Other Calendars

If you want to keep a wider group, such as the office football team, organized and be sure they all know what's happening, use your iPad to set up and share a calendar on one of the free services, such as Google.

1. Open Google in your browser, click Sign in to your Google account. Once logged in, select More from the menu bar, then select Calendar. Rather than share your personal calendar, you can set up a new one. Tap the arrow beside My Calendars and select Create new calendar.

2. Fill in the details. Enter the email addresses of those you want to use it in the Share with specific people section and then tap Create Calendar.

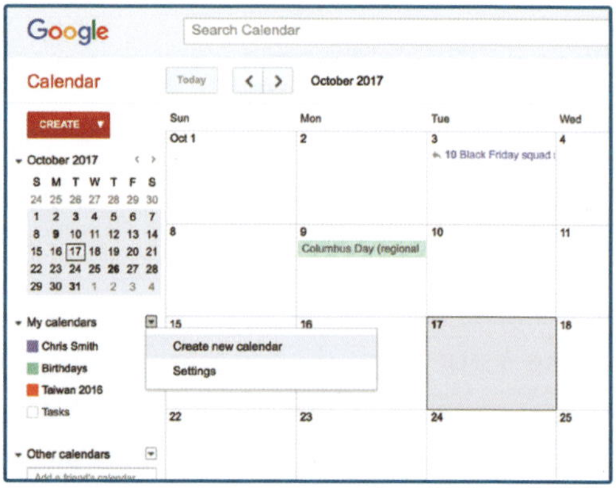

Above: Use your Google account to create a new calendar and select who you want to share it with.

3. Now set up the Calendar app on the iPad. If you don't already subscribe to a Google calendar, tap Settings, then Accounts & Passwords and select Gmail. If your account isn't added tap Add Account, fill in your account details and tap Save.

4. Open the Calendar app, tap the Calendars button and under your Gmail address you'll see the new calendar has a tick beside it. Now enter events, making sure that the name of the shared calendar is the one used in the Add Events box. Now those sharing your calendar will also see the event.

SYNC CALENDARS

Such is the nature of all calendar apps is that they'll sync with your other devices.

Cloud Syncing

Thanks to iCloud, if you have a Mac, the calendar app will feature everything you've added on the iPad and vice versa. If you're on a PC, you can go to iCloud.com to view and edit your calendar. Third party providers like Google, Yahoo! and Microsoft also have cloud syncing capabilities that ensure everything is up to date.

Hot Tip

Your colleagues will need an Apple ID and an iCloud account to accept your invitation to share a calendar.

1. To make sure calendars are being synced, go to Settings, Passwords & Accounts and choose from the accounts list. Make sure the Calendar button is toggled to on.
2. Head to Settings then Calendar and select Sync to choose how far back the events sync.
3. Tap Sync and choose from the options between Events 2 Weeks Ago, Events 6 Months Ago and All Events, to make sure everything you need is available.

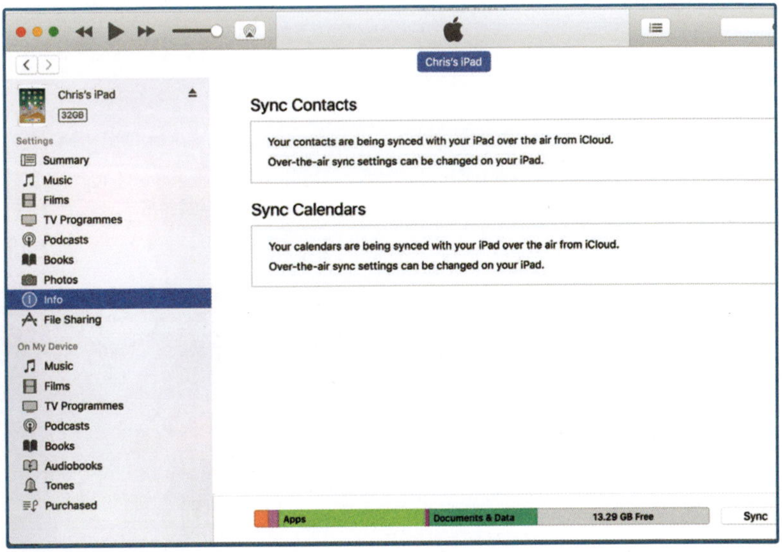

Above: You can choose to Sync your calendars via iCloud or iTunes.

CONTACTS

Your Contacts app is far more than just a list of names and addresses; it is also your social hub from which you can send an email, text or even Tweet.

MANAGE CONTACTS

There are many ways to keep contact details of your friends, family and colleagues up to date.

Import Contacts

If you have your list of contacts elsewhere – in Gmail, webmail or an email program such as Outlook – then you don't want to re-enter them one-by-one. Fortunately, you can import your contacts to iCloud and sync them to your iPad.

1. As iCloud is built into the iPad, all you need to do is to activate it, using your Apple ID. Go to Settings, Your Name, then iCloud, and make sure Contacts is turned on.

2. On your Mac or PC go to your existing mail program or webmail account and export all contacts in a single vCard file. How this is done will vary but the program's help file should explain what to do.

3. Still on your computer, access iCloud in your browser by going to www.icloud.com. Sign in with your Apple ID and password, then select Contacts. Click the Settings button with its gear icon that's in the bottom-left and click Import vCard.

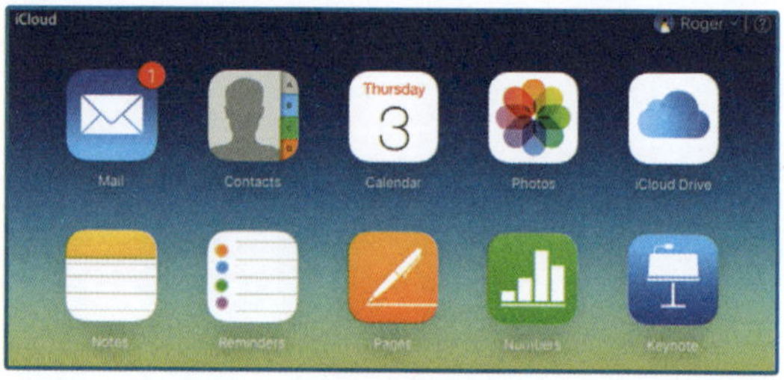

Above: Once you have turned Contacts on in your iCloud settings the app will appear in your iCloud home screen.

4. Browse to where you saved the vCard and select it. This will import the contacts online, which will then be synced to your iPad Contacts address book.

Sync Contacts by iTunes

As an alternative to using iCloud, you can sync your contacts using iTunes, but you can't do both.

Hot Tip

iPad is capable of adding contacts from other accounts like Yahoo! or Google. Head to Settings, Accounts & Passwords and toggle the Contacts switch to on.

1. Connect your iPad to iTunes and select it from the menu, then press the Info tab. Select Sync contacts and you have the choice of keeping all of them up to date or tapping Selected groups and checking the box beside those to sync.

2. The first time you sync with the iPad, you'll be asked if you want to merge the data, replace the contacts list on the iPad or replace the contacts on your computer with the information on the iPad.

3. You can sync contacts data from the Address Book or Microsoft Outlook on the Mac or Windows and others.

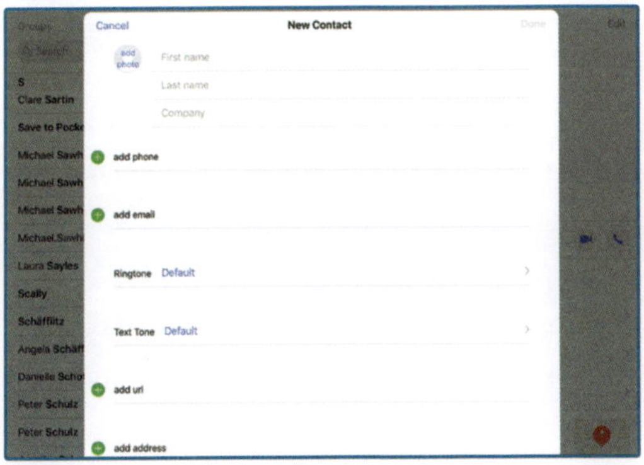

Above: Manually add contacts to your iPad by filling in the various details and tapping Done.

Add Contacts Manually

In order to add a contact directly to the iPad, tap the Contacts app to open it, then press the + button. A blank form appears. Enter the details, tapping the return key on the keyboard to move between fields. Tap the green button beside add field, and there are options to add a contact's nickname, the phonetic pronunciation of their name, birthday, Twitter handle and so on. Tap Done when finished.

Locate Contacts

As your popularity grows, so will your address book, which makes it difficult to find the contact you're looking for. Here is what to do to navigate through your contacts quickly.

- **Search**: tap the Search field and use the keyboard to start typing the name. Notice that only those names that contain the letter will appear. As you type more letters, the list narrows.
- **Tap the initial letter of the contact**: from the tabbed list on the left of the page to jump to that point in your contacts book.
- **Ask Siri**: for example, say, 'Find Thomas Smith' or if you have established your relationship with some of your contacts, ask: 'Find Mum,' for example.

Hot Tip

Don't worry about formatting, such as putting capital letters at the start of someone's name or dashes in phone numbers, as Contacts handles these automatically.

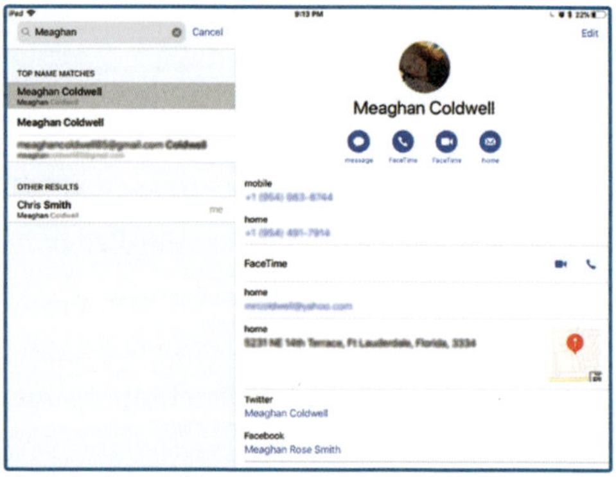

Above: Search your iPad contacts by tapping search and beginning to type the name you are looking for until it appears in the list below.

Set up Relationships for Siri in Contacts

On iPad 3 and later, Siri can use Contacts to send text messages or emails, but it is much easier if it knows who are the key people in your life.

- **Tell Siri who you are**: Go to Settings > Siri & Search > and ensure Siri is switched on. You'll see a menu option that says My Information – from there, select your contact details.
- **Add your relationships**: Whether it's your boss, girlfriend, mum or big brother, let Siri know the link to individual contacts by saying, for example: 'Vicky Alexandra

is my daughter.' Siri will ask you to confirm the information.

- **Dealing with a large family**: It could be confusing if you have several daughters, so you may have to be more specific about the relationship, such as oldest daughter or youngest daughter.

Add Relationships Manually

Tap the Contacts app to open it, select the name you want and then the Edit button. Tap on add related name field. Tap the label name to change this to the right relationship, such as brother, sister, friend, manager, assistant, partner etc., and then tap the name field to type the name or tap the information (i) icon to select the contact from your list. Tap Done when finished.

Above: Add relationships manually by going to add related name and entering the relevant details.

Hot Tip

If the right label to describe your relationship is not listed, create it yourself. Scroll down the list of label names, tap Add Custom Label and enter the name you want.

USING CONTACTS

Once you have family, friends and colleagues set up it's easy to get in touch with them, direct from the Contacts app.

Sending a Message through Siri

When you have let Siri know who your key contacts are, you can simply speak your message. For example, tell Siri: 'Text my boss I'm running late for the meeting.'

Siri will locate the contact and ask you to confirm the message. If it's correct, tell Siri to 'Send.' Say, 'Change it' to alter the message or 'Cancel' to abandon it.

Off the Page

- **Save to memory**: tap-and-hold a name or phone number and you can copy it to memory, so it's easy to add to an email or message.

- **Send an email**: tap an email address, and it opens a new email with the address already filled in. Just add a subject line and your message.

- **Share contact**: this opens the Share box, so you can send a new message with all the information about the contact saved as a vCard. You can send the contact details via iMessages, by email, text, or to an online storage account, such as Dropbox or Evernote. If you have saved any personal information with this contact, it will also be included.

- **Send a message**: select the number to use to send a text message.

- **FaceTime**: this button shows only if you have FaceTime activated. To do this, go to Settings, FaceTime and turn it on. Tap the button, and it starts a video call.

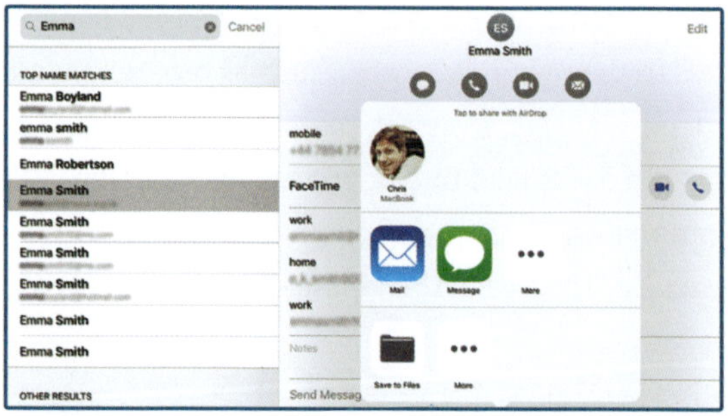

Above: Share your contacts by sending an automatically compiled vCard.

SOCIAL MEDIA CONTACTS

On iOS 10 and before Twitter and Facebook are built-in apps. This means you can add friends' Twitter handles as well as other details to their entries in Contacts.

Add Twitter

There's nothing to stop you adding Twitter details when you enter a contact's details but there is a much quicker and more certain method.

1. Go to Settings and tap Twitter. Assuming you have set up your account (*see* page 79), tap the Update Contacts button. This will compare email addresses and phone numbers from your Contacts with those used in Twitter.

2. Any matches, and Twitter usernames and profile photos will be added to individual contact details. You'll see the progress bar while it's happening, and then the number of contacts updated.

3. Tap Contacts and you'll see that several will include a Twitter username and the avatar – or profile picture – they use.

Hot Tip

If you have iOS 11 then the Facebook and Twitter integration of previous iOS versions is gone. This means you can't get in touch with your social media friends directly from the Contacts app, but on the plus side your contacts book is far less cluttered.

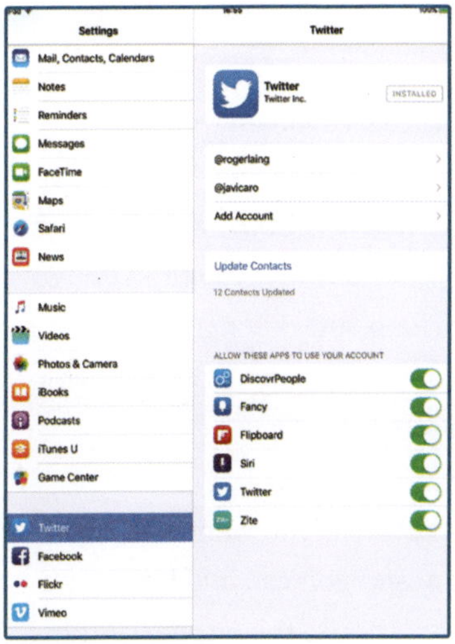

Above: Go to Settings, Twitter to update your contacts with their Twitter usernames and profile photos.

Tweet from Your Contacts

Tap your contact's Twitter username and you're taken to their Twitter page, showing all their latest posts and enabling you to Follow them, if you don't already. You can then tap the quill icon in the top right-hand corner to open a tweet box that's already addressed to them.

Add Facebook

Facebook works in a similar way to Twitter, above. It also adds a profile photo and marks it with a small Facebook logo.

Facebook has its own messaging service and will try to use this as the default email address, rather than the one used to sign up for the service. It adds this Facebook address to the contact's details.

REMINDERS

While you can use Notes to create your to-do lists, Reminders goes a step further. Not only does it let you list your tasks and check them off, it also provides a timely alert when you have something to do.

SET UP REMINDERS

Reminders help you to organize daily life by setting up a list of all you have to do. As with Calendar events, you can set these up with dates and alarms when they have to be done or simply list them with no prompt.

Setting up Reminders: Step-by-step

1. Tap the Reminders app, which is now built in to the iPad operating system, and then tap the + sign beneath the iCloud reminders.

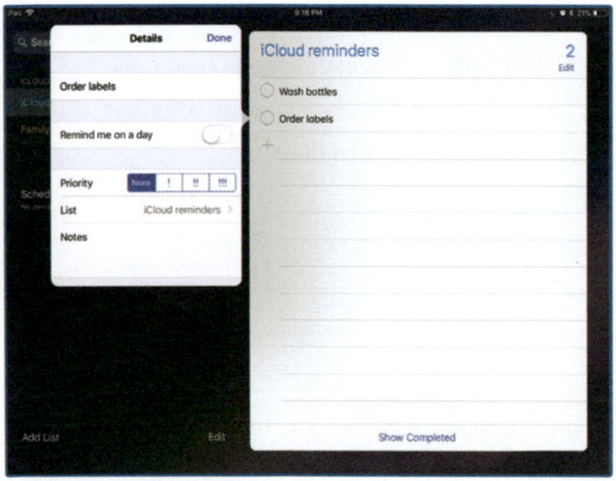

Step 2: After opening the Reminders app, you can add new reminders by tapping the + sign. Use the virtual keyboard to type your list.

2. Using the virtual keyboard that appears, type in your item 'to do', such as buy some bread or pick up kids from swimming and then tap the Return key. The titles don't need to be long, just descriptive enough to remind you what has to be done. To edit them, just tap again.

3. Add more details if you want. Tap the info button, and you can add Notes. You can also choose the priority – from high to none – as well as choose which list to add it to.

4. That's where you could leave it. Many to-do apps offer simple checklists that rely on regularly checking what to do next. Reminders goes further and will let you know when something needs doing. Tap the reminder in the list, then turn on Remind Me On a Day.

5. Tap on the date and time and use the dials to specify when you want the reminder, and then tap Done.

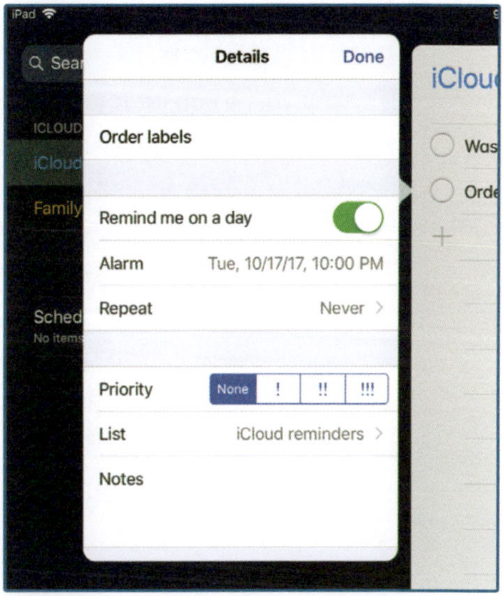

Step 3: Tap the info button to add more details to your 'to do' item in the Notes box, set its priority and choose the list to add it to.

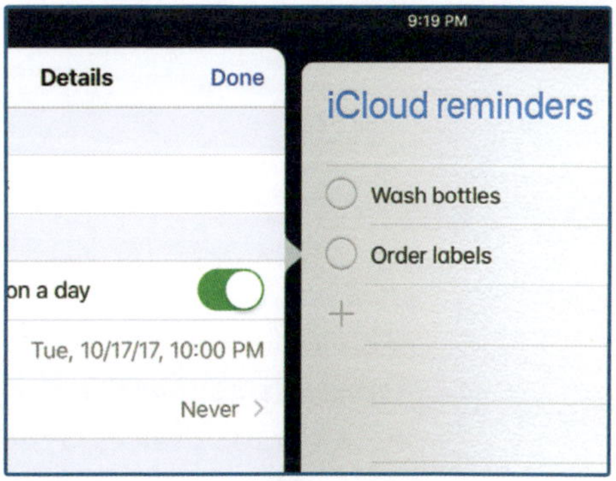

Step 5: To set alerts for your reminders you can choose a date and time using the dials.

Create New Reminder Lists

When you create a reminder, it is added to the list in Reminders. For easier organization you can create your own 'to do' lists with more meaningful names, such as Family, Work projects and so on.

Tap Add List in the panel on the left, choose whether to add it to your iPad or iCloud account and then write in the name using the on-screen keyboard.

Repeat Reminders

Enter keywords in the Search box in the top-left, and a list of any completed and outstanding 'to-dos' appears. Tap one to select it. Tap Scheduled to see all items that are due today as well as any that are overdue.

Search Reminders

Enter keywords in the Search box in the top-left, and a list of any completed and outstanding 'to-dos' appears. Tap one to select it. Use the mini-calendar in the left-hand panel to look for all reminders due on a certain date.

DICTATE REMINDERS

If typing your to-do list is just another task you'd rather do without, get Siri to fill it in for you if you have an iPad 3 or later.

Timely Reminders

Tap-and-hold the Home button to access Siri and then say what you want to be reminded about – and when. For example, 'Remind me to book the restaurant for 7.30pm.' Before you say or tap Confirm, you can change the details by saying, 'Change the time to 8pm' or say, 'Cancel' to delete the event.

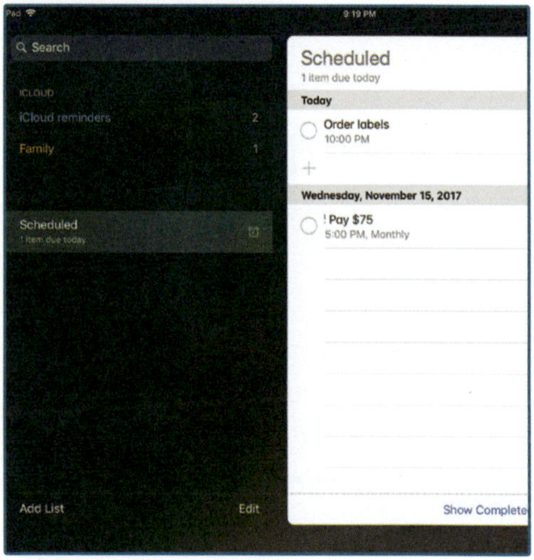

Above: Tap Scheduled and you can quickly and easily view which Reminders are due today or overdue.

Choose Your List

The reminder will be added to your default list, which is typically Reminders. To change the default, tap Settings, then Reminders and Default List. You can also tell Siri where to add your reminder. For example: 'Add butter to shopping list' or 'Add book DJ to party list.'

Hot Tip

Through iCloud you can sync Reminders, so they'll appear on your other iOS devices, as well as on your Mac (via Reminders app) or PC desktop computer (via iCloud.com). Go to Settings then iCloud and turn on Reminders.

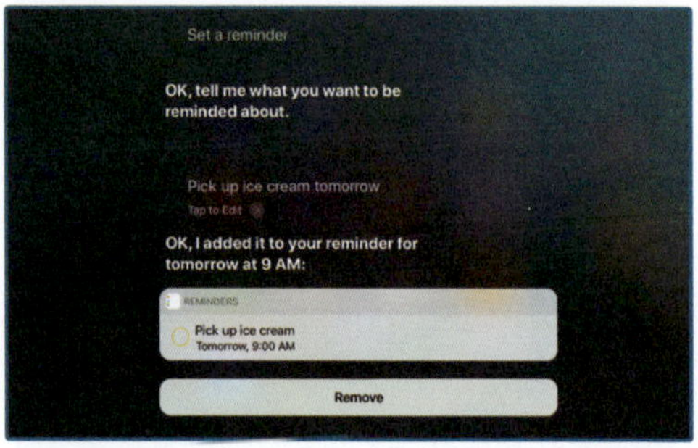

Above: You can use Siri to remind you of items on your to do list, and help with other tasks such as recording your shopping list as you dictate it aloud.

COMPLETED TASKS

When a task is done, there's a tremendous sense of satisfaction from being able to mark it off as completed. Although it's finished, you can still review it. However, when your lists start to get too crowded, you'll want to remove tasks for good by deleting them.

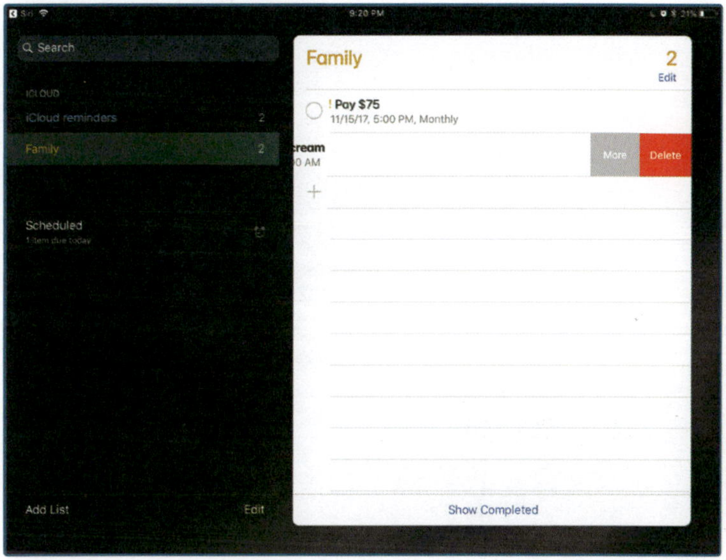

Above: To delete reminders swipe right to left and tap Delete.

Complete Reminders

Select a list or date from the left to view your reminders. To mark a task as completed, tap the checkbox beside it. Tap Show Completed, and you'll see, in date order, all the tasks you've finished. Hide this again by tapping Hide Completed.

Hot Tip

If you have created a new reminder list you no longer need, tap the top-left Edit button, tap the red button beside the name of the list to remove and then press the Delete button. When you remove a list, it also deletes any remaining reminders.

Delete Reminders

Select the to-do list and you can delete individual items by swiping across the entry from right to left and tapping the red Delete button.

To delete an entire list, select it from the panel on the left, swipe from right to left and press Delete.

ADVANCED iPAD

CUSTOMIZING YOUR iPAD

Make the iPad your own by modifying the background and changing the ways different apps and controls work.

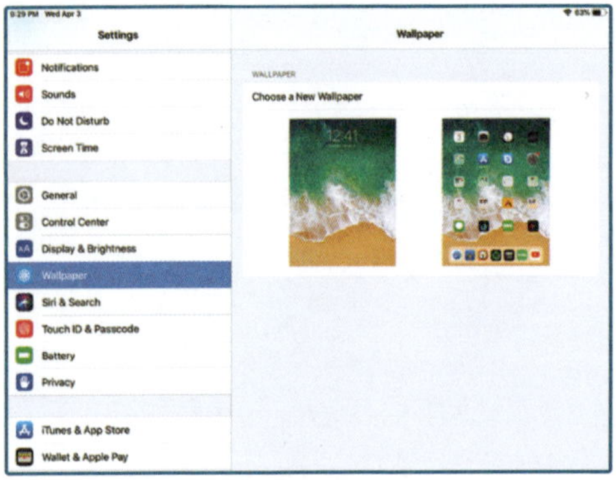

Step 1: Select Wallpaper from the Settings menu to display icons previewing the current wallpaper.

Step 2: Tap the icons to select a new wallpaper image from the pre-supplied options or your own photo albums.

PERSONALIZING THE EXPERIENCE

Keep the pictures that mean the most to you – family, friends or landscapes – as your background, associate different sounds to individual events and set up your iPad to work the way you do.

Changing Wallpaper: Step-by-step

The wallpaper for your iPad is pasted to your Home screen and on the Lock screen.

1. In order to change it, tap Settings and then Wallpaper. The large icons under Wallpaper preview the current wallpaper.

2. Tap this and select Choose a New Wallpaper to choose an Apple-supplied image or access one of your own photos from the albums below.

3. Select the image you want and see it full view. If it's one of your own photos, you can adjust it to fit the screen. Tap and drag the image to centre on the part of the photo you want as your background.

You can also pinch to enlarge or reduce the size of the photo.

4. Tap Set Lock Screen to use it as the wallpaper there or Set Home Screen if you want it to be the background for that screen. Set both will use the same image as wallpaper on both screens.

Sounds

Make your iPad operate as noisily or quietly as you wish by turning on or off the sounds that go with different events, such as tapping on the keyboard.

1. Tap Settings and then Sounds. At the top is the slider that controls the volume on incoming FaceTime calls and other alerts. When Change with Buttons is turned on, the slider also controls the Alert volume. When turned off, the volume for each is set separately.

2. Go through the list, and you can change the sound that plays with individual events; for example, the tone you hear each time you get a new email, a calendar alert or a reminder.

3. Turn the Lock Sounds on, and a sound plays when the Lock screen is unlocked. Similarly, switch Keyboard Clicks on if you want to hear a click each time you tap a key on the on-screen keyboard or off if you prefer not to.

Step 4: To set an image as your Lock Screen background tap the Set Lock Screen option.

Above: Adjust options in the Sound Settings list to customize which sounds your iPad makes.

Hot Tip

Rather than stick with the limited choice of Alert Tones supplied, you can create your own.

A world of tones

If you're unhappy with the default tones available from Apple, there are a couple of ways to spice things up. You can create a little jingle in GarageBand and save it as a tone, or you can access the Tone Store on iTunes and select from loads of options.

Create Tone in GarageBand

Follow the steps outlined on page 174 to create a tune in the GarageBand app. Then do the following:

1. When complete, return to the My Songs menu and press and hold the song you want to turn into a tone.
2. Select Ringtone, give it a name and select Export.
3. You'll immediately have the opportunity to set as a ringtone, text tone, or assign it to a contact. Alternately, it will appear at thew top of the Ringtones section when selecting new tones for specific apps.

Above: Adjust options in the Sound Settings list to customize which sounds your iPad makes.

Hot Tip

Want to know who's contacting you without looking at the iPad? Set a custom Ringtone or Text Tone. Head to Contacts, open a contact card and tap Edit to assign sounds.

Tone Store

Alternatively you can buy ringtones from the iTunes Store. Tap Settings, Sounds, Ringtones, Tone Store for a huge variety of songs and sounds from your favorite TV shows and movies. You can preview and buy these in the same way you purchase a song in iTunes. All of your purchased Tones will appear as options when choosing sounds.

Date and Time

It's easy to change the time and date. Go to Settings, General, then select Date & Time.

- **24-Hour Time**: turn this on if that's your preference and the iPad will display that time format (13:12 instead of 01:12 PM) in the status bar at the top of the screen.
- **Set Automatically**: turn on and the iPad will get the correct time based on your Wi-Fi or mobile connection. If you turn this off, you'll see the option to set it manually.
- **Time Zone**: tap this and in the Search box type the first letters of the nearest city. Select it from the list underneath, and it will automatically enter the time and date.

Hot Tip

Get the time around the world with the Clock app. Tap to open and select the World Clock tab. Tap any clock face to open the Search box for a city you want.

Modifying the Keyboard

The more you use the iPad, the more you'll come to rely on the on-screen keyboard. Fortunately, you can get it to adapt to your way of working and add your own short cuts. Go to Settings, General and then press Keyboard.

- **Auto-Capitalization**: automatically capitalizes those pesky first letters of a sentence or name that you may forget to do.
- **Auto-Correction**: the faster you tap, the more likely you are to make mistakes. This will automatically correct common errors.

- **Check Spelling**: always handy when you're writing an email to the boss.
- **Enable Caps Lock**: by default this is turned off. When it's turned on, you can double tap the Shift key to activate it, so that everything you write is in capital letters.
- . : looks strange but is very useful. By double-tapping the space bar you can automatically add a full stop and a space at the end of any sentence.

Changing Keyboards

From the Keyboards menu in General Settings, tap Keyboards, Add New Keyboard to add more keyboards to your iPad or change the layout to match your language or country. To swap between Keyboards, tap the Globe icon on the bottom row of keys of the on-screen keyboard. This is also where you can add third-party keyboards like Google's Gboard.

Split Keyboard

You can split the keyboard to different sides of the screen in order to see more of the screen while performing other tasks. Press and hold the keyboard icon in the bottom right corner of the keyboard and select Split. You can also select Undock to move the keyboard on the screen.

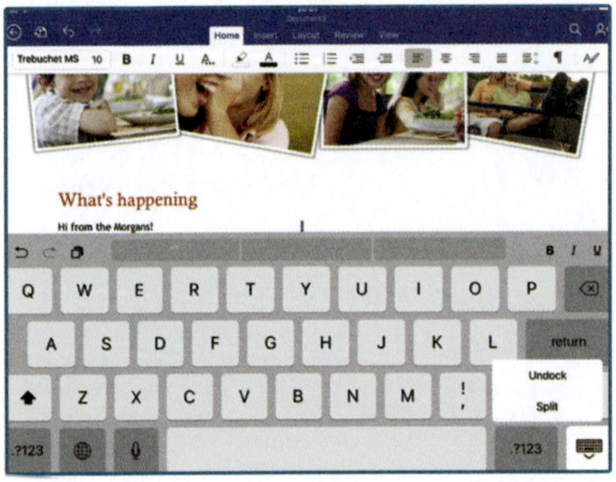

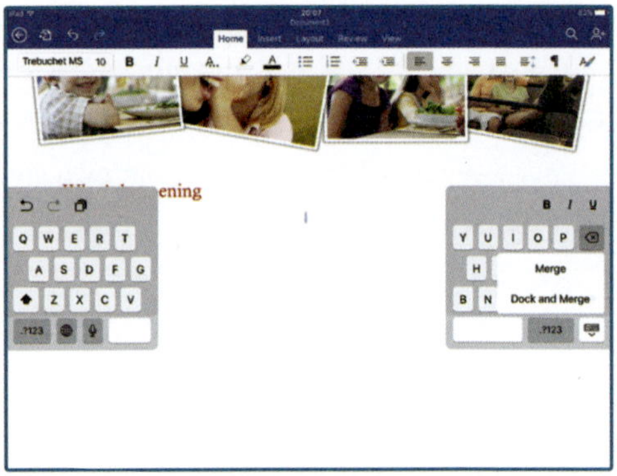

Above: Split and merge your keyboard by tapping the keyboard icon and selecting Split (left) and return to single keyboard by tapping the icon and selecting Dock and Merge (right).

Short Cuts

These can save a lot of time if there are several common phrases you use in Word documents or emails. Under General, Keyboard, Text Replacement there's one shortcut already written. Type omw and On my way! appears. To add your own, such as a tagline to add to your emails, tap Edit then the + button. Write out the full phrase and then add the letters you want to use as a short cut.

SUSPENDING NOTIFICATIONS

Do Not Disturb will silence alerts and FaceTime calls for a period of time that you set. A moon icon is shown in the status bar at the top of the screen when it's active.

Turn on Do Not Disturb

This prevents notifications from lighting up your screen or making a sound – but only when your iPad is locked or sleeping. To turn it on go to Settings, then Do Not Disturb and choose from the various options. You can also quickly access the setting in the Control Centre by tapping the moon icon. When DND is enabled you'll see it reflected on the lock screen.

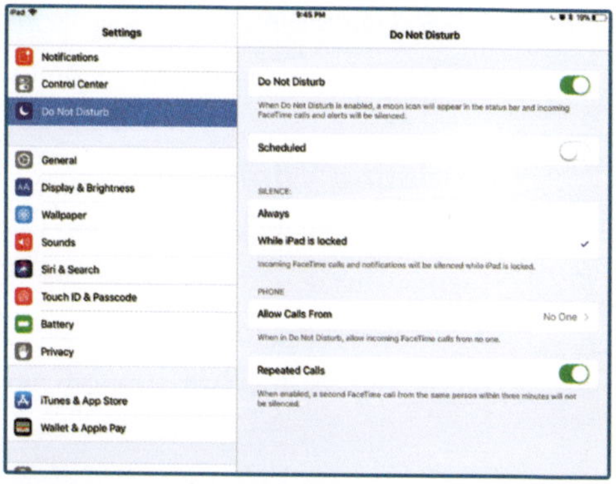

Above: Customize your Do Not Disturb settings via the Settings menu.

- **Scheduled**: lets you select the quiet hours, the automatic time period when Do Not Disturb operates. For example, this could be at night from 22:00 to 07:00 when you're likely to be sleeping.
- **Allow Calls From:** this creates the exceptions to the Do Not Disturb rule and allows incoming FaceTime calls from your Favourites or selected Contacts.
- **Repeated Calls**: if someone's calling you urgently, they can get through. By turning this on, the second call will ring through if the same person calls twice within three minutes.

iPAD'S OPERATING SYSTEM (iOS)

iOS is Apple's operating system for mobile devices such as the iPad, iPhone, iPod touch. iOS is regularly updated with new features and once a year there's a major new version.

Updating to a New Version

Above: You can update your iPad directly from your iPad by going to Settings > General > Software update.

Each new version of iOS fixes some problems, such as security patches for Safari, as well as adding new features. Because some of these additions, such as Siri, depend on a lot of processing power they are not available on all versions of the iPad. For example, you can only upgrade the first generation iPad to run iOS 5 (currently version 5.1.1). The iPad 2, iPad 3, and the first-gen iPad mini cannot be updated beyond iOS 9. All other iPads can be upgraded to run the current version, iOS 12, and later. Even so, there are some physical differences that mean that not all features in iOS 9 are available on each model – for example, Siri can't run on iPad 2.

Updating Wirelessly

You'll receive a push notification when one is available, but to check, tap Settings, General, then Software update. This shows the version number and if an update is available. If there is a newer version, follow the on-screen instructions to download and install the update. If your battery is less than half-strength, you'll be warned to connect your iPad to a power source.

Updating via iTunes

Connect your iPad to your Mac or PC and click on your iPad's name in the top menu bar, then the Summary tab. You can see the version the iPad is currently running and whether it's up to date. If an update is available you should receive a notification in iTunes asking you to download and install the update.

BROWSER SETTINGS

While you control the way you browse the web through Safari itself, some of the default settings, such as your search engine of choice, are changed elsewhere.

Changing Safari

Go to Settings and tap Safari in the list on the left-hand side.

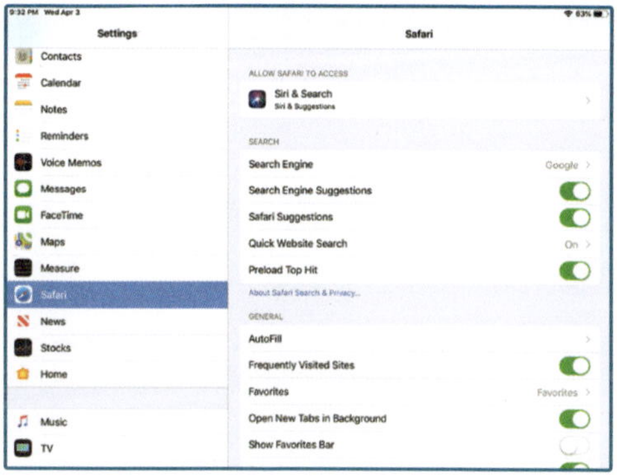

Above: Select Safari from the Settings menu to alter your internet browsing settings, such as turning on AutoFill and adjusting how new tabs are opened.

- **Search engine:** Google is the first choice of most, but you can change this to Yahoo! or Bing.
- **AutoFill:** repeatedly filling in the same information on web forms is a nuisance. Turn AutoFill on and it will use your info from the Contacts app or other forms you've previously completed. If you turn on Names and Passwords, Safari will remember the username and passwords used to access some websites.
- **Open New Tabs in Background:** turn this on and when you tap for a new page, it appears in the background while you stay on the page you have open.
- **Show Favourites Bar:** turn this on and Safari will display the bookmarked sites you have saved as Favourites.

GENERAL SETTINGS

Select General from the list of settings, then About. Tap Name and enter a new one for your iPad. This is used when you connect to iTunes or sync your apps with the computer.

You can also see the Capacity of your iPad, while Available shows how much space you have left. This section also lists how many songs, videos, photos and apps you have stored.

App Settings

Most apps downloaded from the App Store have settings that you can change to customize the way they work. Typically, these are applied within the app itself. There are other, more general settings, which apply to an app, that are controlled through the iPad's Settings app.

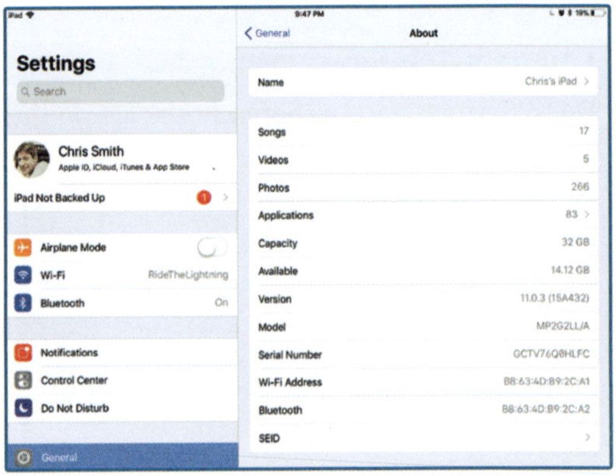

Above: Select General, About from the Settings menu to enter a name for your iPad and view its remaining space capacity.

1. Tap the Settings app on the Home screen. On the left, underneath the list of built-in apps, are the other apps that have additional settings.

2. Tap them to see what's available. Some of them have very little information – for example, the BBC iPlayer simply gives a version number.

3. Others offer a more settings that you can change. For example, from Settings > Google Maps you can control when the app can access your location and whether the app should refresh in the background.

4. Once you have changed a setting, tap the button at the top to return to the previous screen.

Hot Tip

Even though your iPad is described as 16GB, 32GB, 64GB, 128GB and 256GB the Capacity shown is always less. For example, a 64GB shows as 57.2GB. The difference is taken up by the operating system and other files that make your iPad work.

TROUBLESHOOTING

While most problems on the iPad are easily resolved, there are times when you'll have to dig a little deeper to get the best performance and keep it running smoothly.

CONNECTIVITY

For most people Wi-Fi is the main way they connect the iPad to their home network. When it goes wrong, there are a series of steps to take to try to sort the problem.

Wireless

Check initially that the problems aren't with your Wi-Fi network. The easiest way is to see if other devices are able to connect and working properly. If they're not, restarting your router might sort out the glitch. If the problem is just on the iPad, try the following.

- **Turning on Airplane mode**: tap Settings then switch the button beside Airplane Mode to On. After a few seconds turn it Off. This will force the iPad to quit the network and try to reconnect.
- **Restarting Wi-Fi**: tap Settings, then Wi-Fi, select the network you were connected to and tap the Renew Lease button.
- **Re-entering the network settings**: follow the same path as the restart but this time tap Forget this Network. Then hard reset the iPad by holding down the Home button and Wake/Sleep button together

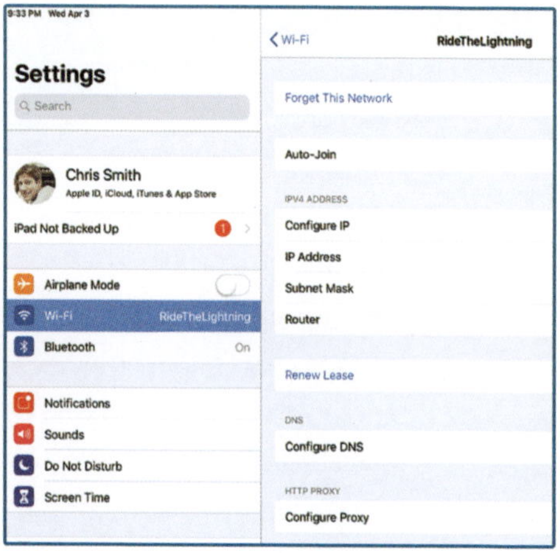

Above: Restart your Wi-Fi by tapping Renew Lease or Forget this Network and then resetting the iPad.

until the iPad restarts and the Apple icon appears. Tap Settings, Wi-Fi and re-enter your network settings.

- **Resetting the network**: Go to Settings, tap General, then Reset and press the Reset Network Settings button.

SYNC PROBLEMS

Given the complexity of the task, there are surprisingly few problems with syncing your iPad – and those there are can be quickly resolved.

App Download Problems

Apple removed the ability to sync apps to devices with iTunes on your PC back in 2017, so all downloading has to be done on the iPad itself via the App Store. If you've downloaded them before, you should see them in the Purchased section, where they can be easily re-downloaded. Open the App Store, tap your profile picture and hit Purchased > My Purchases > Not on this iPad to find them. If the download isn't successful, here's what you can do.

- **Make sure you're running the latest version of iOS**: some apps can run only on the most advanced version of the operating system. To see if an upgrade is available, go to Settings, General, then Software Update.

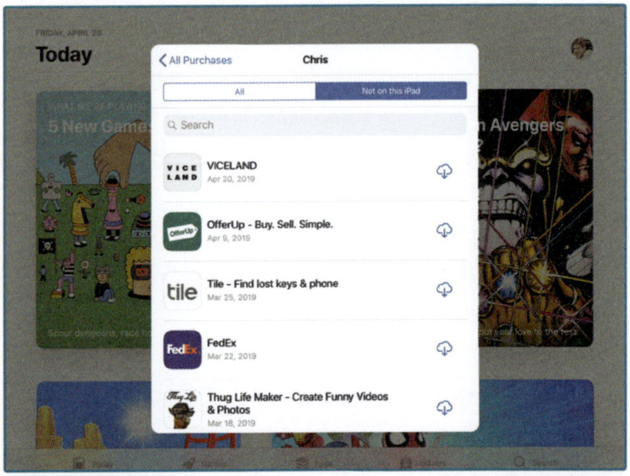

Above: The 'Purchased' section of the App Store keeps a record of all the apps you've previously downloaded for your iPad.

- **Look to see if you have enough space**: particularly if there's an error message in iTunes or the app isn't fully downloaded during a Wi-Fi sync (the app's icon will appear dimmed on the screen and the progress bar will be blank).

- **Make space for new apps**: apps are compressed for downloading and then expanded during installation, so even if you have space to download the app, there may not be room for the full app. Back up your iPad, then try deleting similarly sized apps and try again.

Hot Tip

TV shows and movies will probably take up the most space on your iPad. Rather than download them, stream them from your computer to your iPad using Home Sharing.

Where Are My Apps?

The iPad does its best to keep available space open by removing apps you don't use often but retaining data for when you want to re-download them. Apple calls this Offload Unused Apps. If you enable this tool within Settings > iTunes & App Store you may notice that apps on your home screen are greyed. Tapping them reinitiates the download.

Sync Problems with iTunes

Syncing by Wi-Fi or cable with iTunes is very convenient, until you find that your iPad appears to have vanished.

- **Syncing by Wi-Fi**: it may be a simple problem of the network having crashed momentarily. Switch Wi-Fi off and on on the iPad by going to Settings and toggling Airplane Mode on then off. You may also have to relaunch the Wi-Fi connection on your Mac or PC.
- **Restarts**: first try closing and then re-opening iTunes on your Mac or PC. If this doesn't work, restart your iPad and Mac or PC.

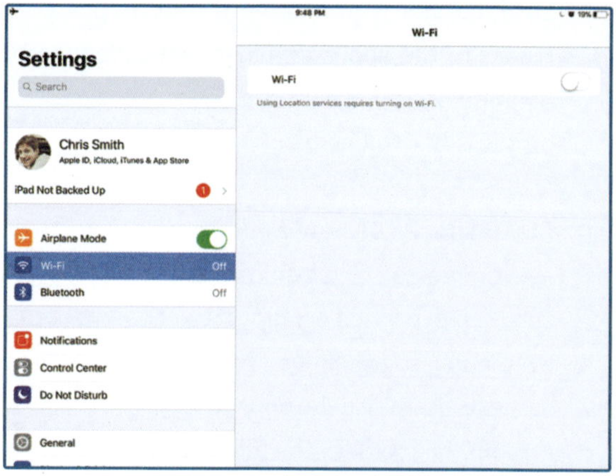

Above: If your internet crashes, you can toggle Airplane Mode on then off in your Wi-Fi settings to reconnect it quickly.

- **Syncing by cable**: if you're struggling to connect your iPad to your computer to sync via iTunes, the cable might be the culprit. Some cheap, low-powered cables won't connect, while others wear down over time. Try a different cable, or try a different USB port to see if that makes any difference.

Sync Problems with iCloud

Remember that details you enter in your calendar or new bookmarks aren't synchronized instantly. You should only worry that there's a problem if nothing is syncing.

- **Are you on the same network?**: make sure that you are using the same Wi-Fi network and account details for iCloud on your Mac and iPad. If necessary, try deleting and re-entering the information.
- **Make sure that sharing is enabled**: on the iPad go to Settings, iCloud, then Account. You should also check that the various services – Mail, Contacts, Calendar, etc. – are turned on and set to sync.

iPAD BEHAVING BADLY

Sometimes, even the very best things go wrong: when the iPad freezes, apps crash or are not performing, try these steps, which are progressively more severe, to resolve the issue.

- **Quit the app**: if an app freezes or refuses to do as you want, try closing it down completely. To do this, double-press the Home button to open up the multitasking bar, then swipe up to remove the app's preview screen. This shuts down the app.

- **Check for app updates**: if an app is behaving badly, the developers may have pushed out an update. Go to App Store and tap Updates to see those waiting for you. Alternatively, for ease, you can turn on Automatic Downloads for Updates in the iTunes & App Store section of the settings menu.

- **Restart iPad**: as with many an electrical device, simply turning the iPad off and then on again can do wonders. Hold down the Sleep/Wake button at the top and when the Power-Off slider appears, slide it across to shut down the iPad. Press the Sleep/Wake button again to restart the iPad.

- **Reset iPad**: this clears most problems. Press-and-hold the Home button at the same time as the Sleep/Wake button at the top and continue to do so until the iPad restarts and the Apple icon appears.

Above: If an app crashes double-click the Home button to get to the multitasking bar. Swipe to close down the app.

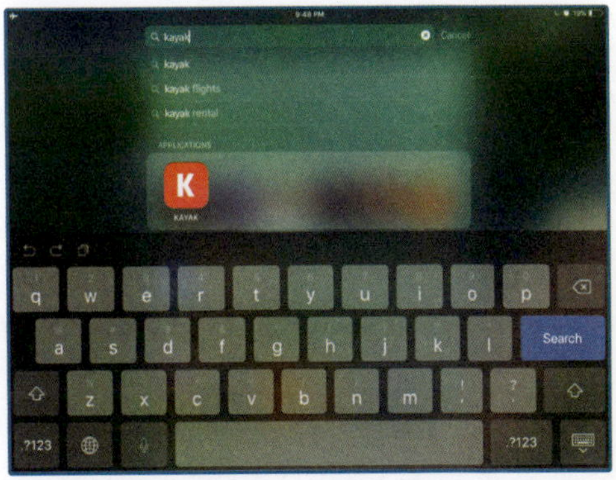

Above: Search for lost apps using the Search bar in within the Today screen. It can be found by swiping down from the home screen, or swiping all the way.

- **Restore iPad**: whatever has gone wrong, now you can try to get round it by rolling back to the most recent backup you have for the iPad. Connect the iPad to your Mac or PC, select it from the top menu bar in iTunes and then press the Summary tab. Click Restore iPad. Select the most recent backup to restore your software and settings.

- **Recovery mode**: if Restore fails to complete, the iPad stops responding or continually restarts but never reaches the Home screen, then this is the ultimate step.

1. Connect the USB cable to your computer's USB port but don't yet attach it to the iPad.

2. Turn off the iPad the normal way. If it doesn't turn off, press and hold the Home button and Sleep/Wake button until it does.

3. Press and hold the Home button and connect the iPad to the USB cable. Continue to hold until you get a Connect to iTunes screen.

4. Release the Home button and open iTunes. You should see a message that it is in recovery mode. All your content on the iPad will be erased but once it has been recovered you can restore your settings from a previous backup in the normal way.

Hot Tip

Help! Can't find a new app? There's room on your iPad for 11 pages – Home Screens – full of apps. After that the apps will be there but the only way of finding them is to use Spotlight and search by name. Longer term, think of rearranging your apps in folders.

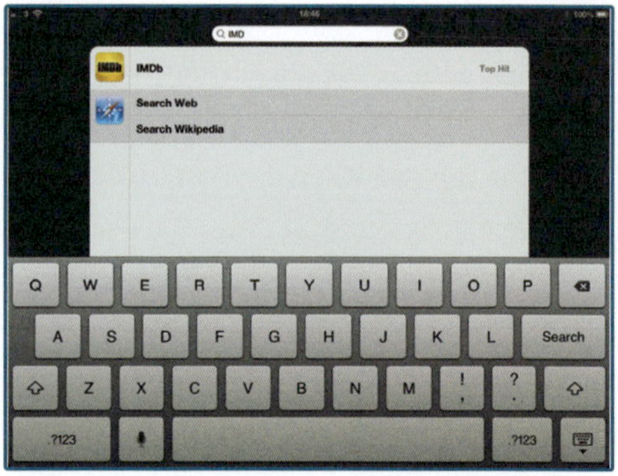

Above: Search for lost apps using the Spotlight bar which can be found by swiping to the right of your Home Screens.

POWER

You can do so much with your iPad, but as you do more, you do put pressure on the battery. There are ways to conserve power, so you have the energy you need.

Charging Tips

The best way to charge the iPad is to plug it in and leave it alone until replenished. You can use in the meantime, but this will place strain on the battery and add hours to the overall charging time.

Hot Tip

Strangely, fully charging your iPad and then using it until the power's right down is a good way of improving battery performance. You should try to do this at least once a month.

- **Recharge the battery**: the best way to recharge the battery is to use the Apple-supplied power adapter to connect the iPad to a power source and turn the device off or put it in sleep mode.

- **Drained battery**: an empty battery doesn't have enough power to show the Home screen, so if your iPad screen is blank when you turn it on, it may have no battery charge. Plug it in and you'll see an indication the iPad is recharging. From here, give it about ten minutes before trying to turn it on again.

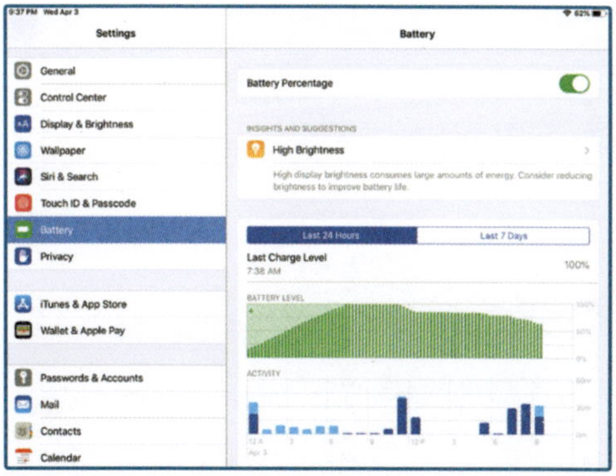

Above: Battery in Settings shows the proportion of battery used by each app in the last 24 hours.

- **iPad USB adapter**: only use the iPad USB adapter. Although others, such as the one for the iPhone, look similar, they are not powerful enough to charge the iPad efficiently.

- **Not Charging**: you may see the message Not Charging on the iPad status bar, typically, this is when you're trying to charge the iPad through the

USB port on your computer. Some older machines don't supply enough power to charge the iPad this way.

- **Battery percentage indicator**: turn this on so you can see how much charge you have left. Tap Settings, Battery and turn on Battery Percentage.

- **Battery Usage**: also under the battery settings you can see how much power individual apps have taken over the last 24 hours and shutdown the energy-guzzlers. You can also see usage since your last full charge.

Saving Power

Some features consume more battery power than others and you can conserve energy by turning them off when they're not in use.

- **Sleep mode**: is the ultimate way of saving power when the iPad is not in use. Activate it by pressing the Sleep/Wake button at the top of the iPad.

- **Alter screen brightness**: tap Settings, then Display & Brightness and move the slider to the left.

- **Turn off Wi-Fi and Cellular**: as your iPad will always try to maintain a connection to a network, you may want to turn these off when you're in areas with low or limited coverage. Go to Settings, Wi-Fi and turn Wi-Fi off. For mobile go to Settings, Cellular and turn off Cellular Data.

- **Minimize location services**: such as Maps, which can rapidly reduce battery

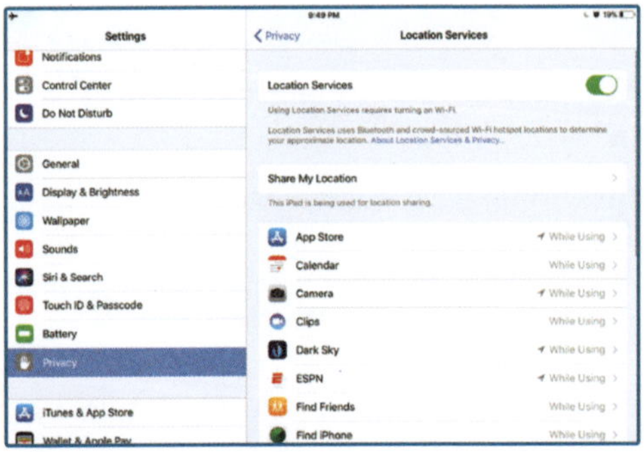

Above: Turning off location services you are not using will make your iPad battery last for longer.

life. Go to Settings, Privacy and turn off the Location Services you don't want.

- **Switch off Bluetooth**: if you're not connected to a Bluetooth speaker or a fitness tracker, then you can turn Bluetooth off to help conserve battery life. Head to Settings, Bluetooth.

- **Switch off push notifications**: some apps are constantly checking when new data is available and will send an alert – push notification – when it is. To disable this, go to Settings, Notifications and turn off notifications for individual apps. Similarly, turn off Push Mail when you don't need it or don't want to be disturbed by it. Go to Settings, Passwords & Accounts, Fetch New Data and set Push to off.

- **Fetch data less frequently**: instead of having them push new messages to you, you can get applications such as Mail to fetch new data wirelessly after a specific time interval. The shorter the interval, the more frequently data is fetched and the quicker the drain on your battery. Save power by going to Settings, Accounts & Passwords, Fetch New Data. Set the Fetch period to a longer time interval, such as hourly.

Above: Turn off Push mail notifications and change the Fetch frequency to Manually to stop the app gathering new data so often, thus saving battery.

Hot Tip

While you can lower screen brightness through the Settings app, iBooks has its own brightness control which lets you dim the screen even more.

RUNNING OUT OF SPACE

Even at 64GB to 256GB the larger capacity iPads don't offer much storage space compared with a computer. With new apps doing more, they are becoming larger and it's very easy to fill the available space on your iPad quickly.

Managing Storage Space

If you are running low on storage, there's a quick way of finding out what apps are using the most space, so you can delete those you don't use often.

1. Tap Settings, General, iPad Storage. The iPad lists your apps and the amount of space each one takes. Tap an individual app, and you'll get a breakdown of the size occupied by TV series plus individual movies and clips.

2. In most cases, the app itself takes up little space. Most of the storage is for documents and data, such as photos, videos, music and files. Before deleting an app completely, it's worth checking if it contains files that you could delete.

3. Tap the Usage button to return to the previous screen and then Show all Apps to see a full list of the size of each app.

4. If you decide to delete the biggest apps that you don't use: tap on the app then press Delete App.

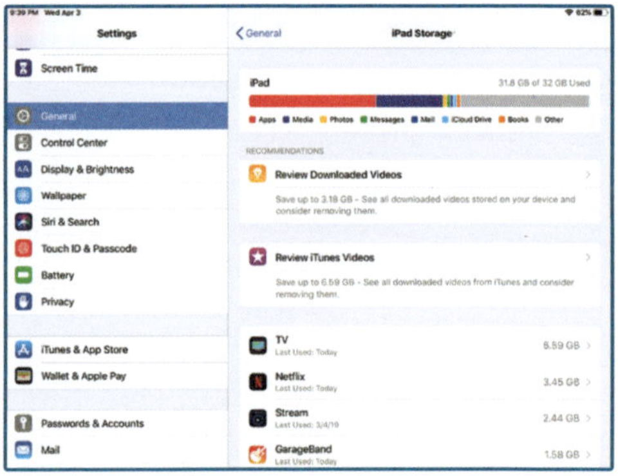

Above: You can check how much storage space individual apps are taking up by tapping Settings, General, iPad Storage. Free up space by deleting those apps which you don't use very often.

Hot Tip

Not all apps can be deleted, including those built into iOS, such as the Photos app.

Storage Recommendations

We mentioned Offload Unused Apps a couple of pages back. This is a great way to free up some space without losing data. When accessing the iPad Storage settings you may see a recommendation to enable this setting, which informs you how much space you'll save. However you'll also get other pointers. For example, you may see options to Review iTunes Store Videos, which tells you how much space is being used.

ACCESSORIZING

There are accessories for your iPad that enhance its look, protect it from everyday knocks or, like the wireless keyboard, extend the way it works to make it even easier to use.

COVERS

From the colourful and zany to the highly functional smart covers, there's plenty of choice when it comes to cases for your iPad. Search online if you are interested in purchasing any of the accessories that follow.

Smart Cover

Through a series of magnets Apple's smart cover sticks to the side of the iPad. Another set of magnets attach it to the screen, so that opening the cover wakes up the device and closing it puts the iPad to sleep. Inside the micro-fibre surface helps keep the screen clean. The cover also folds into a triangle to create a small stand for the iPad. This is suitable for the iPad 2 and above.

Above: The Case-E kid-friendly case from Speck.

Case-E

If your iPad is going to be used by a kid, you might want to grab a case with a little more protection. The Speck Case-E will ensure your iPad survives drops from up to six foot in the air. It's made from EVA foam, so it's also soft and comfortable to hold.

Leather Portfolio

Go eco-friendly but stay smart with these recycled leather cases for the iPad, which also double as stands. Find the Proporta Recycled Leather Eco Case at www.proporta.com/smart.

BookBook

Should you want to disguise the ultimate modern tablet as a vintage book, these leather hardback cases are for you. They also double up as a typing and display stand and some have slots for your credit and debit cards.

STANDS

If you don't want to cover up the elegance of the iPad itself, go for a stand which lets you view the screen hands-free, even watch videos in bed or attach it to a microphone stand for making a speech or presentation.

Compass 2

The Compass 2 stand from Twelve South is a compact option that will prop up your iPad at a number of angles. It's easy to unfold and won't add too much weight to your work bag. It also works in portrait and landscape.

Left: The Compass Pro stand is compact and highly adjustable.

Hot Tip

If you're working on the iPad for a while – watching a movie or playing a game – it can get quite hot, so use a stand or place it on a magazine or tray if you have it on your lap.

Boss Tab

If you think your tablet is going to remain in the same place, such as on your desk or your bedside table, you may want to consider a more sturdy holder such as the wide range of options from Boss Tab (www.bosstab.com). Depending on which you choose, you'll be able to rotate the tablet in the direction of your choosing too.

Swingholder

This is designed to keep the iPad at eye-level, whether you're on a treadmill in the gym, lying down in bed or standing on a stage. Based on a microphone stand, it has a weighted base and adjustable swing arm. However it is relatively expensive compared to other stands. Find the Swingholder on Amazon.

SOUND

Share the music on your iPad at a family get together or in the office by streaming it wirelessly to an external speaker or listen through your headphones to songs playing on the iPad in your backpack.

Above: The UE Boom speaker range can be used to wirelessly stream music from your iPad if Bluetooth is enabled.

Wireless Speakers

As portable as your iPad, the excellent UE Boom speaker range can stream music wirelessly from any Bluetooth-equipped iPad, while the more expensive Bose SoundLink uses Apple's wireless technology AirPlay for what the manufacturers state is clear, room-filling music. Find these speakers at the Apple Store.

Headphones

No wires needed with Bluetooth-connected headphones, like these ones from Beats. As most manufacturers offer Bluetooth-enabled headsets that would work with the iPad, make your choice on comfort, sound quality and reliability. Find these headphones at the Apple Store.

Above: The Beats Solo3 wireless earphones are Bluetooth-enabled, allowing for easy wireless access to the music stored on your iPad.

INPUTS

While the iPad's touchscreen is great for writing email and such, for longer pieces of text a proper keyboard is much faster and more convenient. And if you want more precise handwritten text or drawings, there are iPad pens to help.

Keyboard Case

Some accessories perform double duty, such as the Logitech Slim Folio Case with Integrated Bluetooth Keyboard (a mouthful, we know). This folio case features a built-in Bluetooth keyboard with dedicated iOS shortcut keys that'll take you to the home screen, access Siri or control media playback.

Above: The Smart Keyboard for iPad Pro and the 2019 iPad Air acts as a case and a keyboard for your iPad.

Smart Keyboard

Designed for the iPad Pro, it acts as a full-size keyboard when needed or slim lightweight cover. It is powered by the Smart Connector on the iPad Pro which allows for a two-way exchange of power and data.

Bluetooth Keyboard

More traditional keyboards use Bluetooth. This is a short-range wireless technology that will connect two devices up to about 30 feet away. Because it doesn't need a line of sight connection, it works well with headsets, speakers and particularly keyboards.

- **Apple**: offer a wireless keyboard, which works with Macs too. Slim and compact, it takes up about a quarter less space than the normal full-sized keyboard. Battery-powered, it will switch off automatically to save power when you're not using the keyboard and then restart instantly when you start typing again. Find the keyboard at the Apple Store.

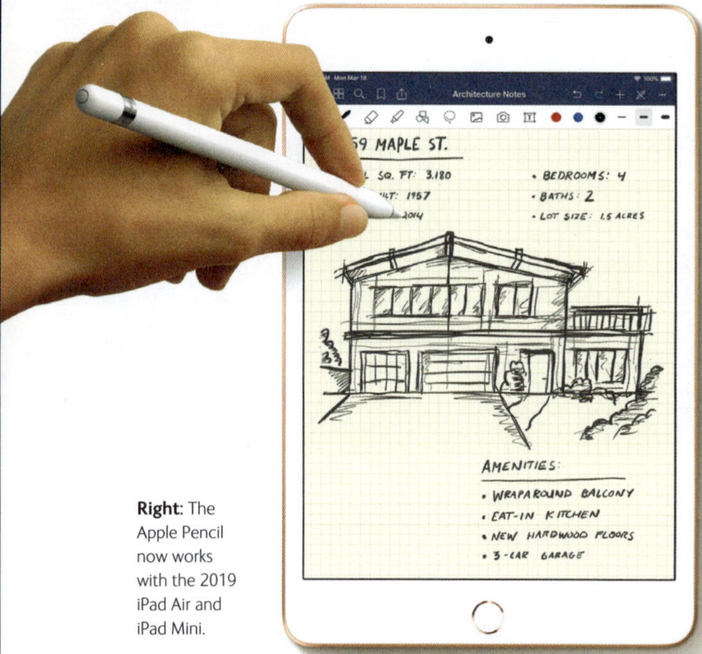

Right: The Apple Pencil now works with the 2019 iPad Air and iPad Mini.

Apple Pencil

The iPad Pro series also saw the introduction of the Apple Pencil. It allows greater precision for intricate drawings and enables you to annotate or sketch in a variety of apps, such as Notes. Alternatively, the Cosmonaut is a crayon-sized stylus, with a large rubber barrel, that feels like a marker pen but is great for sketching out ideas. Find the Cosmonaut at www.studioneat.com.

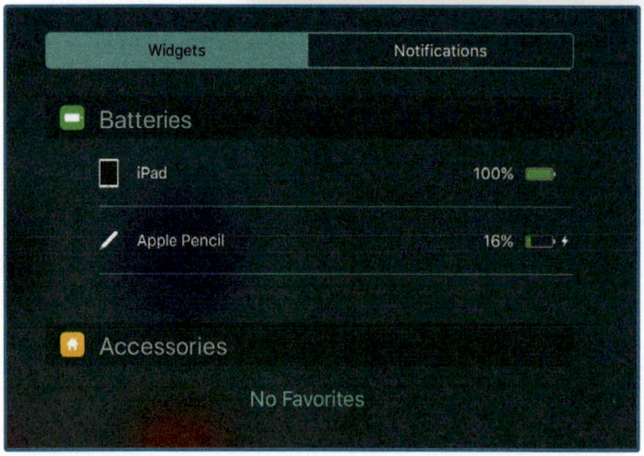

Above: To check on the battery status of your iPad and Apple Pencil, you can use the new Battery widget on your iPhone or iPad. Just swipe left to right from your Home screen to view the Today screen.

Hot Tip

Extend the usefulness of your iPad's cameras with Photojojo's fish eye, wide angle and telephoto lenses that attach by a magnetic ring (photojojo.com).

SECURITY

Given the range of all that you can do on the iPad, from your accounts to buying and selling on the web, there are a number of security measures that can help you keep your private information confidential.

iPAD PROTECTION

The simplest way of keeping your information private is to use password protection – but if Touch ID or Face ID is available on your iPad you should use it to keep your iPad secure.

Locking Your iPad: Step-by-Step

1. Go to Settings, then Touch ID & Passcode or just Passcode if you don't have a device with Touch ID.

2. You'll be asked to enter your passcode, if you established one during set up. This will have been 4 or 6-digits depending on your preference. If you didn't establish a passcode during setup, Tap Turn Passcode On and you'll be asked to enter a 6-digit number. You can change this back to a 4-digit code if you want.

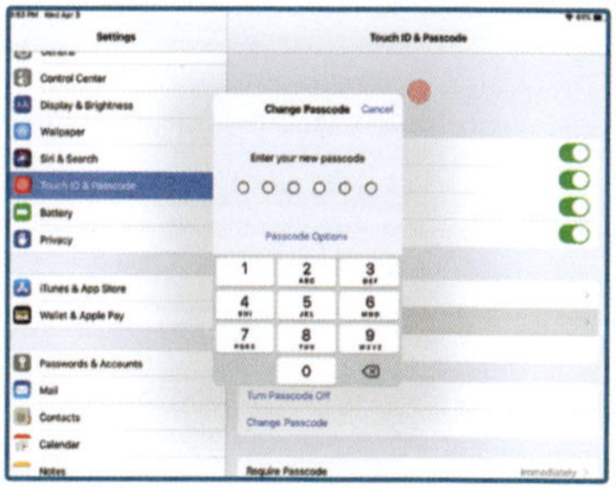

Above: Turn on the passcode option within the general settings menu to increase iPad security.

3. If no Touch ID is enabled you can select Require Passcode. from more than four hours to immediately, before the iPad locks. The shorter the interval, the more secure it is. If you have Touch ID enabled, this setting will default to immediately.

4. Even when the iPad is locked, there may be certain services you want to use, such as asking Siri to set a Reminder. Under the Allow Access When Locked section, choose which apps you want to be available in the background.

5. Speaking of Touch ID, if you didn't set this up, you should certainly do so here. After establishing a Passcode, you can select Add Fingerprint (this is also possible if you want to add more than one digit or have other people in the home that use the iPad). Touch the Home button with a finger and rest it there until you feel a vibration. Repeat the onscreen instructions until the fingerprint is registered.

6. If you have a new iPad Pro (11-inch or 12.9-inch 2018) which doesn't have Touch ID, you can set up Face ID to unlock the iPad using your face. On these models you'll see Face ID & Passcode as an option in Settings. Choose Set-up Face ID.

Apple Pay

If you have an iPad with Touch ID, you can pay for goods and services in apps and on the web using your fingerprint thanks to the Apple Pay platform. Using Apple Pay is more convenient than entering your card details each time and it's all more secure. Because Apple Pay sends a one-time payment token to the retailer, the store actually never has your card details.

Loads of apps and websites offer Apple Pay as a payment option. You'll be presented with the option during checkout or you'll see the Apple Pay logo, which you can tap to continue. Once selected, you'll see a pop-up menu with the transaction details. Then all you'll need to do is authenticate the payment with Touch ID and you're all set. In order to set up a payment method for Apple Pay, head to Settings Wallet & Apple Pay and then select Add Card.

Auto-Lock

You can automatically lock your iPad or turn off the display when it's not in use. Go to Settings, Display & Brightness and then Go to Settings, General then Auto-Lock and select the time delay before it switches off, which varies from 15 minutes to 2 minutes.

Encrypting iPad Backups

If you choose this option, passwords for different accounts, such as Mail, will be stored and you won't need to re-enter them individually if you have to use the backup to restore the iPad.

Instead, there's one master password you need to restore the backup. To encrypt your backups go to iTunes, select the iPad, then the Summary tab and check Encrypt iPad Backup.

iCloud Security

When your personal information is sent from your iPad to iCloud over the internet, it is encrypted, employing the same level of security as that used by major banks. It is also stored on Apple's servers in an encrypted format. That way, your data is kept private and protected from unauthorized access while it's being transmitted to your iPad and when it's stored on iCloud. Apple recommend you use a very strong password with your Apple ID that is used for accessing iCloud. It should be a minimum of eight characters and include various characters.

FIND MY iPAD

Whether your iPad has been stolen or you've mislaid it, you can track it down, provided you've already set up Find My iPad.

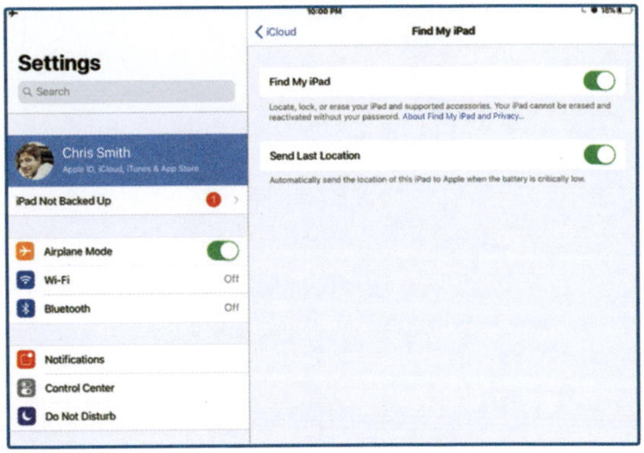

Above: Turn on Find My iPad in your iCloud settings to ensure it can be tracked via Location Services.

Find Your Device

1. To start tracking of your iPad, go to Settings, Your Name, iCloud and turn on Find My iPad.

2. As soon as you've done this, a permission box opens, asking you to confirm you are happy for the iPad to be tracked and its location shown on a map. Tap Allow.

3. You can download the Find My iPad app (called Find My iPhone) from the App Store and use this on another iDevice, such as iPhone, to track your iPad. Once it's downloaded, log in using your iCloud username and password.

4. Alternatively, you can log in direct through Find My iPhone on the iCloud website. Go to

www.icloud.com and use your Apple ID to sign in. Click on Devices, and any that can be found are shown with a green pin on the map. Those that can't are red.

5. Click on the pin, and it shows you the last time the iPad was tracked to that address. Click on the information button and a new window opens.

Other features of Find My iPad include:

- **Play Sound:** sends a strange bell-clanging noise to your iPad – handy if you know it's in your home somewhere, but you have misplaced it.
- **Lock:** lets you lock your iPad remotely, with a four-digit passcode if you haven't set one already, which is useful if you've left it at work or a friend's house.

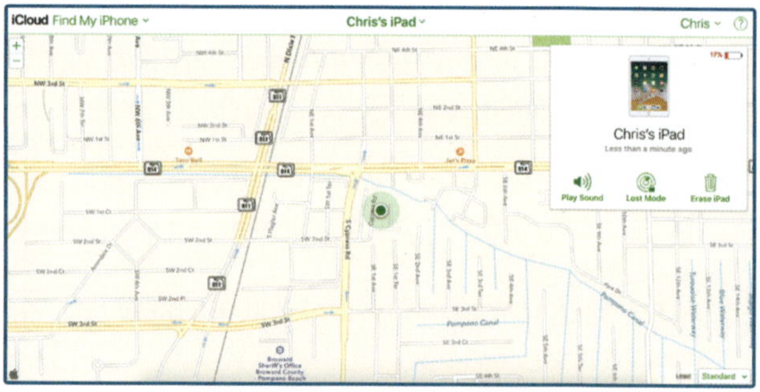

Above: You can choose actions for when your iPad has been tracked, for example playing sounds, locking it remotely and erasing its content.

- **Erase iPad:** the nuclear option if you believe it has been stolen, this wipes out all the iPad's content, including your private, sensitive information and restores the device to the original factory settings.

LIMITING ACCESS

If you don't want every user to have full reign over your iPad, you can limit the areas they can access.

Hot Tip

For Find My iPad to work, it has to be turned on at all times, which will use some battery power, but it does offer great peace of mind in case anything happens to your iPad.

Setting Restrictions

Tap Settings, Screen Time and then select Content & Privacy Restrictions, which enables you to block inappropriate content if your kids are using the device. The Screen Time feature is new in iOS 12 and is designed to help monitor iPad usage and improve digital health. However, it's useful for controlling who can access what.

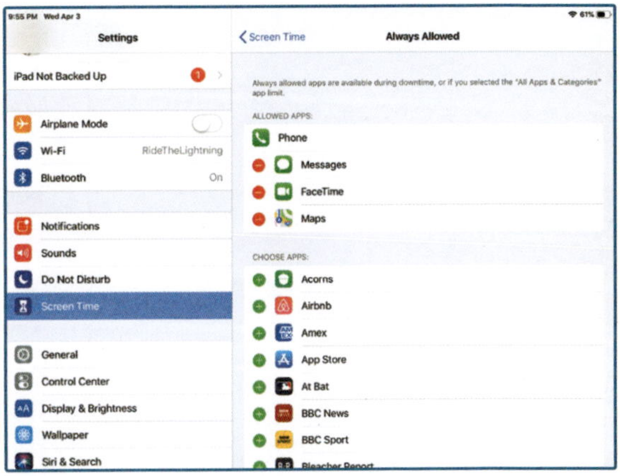

Above: Set up restrictions to limit access to parts of your iPad.

- **Restrict Apps**: if you turn off any of the apps listed under the Allowed Apps menu – which include Safari, Camera and apps that use it, FaceTime, iTunes Store, Book Store and Siri – they can only be used by someone who knows the password.
- **Disable Installing of Apps**: Under Settings, Screen Time, Content and Privacy Restrictions, iTunes & App Store Purchase you can prevent children downloading content and buying it online. You can disable installing of apps and in-app purchases by always requiring the password. You can prevent apps being deleted here too.
- **Avoid Explicit Language**: within Screen Time, Content Restrictions you can block naughty words, with Siri using asterisks and beep sounds to cover any unfortunate words that may slip out during dictation.
- **Set Content Restrictions**: for music and podcasts, books, movies, TV shows, and apps, according to the country you select from the list. Any content outside of the ratings you select won't be shown on the iPad.
- **Web Content**: Within Content Restrictions, select Web Content and choose between Unrestricted Access, Limit Adult Websites and Allows Websites only.

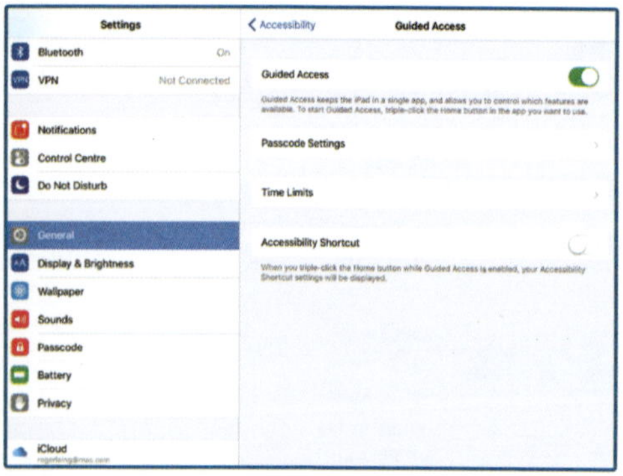

Above: Turn on Guided Access to use kiosk mode to limit your iPad to a single app when needed.

Guided Access

If you want to share a single presentation, use your iPad solely as a photo frame during a party or have your child focus on a single game, then you can use kiosk mode. This limits the iPad to a single app, with you controlling what features are available.

Tap Settings, then General, Accessibility, Guided Access and slide the button to On. Set a passcode to use. Select the app you want to use, triple-press the Home button, adjust the settings and press Start.

PRIVACY SETTINGS

You can control which apps have access to your personal information in your contacts, calendars, reminders and photos, as well as Twitter and Facebook.

Controlling Access

The first time an app tries to access your personal information, a pop-up box will ask if you allow this or not. Whatever your response, the decision stands and the app won't ask again. However, you can change your mind.

To change your privacy choice, go to Settings, Privacy and select one of the apps from the list, for example Contacts. Here you'll see a list of apps, such as Skype or Find Friends, that have asked to access this personal information. You can allow or disallow access by switching the button to On or Off.

Hot Tip

If you want to wipe the slate clean and start again, you can reset all your privacy warnings. Go to Settings, General, Reset and tap Reset Location & Privacy.

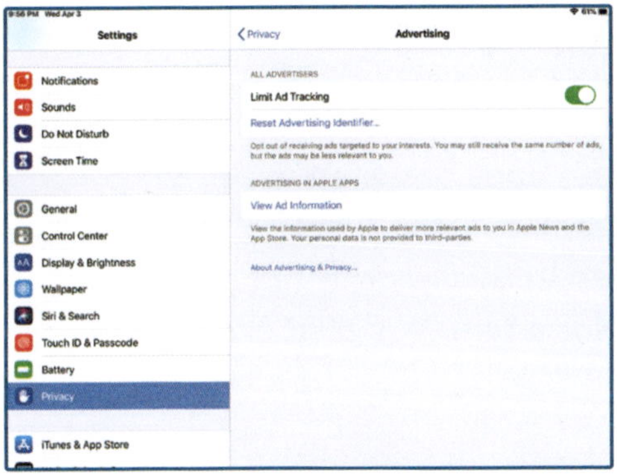

Above: Activate the Limit Ad Tracking setting to prevent online advertisers from using your web data to target you specifically.

Hot Tip

You can have more than one VPN connection and switch between them on the VPN settings page. A VPN button appears in the status bar when you're using the secure connection.

Stop Ad Tracking

This prevents advertisers using your web usage data and cookies (which have information about the sites you visit) to target specific ads to you.

To turn it on go to Settings, Privacy and scroll down to Advertising, then turn on Limit Ad Tracking.

Fraudulent Website Warning

Go to Settings, Safari and scroll down to turn this on. This checks websites you visit against a public database of problem sites. If you follow a link to one of these sites, you get a warning, so you can stop loading the page.

VPN

Connect securely and privately to your office network, via the internet, using a virtual private network (VPN).

Setting up a VPN Connection

Go to the Settings app, select VPN and and then Add VPN Configuration.

In the window that opens enter your network settings, which you will need to get from your IT department (or copy from your Mac or PC if you already have a VPN set up on your computer). When complete, tap Save.

100 BEST iPAD APPS

There are more than a quarter of a million apps designed exclusively for the iPad in the App Store. Many are brilliant, some not so. Here, in line with the different categories covered in this book, is our pick of the essential apps (excluding built-in apps) for a fantastic iPad experience.

Communication

1. **Facebook**: The official app for the world's largest social network.
2. **Friendly for Facebook**: An alternate way to access Facebook.
3. **Twitter**: All you need to go a-tweeting.
4. **Snapchat**: Send 'Snaps' to your followers and update your 'Story'.
5. **LinkedIn**: Keep in touch with your professional network.
6. **WhatsApp**: Hugely popular instant messaging app that allows you to connect with non-iOS users via the internet.
7. **WeChat**: Another popular instant messaging app.
8. **Skype**: Instant message, voice or video call to friends and family around the world.
9. **Find My Friends**: Stalk your friends and family.
10. **Tumblr**: Update your personal blog and connect with your friends in the blogosphere.
11. **Slack**: Robust productivity tool lets you send instant messages to your work colleagues.

Connectivity

12. **VNC viewer**: Manage your PC or Mac desktop remotely from your iPad.

Photos

13. **Google Photos**: Backup all of your photos to Google's servers so you can free up space on your iPad.
14. **Adobe Photoshop Express**: A scaled down version of the desktop app, ideal for quick edits.
15. **Pixelmator**: One of the best photo editing apps.
16. **Shutterly**: Get prints and create gifts from your photos.
17. **Brushes 3**: The painting app that's so good that artist David Hockney uses it.
18. **Instagram**: iPhone version of the fun social network for taking and sharing photos.

19. **Pic Collage:** Create collages from multiple photos to share on social media.

20. **Affinity Photo:** Expensive, but in terms of features, it's an unrivaled photo editing app.

21. **FaceTune 2:** Touch up your selfies and give yourself a celebrity airbrush.

22. **Lifecake:** Private photo sharing with small groups of family.

23. **ComicBook!:** A fully featured app for creating comic books.

24. **PhotoSync:** Wirelessly transfers your photos and videos.

25. **Flickr:** Lets you browse, upload and share photos on Flickr, as you would on the website version.

26. **Postsnap:** Create holiday postcards and send them back home.

27. **Flipagram:** Get your photos ready for social sharing with filters, effects and music.

TV, Movies and Music Video

28. **YouTube:** No longer a built-in app, but you can still get access to one of the world's greatest collections of videos.

29. **Vimeo:** Designed for watching, creating and sharing videos on the Vimeo site.

30. **iMovie:** Movie-editing for the touchscreen.

31. **Skyfire Web Browser for iPad:** The browser that does let you watch Flash videos on the iPad.

32. **Netflix:** The subscription service for watching TV and films on your iPad.

33. **Matcha – Find and Watch Movies & TV:** Personalized guide for video services.

34. **NowTV:** Get on demand access to Sky TV content without a satellite subscription.

35. **Crackle – Movies & TV:** Watch free Hollywood movies and TV shows.

36. **BBC iPlayer:** Watch and listen to BBC TV and Radio.

Books/News

37. **iBooks:** Apple's ebook reader and bookstore.

38. **Google Play Books:** Provides access to millions of books – free and paid-for.

39. **Kindle:** Reader for Kindle books, newspapers, magazines and more from the Amazon store.

40. **Newsweek:** Digital editions especially created for the iPad.

41. ***The Guardian* and *Observer* iPad edition:** The newspapers re-imagined for the iPad.

42. **MailOnline for iPad:** Standalone app with customizable international editions linked to the UK's number one newspaper website.

43. **BBC News:** Breaking news from around the world.

44. **Reuters News Pro for iPad:** Professional-grade news and market data.

45. **Early Edition 2**: Edit your own newspaper.

46. **Feedly**: RSS app that lets you see updates from all of your favourite apps in one play.

47. **Flipboard: Your Social News Magazine**: Personal magazine combining international news sources and your social networks.

48. **Pocket**: Lets you save content from the web to read later.

49. **ESPN**: Results and news from sports leagues around the world.

50. **Zinio**: Buy and read magazines on your iPad.

51. **Instapaper**: Save your favourite articles in an easy-to-read format

52. **ComiXology**: Read comics from all of the top publishers on your iPad.

Reference/Lifestyle

53. **Shakespeare**: The complete works.

54. **Encyclopedia Britannica**: If you don't trust free encyclopedias, this offers a rolling monthly subscription to one of the most respected reference sources.

55. **Wikipanion**: If you do trust free encyclopedias, this is a faster and easier way to access Wikipedia.

56. **Google Earth**: Fly around the planet from your iPad.

57. **Google Maps**: An alternative to the built-in Apple Maps app.

58. **Dark Sky**: A brilliant alternative to the Apple Weather app with up to the minute forecasts.

59. **World Atlas HD**: World maps designed for the iPad.

60. **NASA App HD**: Explore the universe from your iPad.

61. **National Geographic Magazine-International**: The magazine plus special interactive content.

62. **WebMD**: Health information and symptom checker for the hypochondriac in you.

63. **Epicurious**: Recipes for foodies.

64. **TripAdvisor**: Hotels Flights Restaurants and candid reviews by fellow travellers.

65. **TripDeck**: When you've decided where you're going, this is your itinerary organizer. iPhone app.

66. **Etsy**: Purchase arts and crafts supplies as well as lots of different handmade items.

Entertainment

67. **Podcasts**: Manage your podcasts.

68. **Spotify**: Access millions of songs free or subscribe.

69. **Last.fm Scrobbler**: iPhone app for access to the music recommendation site from your iPad.

70. **Vevo HD**: High-quality music videos.

71. **TuneIn Radio Pro**: Listen to and record music, sports and news radio around the world.

72. **Tidal**: High resolution streaming for audiophiles.

73. **Amazon Prime Music**: Stream your favourite tracks directly from Amazon Prime.

74. **GarageBand**: Your own recording studio.

75. **Angry Birds**: Destroy greedy pigs in a number of environments.

76. **Minecraft**: Build and show off your creations to the world.

77. **Scrabble**: The word game designed just for the iPad.

78. **Super Mario Run**: Nintendo's most loved character is finally available on iOS.

79. **NBA Jam**: Fast paced 2-on-2 arcade style basketball.

Work

80. **GoodReader for iPad**: Robust, flexible PDF reader.

81. **Dictionary.com**: English dictionary and thesaurus for the iPad.

82. **Evernote**: Sync notes, to-do lists, documents, photos and more across all your devices.

83. **Dropbox**: Share and sync your docs, photos and videos.

84. **Things 3**: If you don't mind splashing out, this is a fantastic task manager.

85. **Mint**: A powerful personal finance tracker.

86. **Pages**: Word-processor app.

87. **Numbers**: Useful spreadsheet app for the iPad.

88. **Keynote**: Presentation app.

89. **Quickoffice Pro HD**: Edit Microsoft Office documents and view PDF files.

90. **Google Drive**: Create, share and keep all your documents online in one place.

91. **Microsoft Word**: Free access to the world's most famous word processing app.

92. **Duet**: Turn your iPad into an extra display for your desktop.

93. **iTranslate**: Translate words and texts into 50 languages.

94. **Printer Pro**: Wirelessly print from your iPad.

95. **Bento 4 for iPad**: Personal database for organizing contacts, tracking projects and managing lists.

96. **StockManager**: Real-time access to the latest share prices.

97. **MindNote**: Stylish mind-mapping and brainstorming.

Security

98. **1Password**: Remember the master password and 1Password remembers the rest.

99. **Find My iPhone**: Use another iDevice to find your iPad and protect your data.

100. **OmniFocus for iPad**: Fully featured organizer for a busy life.

INDEX